This book is dedicated to you.

Thanks for being curious enough to pick this book up.
Thank you for being interested to learn these fundamental pieces that are crucial to building the world of tomorrow.

Table of Contents

Chapter 9: {Case Study} MakerDAO

Chapter 10: Token Design

Chapter 11: Bonding Curves

Chapter 12: {Case Study} Bancor

Chapter 13: Other Economics Principles

Chapter 18: Fundraising Bonding Curve

Chapter 19: Crypto Insurance

Chapter 20: Crypto Derivatives

Chapter 21: Financial Risks of DeFi

Chapter 22: DAO, The Future of Governance

Chapter 23: Economics of Yield Farming

Chapter 24: {Case Study} Binance

Chapter 25: {Case Study} This Book

Chapter 26: Conclusion

Introduction

Disclaimer: This textbook mentions various projects and protocols. Mentioning them is not an endorsement in any way, shape and form. The general rule of thumb is that the projects are mentioned because they have the highest market capital within the specific category or that they are most relevant to the mechanism discussed. At the time of writing, the projects and protocols were active with an active community.

Nothing is investment advice.

> *TLDR: This book is a guide. Jump into the chapters directly and it will still make sense. You are not obliged to read it from cover to cover to get each chapter.*

This textbook has been a work in progress for three years. It covers a significant range of topics from economics and finance to math and technology. As much as I would hope for you to read it from cover to cover, I have made each chapter of the book independent on its own. This makes it easier for you to jump into specific chapters and information.

This book serves as a guide and manual to help you navigate through the space and understand the fundamentals behind it. More details of "how to navigate the book" can be found in the next pages, depending on who you are and why you are reading this book.

At the end of the book, I created a glossary list with "human explanation". References for each chapter and additional notes can be found at the end of each chapter. You can find additional information like long-form reports under references too.

Enjoy!

Lisa JY Tan

How to Read This Book: Navigation Guide

This book covers the basic fundamentals of token economics. Thus, there are many chapters with plenty of information. This navigation guide serves as a map to find out how to best read the chapters that are most relevant to you.

This book can be split into two main sections. Chapters 1 to 13 focus on economics. Chapters 14 to 25 focus on DeFi and the mathematics of such mechanisms.

If you are a protocol creator

That means you have an idea and you want to turn that idea into a smart contract on blockchain. I recommend that you start this way:

- Understand foundations: 4, 6, 8, 10, 13
- Bonding curve introduction: 11
- DeFi introduction: 14
- Math for DeFi applications: 16 to 20
- Governance: 22

If you are a retail investor

You are probably looking for fundamental analysis before investing long-term with these protocols. Great job looking at fundamentals instead of only market analysis.

- Case study for analysis: 7, 9, 12, 25, 26
- DeFi introduction: 14
- Math for DeFi applications: 16 to 20
- Governance: 22

If you are looking to get educated about the space

Maybe because you want to get a job in the space, you want to learn more to be an investor, you want to consult for projects or you want to start your own project. That is all fantastic.

- Economics for token engineering: 1 to 13
- DeFi and Math: 14 to 25

If you are a regulator

Thank you for not just trying to squash a new evolving system into an old existing system, not trying to put "new wine into old wineskins". Regulation works hand in hand with innovation, to support new systems and new ways of doing things.

- Economic principles of these ecosystems: 6, 8, 10, 13
- Case studies: 7, 9, 12, 25, 26

PART 1: ECONOMICS OF TOKEN ENGINEERING

Chapter 1: Introduction to the Economics of Token Engineering

1.1. Layer 1 vs DApps Protocols

In blockchain and technology systems we can divide the entire system into three layers, Layer 1, Layer 2 and Application Layer. The language that these systems run is called *protocols*. Protocols[1] help the various systems in Layer 1 to speak to each other, and in the application layer to speak to each other.

Layer 1 protocol form the base technology layer. Layer 2[2] are usually resolving scalability problems in Layer 1. Application layers are where specific applications are being used. Layer 1 and 2 are like the iOS or Android operating systems on your phone. Application layer are the various applications that you can download from the App Store or Google Play.

Think of Layer 1 speaking English.
Each system is a group of countries, like the United Kingdom, India, United States, Australia, New Zealand and Singapore. English helps these countries to communicate and trade with each other and to send information to each other. Instead of international trade, systems send data via protocols so that the systems can speak to each other.

Layer 2 speaks English with a twist.
That could be Singapore with Singlish, Jamaica with Jamaican English, Scotland with Scottish English, Ireland with Irish English. At the end of the day, they are still English and use similar grammar and sentence structure. However, the way they express themselves could be quite different from British English.

Decentralised applications (DApps) speak Spanish.
This is a group of Hispanic countries including Spain. They can communicate and trade with each other using the same language.

We also know that English and Spanish can be translated from one to the other. It just requires more effort and a translator. This translator is what we call *interoperability*. It allows for protocols to speak to each other.

Why? Because in reality, the entire digital space is more complicated than just having 2 languages. There are various Layer 1 languages and various Layer 2 languages. If we want to trade and send information or data across all the protocols and layers, we need to figure out the translator, which is the interoperability solution.

Interoperability between Layer 1 protocols alone is a huge topic. Scalability solutions and technological architecture stake is also worth diving into in Layer 2. Specifically, in this book, we will dive into DApp protocols, the math and economics of them.

This means we will focus less on Layer 1 protocols and their problems (like Byzantine Fault Tolerance, Sybil attack, game theoretic impacts of changing rewards to verifiers) or various consensus models for Layer 1.

Instead, we will focus on the mathematical models required to develop the various incentive mechanisms and other economic considerations that impact users' behaviours in a closed looped ecosystem[3].

1.2. Economics in Three Words

Economics is split into two primary domains: macroeconomics and microeconomics. In recent years, the domain of "behavioural economics" has been rising in significance. In addition, there are also varying schools of thought which influence the fundamentals of how one decides economic policies. But at its core, economics is three simple things:

- Incentives
- Punishments (Disincentives)
- Behaviours

Economics in Simplest Forms

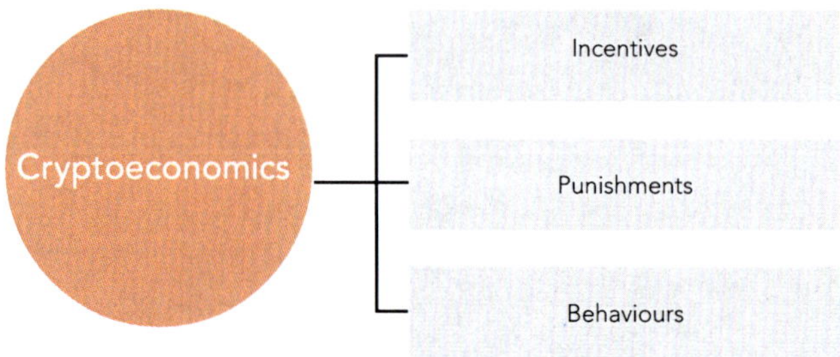

No matter how much the Keynesian[4] school of thought and Austrian[5] school of thought argue, **economics boils down to what incentives drive the desired behaviour of the economy.** Policies seek to intensify incentives or punishments, to change the rational (or irrational) behaviour of participants in the ecosystem.

1.2.1.Token Economy

Similarly, we can take the same principles and apply them in the token economy. The main difference between the physical traditional world and the digital decentralised world (e.g. a token-based economy) is the state of the economy.

1.2.1.1.Open-Loop vs Closed-Loop

The physical traditional world is an open-loop system. The system (aka economy) has no capacity for any state feedback. This gives the engineer (aka policy maker) a limited level of authority to engineer the state towards the outcome desired with a high probability.

For instance, the central bank changes interest rates according to the state of the economy. How the economy reacts is not within the control of the central bank.

On the other hand, the digital decentralised world consists of closed-loop systems which can be defined dynamically through state feedback. This gives the engineer (aka economics designer and systems engineer) the ability to achieve the stability of desired outcomes and behaviours in the system. There is also a greater variety of governance or control over the system in a digital decentralised system.

For instance, central bank digital currencies (CBDC) can introduce more creative incentive mechanism designs. For example, negative interest rates, currency with expiry dates[6] and other innovative mechanisms. These help to engineer and incentivise behaviours towards the desired outcome in the system.

1.2.1.2.Primary Function of a Token

The primary function of a token is to capture the economic value accrued from within the ecosystem. The primary function of a token is not to gain value on the secondary market. i.e. to exist on exchanges to trade. This is possible because such ecosystems accrue economic value. The token captures the value created. Price discovery of the value can be found when the tokens are traded in secondary markets.

Within a token ecosystem itself, the core purpose of a token is to act as the main incentive driver in the network or ecosystem. Each ecosystem has an objective, and a token incentivises participants towards that shared objective. Thus, the economics structure and design consideration of the token becomes a key criteria in achieving success[7].

As much as this book is about tokenising value created, not every ecosystem requires a token. And not every token needs to be traded in the secondary market.

1.2.1.3. Practical reasons to create a token

- Tokens represent a specific financial strategy. You tokenise this strategy so represent the value accrued.
- Tokens represet an underlying asset. You tokenise the underlying asset so this digital asset can now interact with a new technological stack.
- Tokens help with accounting purposes. You tokenise a medium of exchange that rebalances every day and updates the account of users proportionally.
- Tokens help with distribution purposes. You can distribute assets (profits earned, dividends, yield accrued) easily.
- Tokens align incentives of various participants. Money could do that, but there are too many diverse participants. Hence, an ecosystem specific token can achieve the incentive alignment with various mechanisms.

1.3. 10 FAQ About Economics of Token Engineering

Before we begin diving deeper into the topics, it is good to answer a few commonly asked questions regarding the economics of token engineering. Clarifying these doubts make it easier to understand the rest of the book moving forward.

1. What has market design and its variables got to do with the Economics Design framework?

ECONOMICS DESIGN FRAMEWORK

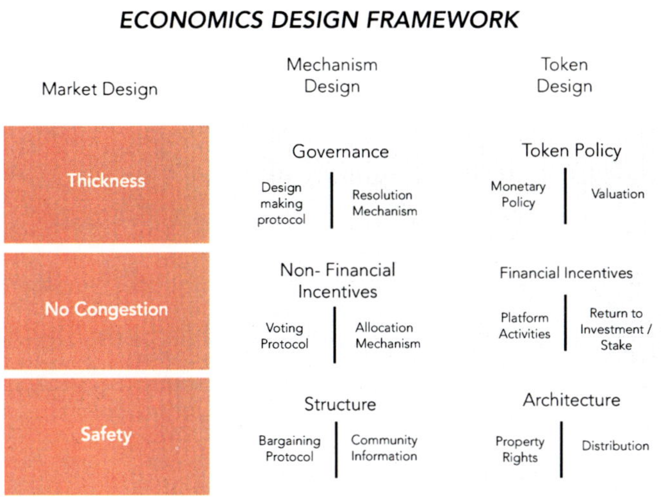

The Economics Design framework is the framework[8] to consider the variables when designing the economics of an ecosystem. I use them when consulting with projects and when doing research analysis on existing protocols.

Market design is the first pillar in the Economics Design framework. A market is the environment which trade happens. Market design defines this environment through design and engineering. This is to ensure that users of the ecosystem trade within the environment. Trade in this aspect could mean exchange of tokens or exchange of information and data.

Mechanism design is the second pillar. Mechanism design is the rules participants need to play by, in this market. It includes governance, non-financial incentives and other structures to update these rules.

Token design is the last pillar. Token design is the rules of the token itself. The rules can be defined with code in the smart contract. The rules could change, as the system grows, or the ecosystem integrates new forms of transactional activities.

2. What are the various token functions?

A token is something that represents value. There are many ways to subcategorise it. For example, token types. There are fungible tokens and non-fungible tokens (NFT).

Another way to categorise tokens are by their functions. There are four primary token functions — **SUMS**. **S**ecurity, **U**tility, **M**oney and **S**table token.

SUMS OF TOKEN FUNCTIONS

Functions	Purpose	Deriving Value	Feature
Security	Represent underlying asset	Valuation pegged to underlying assets	Tradeable assets
Utility	Access an internal network	Valuation from usage in internal ecosystem	Used to only transact within the ecosystem
Money	For Payments: Store of value, unit of account, medium of exchange	Valuation via market or debt	Currency that interacts on-chain and off-chain
Stable Token (Peg token)	Not affected by external volatility	Valuation pegged via underlying assets	Stable token with controlled price level

There are many ways you can define the specific token functions, especially from a legal standpoint, and start specifying what the token can and cannot do. But this is not about that. This table is about the general high-level functions a token can have.

Note: it is possible to have other functions like non-fungible tokens (NFT) and what these could represent. This segment focuses on fungible tokens. A $5 bill is the same everywhere (fungible) but a signed $5 bill by Barrack Obama is not the same as every other $5 bill you see. It is unique on its own (non-fungible).

To emphasise, fungible tokens mean that each token is the same and you can swap one for another. E.g. $BTC. Non-fungible tokens are unique tokens that cannot be swapped for another one. E.g. Digital crypto art or digital entities like Axie Infinity.

Security Token

A token is a security token when it **represents an underlying asset**. Traditionally you determine it using a Howey Test. Just think of it as a token that presents the value of an asset. It could be a tokenised stock, where you own a stock equity of a company. It could be a tokenised property, where you own part of the property. Ultimate, it is a digital representation of the underlying asset. And the fun part is that you can trade it.

Utility Token

A token is a utility token when it is used to **access the platform**. Think of your university giving you credit to book the university's facilities. Or perhaps the airline's frequent flyer programme, where you can access hotel and car rental partners and upgrade your flights in exchange for points (miles) that you have earned. These are tokens used to access the platform (university facilities) or network (network of airline partners). Users of the system use these tokens to interact with each other in the ecosystem.

Money

Money is basically **currency**, something you use to make an exchange with other people. We are talking about liquid money that you make payments with.

Money has three main purposes: store of value, unit of account and medium of exchange. Think of USD, GBP, EUR. With money, there are even more sub-categories. You have physical fiat money issued by a country's central bank, and digital money. In digital money[9], you have cryptocurrency (BTC), virtual money (World of Warcraft's money) and even central bank digital currency CBDC (central bank issued digital money).

Stable Token

Stable Token can have features of security, utility and money, but the main feature is that it is stable by being pegged to something. The value does not change that much when **compared to the value of the something it is pegged to**.

3. What's the difference: Consensus, Allocation, Resolution?

Consensus: general on-chain decision-making that requires consensus.

Resolution: forms of governance such as codes in smart contracts, token curated registries, ways to resolve issues due to incompleteness of contracts.

Allocation: how the asset is given to user(s) via auction market, voting, pricing mechanism, income distribution, access resources of production affect distribution of income, returns or stake in system, and various forms of property rights.

4. What's the difference between Valuation and Token Pricing?

Valuation is usually used in the context of the entire ecosystem. For example, how funds value a specific start-up. In the context of designing economics, it refers to how tokens derive its value. It could be capturing value through transaction fees, it could be through arbitrage on a derivatives market, or it could be in other creative forms.

Token pricing refers to the price of the token, usually via price discovery on the market. This is the price people are willing to pay in exchange for a token.

5. Where does "liquidity mining" or "yield farming" fit in the economics design framework?

ECONOMICS DESIGN FRAMEWORK

Market Design	Mechanism Design	Token Design
Thickness	Governance: Design making protocol | Resolution Mechanism	Token Policy: Monetary Policy | Valuation
No Congestion	Non-Financial Incentives: Voting Protocol | Allocation Mechanism	Financial Incentives: Platform Activities | Return to Investment / Stake
Safety	Structure: Bargaining Protocol | Allocation Mechanism	Architecture: Property Rights | Distribution

Liquidity mining and yield farming generally mean the same thing. It is an incentive mechanism to encourage participation by rewarding native tokens to users.

Liquidity mining and yield farming fit in the Financial Incentives box of Token Design. Liquidity mining in the application layer protocols are the native tokens issued by the protocol when transactions are made, e.g., $UNI issued to Uniswap users. Liquidity mining in Layer 1 is the issuance of tokens to validators in the ecosystem, e.g., $BTC issued to Bitcoin validators.

Everything that has to do with tokens and the monetary value of tokens fall under token design. Market and mechanism designs should not involve a monetary aspect.

6. Where does "game theory" fit into the Economics Design framework?

Mechanism design defines the rules of the system, whereas game theory is the analysis of actions based on the rules.

Game theory is used in the analysis of how people behave in the system. The rules designed in Mechanism Design and Token Design are inputs to understanding how people will likely behave. That is part of game theory.

For example, Nexus Mutual increasing the minimum capital requirement (MCR) is part of mechanism and token design. The analysis of how users reacted due to the increase in MCR is part of the game theory analysis.

7. What monetary policy should I use when I design my token ecosystem?

Monetary policy design of a token depends on your token use-case, token function, and business model.

For example:

1) If your token function is a **currency to facilitate transactions** within the ecosystem you can look into traditional monetary economics to understand the considerations and policy implementations for your token. A good place to start would be "monetary policy instruments" relating to how money is governed.

2) If your token is a currency that is very **vulnerable to external forces** (e.g. stable coin and the exchange rates between token and another currency like USD) you should look at the types of monetary policy that central banks use to govern their currency.

3) If your token represents a **claim to certain assets** on or off the chain, you can look into bonding curves that define token prices as a function of token supply. This requires a few concepts in monetary economics like reserve ratio and considers the impact of inflation.

4) If your token is a utility to **access the network**, the monetary policy here will really depend on the use-case and purpose. For example, if it works like airline miles, there isn't much monetary policy to consider, probably just deflationary measures occasionally. So, it really depends.

In general, a 2% inflation rate[10] is generally regarded as ideal by central banks.

8. Is the MV=PQ[11] mode[12] good enough to define my token's valuation?

Short answer: No.

1) The model is meant to get the price of money.

Your token may not have a "money" function. It's like trying to use a fruit knife to cut a slab of beef. Please use the right tools instead. This model is not the tool for valuation for all token functions.

In fact, this tool (MV=PQ), also known as the Quantity Theory of Money, is used to find the velocity of money. Switching the independent and dependent variables does not mean that the casual effect holds.

2) The MV=PQ model focuses on exogenous (external) variables.

Token ecosystems are amazing because you get to design many endogenous (internal) variables of the token. By that measure, the token's value should be defined in relation to the endogenous variables, not the exogenous variables. This is why token ecosystems are **different** from the fiat world ecosystem. We have comparatively more control of the output, given the input.

9. What are some underlying economic concepts that are fundamental to token economics?

Concepts from matching theory, auction theory, monetary economics, allocation theory, network economics and game theory can help design better and stronger incentives for participants. These concepts help to produce robust stable outcomes, improve inefficient allocations, and improve the efficiency of transactions within the ecosystem.

10. Why is governance so important in token economics?

In a decentralised ecosystem, governance is a crucial consideration in the design of the mechanism.

Governance helps to organise the transactions within the ecosystem through endogenous mechanisms, making it safe for participation and preventing congestion when issues arise. This can take various forms, including legislation and the design of smart contracts.

Governance constrains the ecosystem differently, depending on the token function, use-case and objective function.

There are concerns regarding a high degree of centralisation, inflexible smart contracts, consensus protocols and the regulations and laws of the various judiciaries. But governance should not be limited to just smart contracts[13]. It can also include various resolution mechanisms, consensus protocols and other layers of governance.

Notes

1. Protocols in the technology world are like TCP/IP, HTTPS, FTP, etc. There are endless protocols. Some are governed by international standards agencies like ISO, ITU, and RFC.
2. Layer 2 solutions usually aim at resolving scalability problems on Layer 1 protocols. Some solutions include Sharding, Plasma chain, and Rollups. In general, they resolve scalability problems by aggregating transactions in Layer 2 and then updating the ledger in Layer 1. Think of the difference between using a bicycle to get from Point A to B versus using a plane. The bicycle can only fit one person, while the plane can fit more. Instead of people, think of these people as transaction data. Now, the plane can send more transactional data between the 2 points. This helps transactions to speed up and makes transaction cost significantly cheaper.
3. Here, a closed looped ecosystem is mentioned. In economics this is called an autarky state. In reality, these protocols interact with each other. This is a feature of composability in DeFi. However, it is important to begin with a closed loop ecosystem in mind. If a system is not sustainable or robust on its own, opening the protocol up to composability with other protocols does not add any economic value in the long run. Thus, we begin with considering these ecosystems as closed looped.
4. Keynesian economics is the accepted norm of today. It is based on the usual boom and bust cycle. Government comes in to manage those cycles with regulation, debt and taxation. In this school of thought, economic growth is seen in GDP growth.
5. Austrian economics focuses more on a free market without government, with individuals making rational decisions. That includes savings and spending logically. Economic growth is seen as savings and production rates.
6. Gesell, S. (1958). *The natural economic order*. London: Owen.
7. By success, it refers to token achieving the shared objective.
8. Tan, L. (2019). Token economics framework. *Available at SSRN 3381452.*
9. Peters, G., Panayi, E., & Chapelle, A. (2015). Trends in cryptocurrencies and blockchain technologies: A monetary theory and regulation perspective. *Journal of Financial Perspectives*, 3(3).
10. McKinnon, R. I. (1993). The rules of the game: international money in historical perspective. *Journal of Economic Literature*, 31(1), 1-44.
11. This model is also known as the equation of exchange. In general, it says that the growth of money supply determines the growth of price level in the long-run. That is to say, when central banks print more money, the price level of goods will increase proportionally. It is part of the larger theory called Quantity Theory of Money (QTM).
12. Fisher, I. (1911). " The Equation of Exchange," 1896-1910. *The American Economic Review*, 1(2), 296-305.
13. View this online lecture on Smart Legal Contracts and Legal Smart Contracts by Wong Meng Weng at https://www.youtube.com/watch?v=1Fa_2FXBAjA.

Chapter 2: Evolution of Economics

2.1. What is Economics: An Evolution

Economics is a science. It primarily examines how decisions are made and which alternatives provide the greatest benefits to various stakeholders. It has always been, and continues to be, about the study of allocation of scarce resources (behaviours).

One of the key differences in token economics is to create rules around the allocation of scare resources to affect people's behaviours. We can enforce these rules through incentives and disincentives (punishments).

2.2. Economic Resources

The four traditional economic resources are land, labour, capital, entrepreneurship. These are traditional tangible resources.

In today's digital economic world, a new resource has come into the picture: information (intangible resource).

2.2.1 New Resource: Information (aka Intangible Assets)

BROAD CATEGORY	TYPE OF INVESTMENT	LEGAL (INTELLECTUAL) PROPERTY THAT MIGHT BE CREATED	INCLUDED IN GDP[1]
DIGITAL INFORMATION	Software Developmenent (E.g. Apps, Website)	Patent, copyright design intellectual property rights, trademark	Y
	Database Development	Copyright	N
SYSTEM PROCESSES	Machine learning development		N
	Algorithms		N
	UIUX development and process		N
INNOVATIVE ASSETS	Research and development	Patent, design IPR	Y
	Mineral exploration	Patent	Y
	Entertainment / art	Copyright, design IPR	Y
	Product design	Copyright, patent, trademark	N
OTHER COMPETENCIES	Training and education		Y
	Market research		Y
	Marketing and branding		Y
	Business process engineering and systemisation		N

These are variables and characteristics to consider as we dive and explore this new variable in economics.

FOUR PROPERTIES OF INTANGIBLE ASSETS	• Sunk cost: these are costs that have already been paid for and consumed. • Spill-overs: these can be both positive and negative. It is determined by the secondary impacts and implications related to the intangible assets created. • Scalability: the key feature in an intangible asset is that it has a non-rivalry characteristic. • One person's usage does not reduce the existence of the asset. The asset is also supercharged with "network effects", a positive spill-over. Two people can run the same algorithm without any issues. • Synergies and complementarities: intangible assets can produce synergies and complementarities with other assets, enhancing network effects in the scalability and spill-over properties.
GROWTH OF INTANGIBLE INVESTMENT	• Tech & cost: long run, labour intensive services (designers, researchers) are more expensive than manufactured goods. • Tech & productivity of intangibles: improvement in IT. • Industrial structure: more focused on intangibles today. • Changing business climate: labour market rules, focus on R&D. • Globalisation & growing market size: size of market & scalability.
INTANGIBLE INFRASTRUCTURE	• Institutions (property rights) • Rules • Norms • Common knowledge • Trust
VALUATION PRINCIPLES	• **Net Present Value**: Anticipate value of tomorrow's installed base of customers to determine how to invest today, to attract more customers. • **Network Value**: Value using customers as the major asset rather than figuring out the associated revenue and cost streams. Do this by calculating customer switching costs. • **Stickiness Value**: Valuing information helps to inform decisions affecting customer switching costs (e.g. product design and compatibility decisions).

2.2.2. Evolution in Markets

2.2.2.1 Classic Economic Market

In the classic economic market, we model based on demand and supply to understand how the market behaves. Classical demand and supply are independent of each other. Cost affects prices, which affect supplier's willingness to sell. Consumers are affected by quantity and thus demand for the products. They are relatively independent variables.

2.2.2.2. Information Markets

In information markets, things are slightly different. For this reason, we have to use other ways to signal and understand how markets behave, such as analysing the properties of public goods, externalities, monopolies and government interventions.

In addition, as information markets develop into platformed network economies, the demand and supply modelled is now interdependent. Demand for an asset exists because there is a supply of it.

Let's say a new movie exclusive to Netflix[2] is now available for viewing. This demand exists because there is a supply (the movie) available. Netflix is now an aggregator to match the various demands of users by supplying a variety of movies.

Within Netflix's platform itself, the demand for watching a particular show is interlinked to the movies available (supply).

These platforms play by different rules:

- Restrict access: different subscription tiers give you access to different streaming quality.
- Reduce congestion: using machine learning to predict the type of movies suitable to the specific user based on watch history and recommend the appropriate movies
- Build critical mass and subsidise user growth: allowing accounts to be owned by several account holders and be less stringent about account sharing.
- Enforce rules to punish bad behaviours: screen recording is not allowed on the Netflix app.
- Profit through interdependent supply and demand: Netflix is really about finding the right movie for you to watch, based on your watch profile. By helping you to reduce time looking for a movie you would enjoy, they profit from this small exchange.

This changes the scope of how Economics 101 is taught in school today. This is a new business model. A new economics structure.

2.2.2.2.1.Information as a Public Good

Information is different from classical physical goods in a few aspects. Information can be consumed by two or more people at the same time and they are nonrivals in consumption. This means that there is almost no opportunity cost when it comes to consumption.

For example, you can read an article on BBC and another person can do that at the same time. But if you head to the library and want to read a physical newspaper, you have to wait for the other person to finish reading before you can borrow it and read it.

With that, it becomes difficult to estimate demand for information goods. Hence, we estimate them with data or use proxies to estimate them.

For example, we track how many people are on that BBC webpage to understand how many people demand that specific information the article provides. Or we use proxies to estimate, like trending topics on Twitter, Google, Facebook. They suggest demand for that information.

Example of information markets: insurance, education, marriage market.

2.2.3. Differences between Tangible Resources and Web3.0 Intangible Resources

	TANGIBLE RESOURCES	INTANGIBLE RESOURCES
COST	Lower fixed cost Higher marginal cost	Higher fixed cost No / Low marginal cost
LIMIT	Natural Limit	No natural limit Can be enjoyed by more than 1 without decrease in quantity or amount produced
VALUE	Production Cost	Cosumer value, age of information, time frame
SOLD	Resource removed from previous owner	Resource retained by previous owner
	E.G PHYSICAL BOOK	E.G. EBOOK

2.2.3.1. Characteristics of Resources

For intangible resources like information, data and open-source protocols, there is a large fixed cost for producing the first unit and a low cost for each additional unit. In the near future, we are likely to see zero-marginal cost for additional units produced. For example, forking an open-sourced protocol in the blockchain ecosystem. Or copy-pasting the university notes your friend typed out.

Due to this interesting resource structure, there is no limit to the amount of supply or production of the resource. It can be enjoyed by more than 1 consumer, without a decrease in amount or quality produced. At the same time, in networked information markets, more consumers engaging in the market translates to more benefit each consumer receives from it. We could tokenise this benefit in a token.

Hence, the value of an intangible resource comes in a different form. It is no longer based on the cost of (re)production. The value of information depends on when it is sold, age of information and time sold.

When sold, this information still remains with the seller; e.g. selling you this book does not delete the information from my brain. At the same time, information can be purchased and cannot be returned easily. This information in the book is yours when you consume it and it will not be possible for me to ask you to delete and return the information to me.

Economic cost is calculated by adding accounting costs with opportunity or implicit costs.

2.3. Economics and Technological Evolution

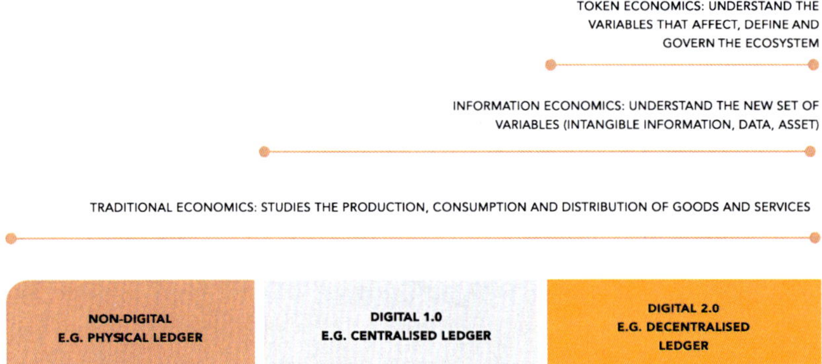

2.3.1. Past: Traditional Economics[3]

In traditional economics we study the production, distribution and consumption of goods and services. We look at equilibriums and calculate when to stop producing more items because that is when we stop making profits. We do this by calculating the cost of items and the revenue we can make from them. We stop producing when the marginal cost is the same as the marginal revenue.

That makes sense, because if your marginal cost is more than your marginal revenue, you make a loss and you would not want to be in that situation. So, if the marginal cost to produce a plate of gyoza is $1 and the marginal revenue you get from selling that plate is also $1, that is the point at which you stop producing more gyoza.

2.3.2. Present: Information Economics

In this evolution, we study how information and information systems affect an economy and economic decisions. Cost of information has a new structure. The main difference is that it is costly to produce, cheap to reproduce.

Take this book for example. This book is a 3-year work project and it has been costly to produce. However, to reproduce it, the printer can reprint it within a few hours.

Hence, cost-based pricing does not work anymore. We need to start pricing according to consumer value, not just production cost. Value based pricing comes from the value of a network, the value of externalities and the value of partnerships.

2.3.3. Future: Decentralised Digital Economics

We are building the future today. Economics is needed to understand the factors that affect, define and govern the ecosystem. As we move towards digitisation, an information economy and the rise in intellectual property (ideas, knowledge, research, open-sourced protocols, algorithms, data), we are also moving the way our economy works.

The information economy will continue to flourish and grow, but there is a new contender in the space: decentralised digital economies. With the digital space moving into decentralised organisations, new issues, variables and problems arise, resulting in decentralised digital economies.

One key challenge is to coordinate decentralised organisations. This is difficult, because everyone has different incentives, objectives and preferences. How can we align them? How can we coordinate agreement between such organisations? These are some of the problems we aim to solve with economics and tokens.

Technology has changed the way economic principles are being applied. The good news is that fundamental economic principles do not change.

2.4. Summary Table

	TANGIBLE RESOURCES	TANGIBLE RESOURCES	
COST	Any input to get output in an ecosystem (usually physical)	Any input to get output in an ecosystem (usually digital)	Self-selecting input to get a desired output in an ecosystem (usually digital with physical representations like art)
LIMIT	Understand the production, distribution and consumption To make better decisions	Understand the new set of variables (intangible information) Better strategic choices involving information tech	Understand the variables that affects, defines and governs the ecosystem To affect the decisions made by the participants
VALUE	Efficiency by analysing when to stop input to get output (MC=MR), pricing structure of inputs etc.	Efficiency by analysing when to stop input to get output (MC=MR), pricing structure of inputs etc.	To govern behaviours by allowing participants to self-select and encourage specific behaviours
SOLD	Supermarkets (Tesco). How much to produce, when to stop producing, how to reduce the cost of distribution (supply chain), how to encourage consumption	Amazon. Allow things to be traded more efficiently. Some centralised rules and guidelines that people have to follow. They make the last calls.	MakerDao. They encourage behaviours (saving / spending) through mechanisms. Rules are voted upon by the community. No one has the last say.
	Hence, production cost is super important (through optimisation)	Hence, trust in the platform is super important (Through network effects)	Hence, governance is super important (through mechanism design)

Notes

1. GDP is gross domestic product. It is the measure of value produced by a country during a period of time. Specifically, it measures the final goods and services being produced.

2. Without Netflix, you would have to

    1. Check what movie is available for screening in the cinema
    2. Decide your movie preference based on limited choices and watch the various trailers to decidewhich of the limited choices will be the best
    3. Check the timings available
    4. There might be no timings available or the preferred seats are not available

3. Economics started off with Aristotle in the 4th century BCE as a philosophy, founded on the theory of value and pricing. In the 16th century, Scruffi (1579) and Daranzanti (1588) continued the discovery with the "metallic" theory of money based on the general conception of value in use. In the 17th and 18th centuries Montanari (1680 & 1683) and Galini (1750) wrote about the theory of money, substantially surpassing these labours.

    Then came Adam Smith, the father of Economics. He wrote about the circular flow of economic life. He was concerned with economic sense and formulation of the economy's phenomenon. He discovered how each economic period becomes the basis for the subsequent one. This process was to understand the technical phenomenon, observe the economic cycle and connect the links between economic causality and gain insights into the inner necessities and general characteristics of economics. This enabled the members of the economic community to repeat the process in the next period.

    Questions he asked included: "How production comes about as a social process", "How it determines the consumption of every individual", "How the latter determines further production", "How every act of production and consumption affects all other acts of production and consumption", "How every element of economics energy completes a definite route year in year out under the influence of definite motive forces".

Chapter 3: Coordination and Incentives

Firms exist because this arrangement makes it easier and cheaper to coordinate with buyers and sellers, compared to free markets. In free markets you have to:

1. Discover what the market prices are
2. Negotiate contract for each & every transaction
3. Figure out of the seller or buyer is trustworthy if you trade at a later date

What makes a good ecosystem? More coordination. Because more coordination means more efficiency.

Free markets work when incentives are all aligned with the different participants (people and firms). Governance and regulations come in when incentives are not aligned and regulations exist to help realign them. This is because participants can find it challenging to coordinate amongst themselves. It can also get very costly in terms of time spent and opportunity cost.

3.1. General Evolution of Coordination

<u>*Past*</u>

Individuals lived their lives within **small tight-knit communities**

Moral impulses, social shame, gossip and empathy provided primary incentives/punishments for individuals to adjust themselves for the common good. These tight-knit communities became an *informal ledger of accountability and trust.*

To some extent, behaviour was constrained by the governance of the community, which took the form of religious or cultural norms. Participants in the community chose to follow (1) an old way of life with informal ledger or (2) a new way of life with social norms set by a higher power (usually a government or religious leader).

Present

Small tight-knit communities have broken down as **scope and scale of trade expanded** beyond the cities and informal ledgers of accountability.

Mass production means low prices. Millions consume these goods. It is now difficult and impractical to boycott such a product. It would be difficult to coordinate such communities.

Merchants trade over long distances with strangers. Hence, personal reputation alone cannot ensure that contracts will be kept. It is difficult to trust strangers. The informal ledger of accountability and trust now becomes *formal legal contracts and regulations*. Government supports trade through contracts and laws and protects the community against the abuse of these through tort law and regulation.

The modern market economy generates significantly more value than the old (moral) economy. Moral economies have a real advantage by being able to reward and punish individual actions that affect the larger community. Modern markets are unable to do so. However, moral economies are unable to account for those participants that are far away.

3.1.1. Moral Economies and Token Economics

Governance, with regulations and ruling, try to enforce and manage moral economies, but it is difficult. It is never as efficient as small tight-knit communities. How then, can we enhance moral economies in the token ecosystem? Can we do this through mechanism design or systems design?

Two possible solutions:

1. Include an added layer to the identity of participants like reputation and ensure that reputation has a more long-term impact. For example, a bad action that affects the ecosystem will be punished for a long time.
2. Have a universal understanding of 'reputation' to have a frame of reference to understand or trust someone without trusting them directly. However, this could mitigate the intrinsic motivation of an individual's action when we start to commoditise all activities. This can also create a dystopian society with social credit scores and ratings.

3.2. Market-Level Coordination

Barter: C2C

This used to be small communities (as mentioned in 3.1) trading with each other. We were able to trust each other because we were in a small tribal community and able to coordinate trade, e.g. apples (summer) for vegetables like celery (winter).

Big corporates: B2C (Tesco, Walmart, Marks & Spencer)

It starts to get harder to coordinate because (1) trade with strangers means having to find ways to trust strangers and (2) it is more efficient to mass produce because of economies of scale. This leads to big corporations because it is more efficient to coordinate between various participants.

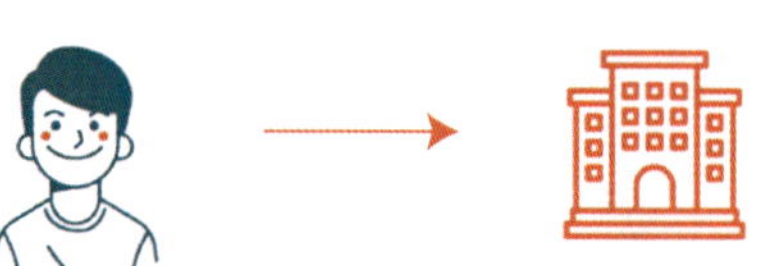

Platforms: C2C (Marketplaces, centralised)

Many individuals create niche products to sell to consumers. Like Amazon, eBay, Alibaba or Etsy. So, we have moved back to a kind of C2C and B2C mix platform. We just coordinate in a different way now. We have centralised marketplaces to coordinate the movement and information of individuals corporate goods and services.

Distributed ledger technology: C2C, P2P

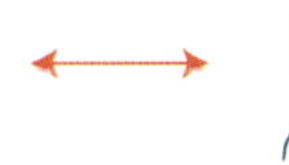

In the beginning of C2C, we could trust everyone. Now with platforms, we trust the platforms instead. After all, they coordinate information much more easily and thus make it convenient for us, the consumers. But we have realised we can take this a step further. What if we don't trust Facebook or Amazon because we don't trust their platforms (e.g. algorithms to match us, privacy issues), but still want to enjoy the coordination and convenience of platforms and ecosystems? That's where decentralisation comes in. We can go back to C2C on a platform we trust and where we enjoy efficiency through coordination without having to rely on big corporations and their centralised power.

3.3. Cooperation

The next big question is: If we manage to coordinate activities, how do we ensure that people will cooperate?

People naturally do not cooperate unless there is an incentive to. This is also where game theory comes in, but we will talk more about that in the next chapter.

Firstly, how do we facilitate cooperation? The best way is to get truthful choices from participants.

Examples where cooperation occurs in the token ecosystem: oracles in decentralised betting, consensus agreements, voting and decision making.

3.3.1.Incentive Compatibility

We can offer the right incentives for people to reveal preferences or types truthfully. If the goal is to make sure the participants are always honest, we can do it in two steps:

1. Ensure that **being honest is consistent** with rationality and intelligent assumptions.
   E.g. users cooperate and agree to increase the transaction fees because it is in line with the purpose of the token ecosystem. Case in point: MakerDao's $MKR holders agree to increase the stability fee to maintain the peg to USD.
2. Offer the right **incentives to reveal preference** or types truthfully. We call this "incentive compatibility".
   E.g. having to stake some tokens when you vote, and new tokens will be redistributed to you if you win the vote. Case in point: Kyber Network's governance token being staked and then deciding on how transaction tokens will be used.

Consistent to the core of this book, we do not deviate too far from the core concept of incentives. But we are looking at new applications and terms for incentives.

There are 2 types of incentive compatibility.

1. Participants being truthful is the best response, irrespective of what other participants say or do. We call this Dominant Strategy Incentive Compatibility (**DSIC**).
2. Participants being truthful is the best response, given their expectation of other participants' choices. We call this Bayesian Incentive Compatibility (**BIC**).

Ideally, we want to evoke the DSIC mechanism. It is not always easy. Thus, the BIC is the next best alternative. An example is to use BIC in improvement proposals and governance voting.

In this approach, a minimum quorum of votes is required to be staked in the improvement proposals before the proposal goes to a governance vote by super-users. Balancer developed a similar voting mechanism smart contract called Snapshot to achieve this.

3.4. [Case study] Coordination and Token Economies: MolochDAO

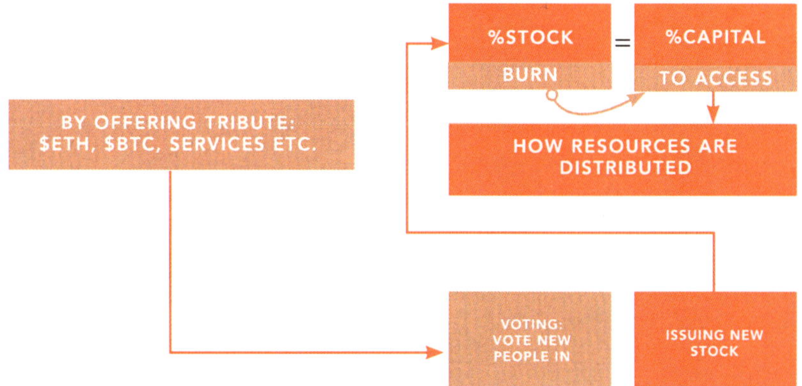

The gist is that MolochDAO aims to coordinate resources for issuing development grants for projects built on Ethereum.

The only way to get access to MolochDAO's capital is to destroy your stock, together with the right to vote on issuing new stock. E.g. if you have 10% of the stock and you destroy your 10%, you get 10% of the capital that MolochDAO currently owns. That is how the resources are distributed and managed.

The only voting on MolochDAO is to vote new people in, and issue stocks to them.

To join and be part of this organisation, you have to ask the existing stockholders to vote and create a new stock for you. If you destroyed your stocks before and want to join the DAO again, the process repeats itself and the existing stakeholders have to re-vote you into the system.

This mechanism also makes it easier for people to leave or defect. If you truthfully do not want to be part of the DAO anymore, destroy your stocks, get the capital and leave. It is easy to be truthful. This is also good in terms of cooperation, because those who do not wish to cooperate will exit. Now, we can have a group of participants who are willing to cooperate.

3.5. Externalities of Incentives

> *"It is not from the benevolence of the butcher, the brewer or the baker that we expect our dinner, but from their regard to their own interest"*
>
> - *Adam Smith*

People behave based on their self-interest. It is important to understand why people do what they do. They do what they do because it is in their self-interest that the cost be borne by someone else[1].

For example, upper management has a secure position and cannot be readily removed. They do not have to worry about job security and can focus on growing the business in the long run. But this incentive could create an externality, where they are shielded from the consequences of poor decision making and are not fired as a result of such decision making. For example, they focus on short-term profits at the expense of long-term losses. The losses will be borne by future management team, for they have long retired.

The solution is to align the interests of agents (upper management) and the principal (the company) so one does not win at the cost of the other.

Two externalities are moral hazard and adverse selection.

3.5.1. Moral Hazard

This is a situation where a **hidden action** occurs. For example, the **agent** has more information than the **principal** and enters the contract with **secret information**. This means that the principal has to pay that **cost**.

E.g. 1: Smokers (agents) are more interested to buy health insurance because they know they will need it in the future (hidden action/secret information). This is bad because the insurance company (principal) has to pay for the medical bills (cost) instead.

E.g. 2: A person (agent) with insurance against automobile theft may be less cautious (hidden action) about locking their car because the negative consequences (cost) of vehicle theft are now the responsibility of the insurance company (principal).

Moral hazard occurs when someone increases their exposure to risk when insured, especially when a person takes more risks because someone else bears the cost of those risks. A party makes a decision about how much risk to take, while another party bears the costs if things go badly, and the party insulated from risk behaves differently from how they would if they were fully exposed to the risk. A possible solution is that the principal creates disincentives to prevent agents from "cheating".

3.5.2. Moral Hazard and Token Economics

There are many examples of moral hazard issues in blockchain and crypto in general. For example, crypto token rating agencies. Crypto token rating agencies are the principals. The agent is the token investors. The investors use the rating information to decide to make an investment.

The rating agencies are meant to rate the risks of these tokens fairly. The information is meant to benefit the token investors as part of their due diligence and research. However, the incentives are not always aligned. The rating agencies have an incentive to be paid by the token issuer and rate the token in a much better rating grade than what it really is. This hidden information is not revealed to the investors.

Investors now take on more risks by following the information by rating agencies. They pay the price (i.e. increased risk) for not knowing the secret information (i.e. the rating grade is inflated).

This is a common moral hazard in traditional finance and credit rating agencies. Although the risks and moral hazards are slightly different.

However, as this book focuses on tokenisation, let's understand moral hazard issues in that context.

3.5.2.1. Rug Pull as a Moral Hazard

> *What is Rug Pull: Rug pull is an unexpected removal of help from someone and leaving the other in a difficult situation. Rug pull in DeFi is where the liquidity provider removes liquidity from the system, leaving users with valueless tokens.*

Rug pull exists in DeFi, especially with decentralised exchanges. Anyone can create a liquidity pool by adding $ETH and a random token in the pool. This provides liquidity for users to trade between the tokens. Rug pull is where the random tokens are added to the pool and remove all the remaining $ETH.

> *Quick Refresher: This is a situation where a* ***hidden action*** *occurs. One party has more information than the other and both enters the contract. After the contract is agreed upon, one of the party has to bear the cost of that hidden action.*

Rug pull is the hidden action by the protocol designer, with the cost being borne by the users. Another method is a secret backdoor in the protocol's codew which allows the bad actor (protocol designer) to steal the funds.

An example is UniCat, a rug pull and scam project with several moral hazards. This protocol, UniCat, allows for a user to earn some new native $MEOW tokens. Wallet transaction approval is required, and the spending limit is automatically set to "Unlimited spend limit permission".

In reality, UniCat, the owner of the scam UniCat project, is a bad actor[2]. They planned to do a few hidden actions even before $MEOW farming began.

1. They did a rug pull and removed liquidity, leaving the market with useless tokens.
2. There is a backdoor in the farming contract to change some settings to allow the owner to withdraw the funds via the "Unlimited spend limit permission" mentioned above.
3. To cover their tracks, a new smart contract is created for each victim which passes the ownership of the farm to a new contract.
4. Each new contract retrieves some funds, swaps them on Uniswap for $ETH and passes them on to the Unicat owner's address.

With this hidden information, you can see that the moral hazard risk is huge in an unregulated tokenised space.

3.5.3. Adverse Selection

Adverse selection is a result of **ineffective price signals** through **asymmetric information** (one party having more information or different information compared to the other).

E.g. 1: Sellers have more information about the situation.

Car mechanics know the problem better (asymmetric information) and can upsell solutions/services when these are not necessary (ineffective price signals). Car owners do not know any better.

E.g. 2: Buyers sometimes have better information about how much benefit they can extract from a service.

An all-you-can-eat buffet restaurant that sets one price for all customers (ineffective price signals) risks being adversely selected against by high appetite and hence, the least profitable customers. The restaurant has no way of knowing whether a given customer has a high or low appetite (asymmetric information). The customer is the only one who knows if they have a high or low appetite. In this case the high appetite customers are more likely to use the information they have and go to that type of restaurant.

A solution is for the party to screen for or use proxies to signal the type of information that the party is lacking.

3.5.4. Adverse Selection and Token Economics

In the crypto world, adverse selection can be seen from a retail investor perspective. These DeFi protocols usually start by having initial funding from a venture capitalist (VC) or through retail investors who are also users of the protocol.
Let's take the example of a decentralised P2P lending market on DeFi.

What are the risks involved in P2P lending? The risk is about balancing the number of lenders (suppliers) and borrowers (consumers). The platform itself takes a cut. These are good risks when you can aggregate the various participants on the platform. Thus, as a platform, it is important to have good branding and exposure to various assets because this is key to balancing the supply and demand of a P2P market.

Now, that is all good. Both are investors, VC investors[3] and retail investors[4], but they behave differently. VC investors are more likely to dig into the nitty gritty aspects of the business as part of their research and due diligence because they have an incentive to do so. They are investing in the protocol for a much longer term. On the other hand, retail investors are less keen on the nitty gritty research and are usually just users of the protocol.

However, this is where a problem arises, the problem of adverse selection. Because the time horizon of interest is different for retail investors compared to VC investors, the liabilities do not match their expectations.

What do I mean? With VC investors, they usually have a mandated vesting period to keep the funds for a period of a few years. With retail investors, however, there are less restrictive mandates of this sort.

Retail investors can dip in and out of the market very easily. They are motivated by the alternatives in the market. DeFi remains attractive when the yields are higher than alternatives in the traditional finance world. However, once the market shifts and blue-chip shares start to gain traction again, retail investors can quickly shift their funds back to traditional finance. Adverse selection in this type of situation creates a 'lemon' market. This is a market which has only low quality (retail) investors in the space.

> *Quick Crash Course: A lemon market is when the quality of goods traded in the market (platform) is reduced in the presence of information asymmetry between buyers and sellers. This results in only lemons being left in the market for sale.*

Notes

1. If everyone recognises that their negative cost affects the social community, this can be very useful information to collectively decide the best way to manage social goods. For example, open source protocols and decentralised finance. The key to success is to align incentives via tokenisation and to have proper governance in place. Proper governance entails power, responsibility and capacity to punish bad actors.

   In designing these tokenised and decentralised systems, we can realign these incentive structures and design the governance (decision making and punishment) mechanisms. Equal power and equal starting points are difficult to come by in the real world. In a decentralised tokenised world, therein lies a solution to these problems.

2. Thanks to Alex Manuskin for the case study. You can read the thread here: https://twitter.com/amanusk_/status/1313070958794727430

3. VC investors are the venture capitalist firms that raise money, collect funds and invest following a mandate.

4. Retail investors in crypto are usually individual investors or protocol users.

Chapter 4: Outcome and Constraints

This book is all about design. Defining and designing the economics of an ecosystem. It is akin to creating your own Newtonian physics on a new planet.

In this chapter we will focus on getting started with design. The first part of the design stage is to define things. We have to define the design space, the objectives, and the constraints.

4.1. Objective

Defining the main objective of the token ecosystem is one of the most important factors in the design process. The objective determines the mechanisms in place, the governance structure, the policies, the protocols and everything in between. Without the objective[1], the incentives and punishments do not mean anything because they do not affect the behaviour of participants in the token ecosystem in a useful way.

The objective is something the ecosystem is working towards. That means all the incentive mechanisms in place exist to achieve the objective.

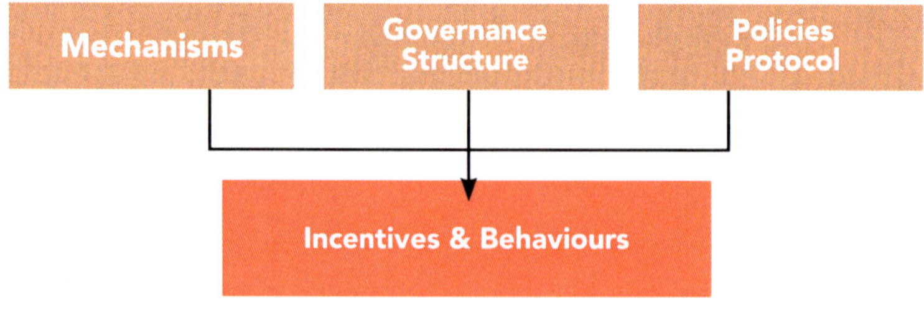

There can be more than 1 objective, but there needs to be 1 main objective.

For example:

- Bitcoin: decentralised cryptocurrency. Any governance, mechanisms and future improvements will be made with the idea of that objective in mind. So it's rather unlikely that Bitcoin will change its focus to become a stable coin and peg it to USD. They **can** do that, but they are not likely to do it, because it is not part of their main objective.
- Ethereum: world's largest computer. Hence, ethereum is focused on research, DApps, new mechanisms, getting more dapps on their blockchain, etc. That's because it is aligned to the main objective of being the world's largest supercomputer.
- MakerDAO: a stable coin AND governance to create this stable cryptocurrency. Since there are two objectives, there are two tokens (coins) in this ecosystem. Each token only has 1 main objective. It is not possible for 1 token to have two objectives because then you would have no idea which to focus on. You have $DAI (stable coin) and $MKR (governance coin) in the MakerDAO ecosystem.

As mentioned earlier, there are many different objectives in the token ecosystem but there is only one main objective, followed by less significant ones. This is important, because we design the token economics model around the ecosystem with the purpose of optimising that main objective.

4.2. Constraints

Constraints are necessary to limit the scope of the token ecosystem. Otherwise, there are too many factors to consider in the model, and it will be difficult to design and implement it.

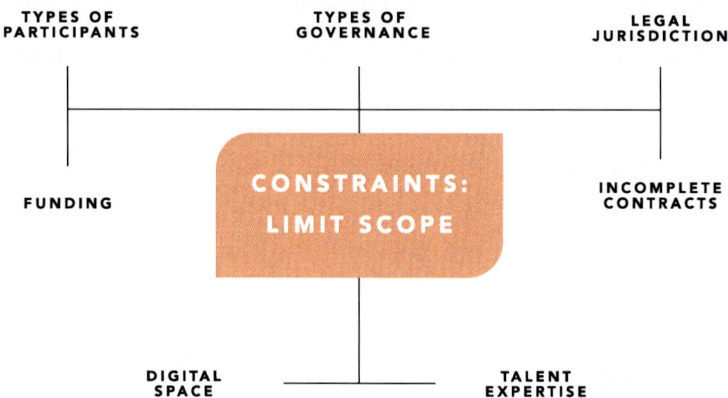

Common constraints:

- Type of participants this token ecosystem is for.
- Space: both digital space and physical legal jurisdiction space in which the project is located.
- Talent and expertise of the designers, developers and builders.
- Type of governance desired: depending on the token function, use-case and objective function, the degree of governance centralisation needs to be considered.
- Incompleteness of contracts: some contingencies are difficult to foresee or describe in advance and may be too complicated to be incorporated into (smart) contracts.

4.3. Design Process

When both objectives and constraints are in place, this is where the design process begins. Economics design merges with systems design to deliver the objectives, given the constraints.

4.3.1. Why is this important?

Having a main objective is key to designing better incentives and mechanisms to affect the behaviour of participants. The design process is split into 2 layers: economics design and systems design.

> *If classical economics is bounded rationality, quantum is unbounded rationality, then economics design is bounded irrationality.*

In economics design, there are three pillars that we will be talking about, market design, mechanism design and token design. They come from the core traditional economics concepts in micro and macroeconomics. They speak to the rationality in people.

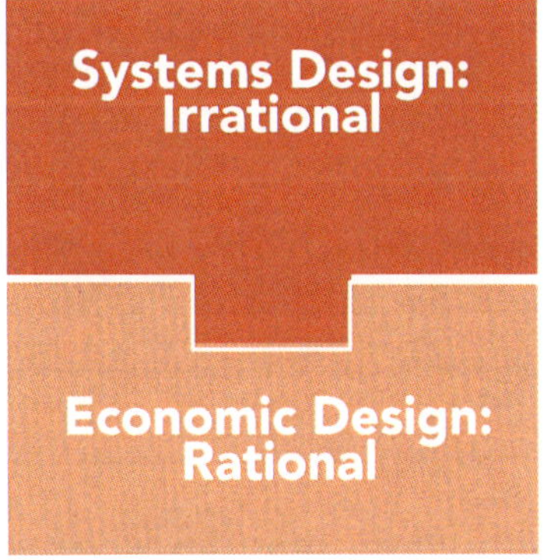

Systems design mixes behavioural economics, consumer psychology and UIUX design to create systems that speak to the irrationality in people.

Thus, we have difference incentives to speak to different parts of our brains, the rational and irrational sides.

Notes

1. In Alice in Wonderland, when Alice asked the Cheshire cat which direction she should take, the cat asked where she was going. And since she did not know where she was going, any direction would not make a difference. Similarly, if the objective is not defined, any incentive and punishment works since it would not make a difference to the unknown objective.

Chapter 5: Seven Wonders of Token Economics

Economics is a huge topic, so token economics is not any different. Token economics can be divided into many concepts, theories and classifications.

Token economics sounds complicated, but it does not have to be. Before we dive into the various design pillars, let's get you started on the seven[1] wonders of economics concepts, the explanation, real world examples and crypto examples.

At this stage, we are just taking existing economic concepts in the physical real world to the digital crypto world. Hopefully, this will inspire you to understand the power of economics in distributed ledger technology (DLT) and inspire you to learn more.

5.1. Network Effects

You hear this all the time. People keep saying that it is all about network effects. Yes, it is true. Network effects are part of the new economies of networks we talked about. Network effects help to speed up mass adoption.

What are network effects?

Basically, the more people use it, the more valuable the ecosystem is. As you can imagine, network effects are closely linked to scalability.

But this is not the same as viral effects! They have different objectives and different playbooks. A network effect is a type of defence that you can build up.

There are many types of network effects. We will start with 2-sided network effects, since most token ecosystems are 2-sided platforms.

Communication

Having a telephone is great, but if you're the only person in the world with a telephone, there is no value in having one.

Our methods of communication have changed with tech. It used to be landlines to pagers to mobile phones. Then came IM like MSN, Yahoo Chat. And today, we have so many possible communication apps.

What communication apps do you use? I use WhatsApp, Telegram and Twitter. Not because I enjoy giving my data to Facebook via WhatsApp, but because people are on the app. The communication app is only valuable if I can speak to people on it.

I have one problem though. WhatsApp is banned in China so I can't speak to my Chinese friends. Instead, we use WeChat. Otherwise, I have to email or snail-mail them. The communication app is more valuable when your network is on it.

Other communication apps include KakaoTalk (Korea), Line (Taiwan, Thailand, Hong Kong), Facebook Messenger (Vietnam, Cambodia, France), iMessage (USA). These apps are also more valuable in certain regions of the world, as more of the community is on that communication app.

Due to scalability properties with network effects, many firms want to dominate the market with network effects. But it is tough. As mentioned, there are different types of network effects.

A simple summary of the various **types** of network effects:

- Direct: trains, roads and highways
- 2-sided: uber, airbnb, tinder
- Data: google, waze, amazon (data is central to product's value)
- Technology performance: VPN, bittorrent
- Social: language, beliefs, religion, currency, conspiracy theories[2]

Once a company builds up their defence with network effects, we see the common outcome of a small number of dominant large companies.

What then, are the network effects in the token space?

In the digital space, businesses looking to compete with owners of scalable assets are in a tough position. It is a winner takes all scenario. Look at Ethereum and its network to promote Ethereum to the mainstream for adoption and its supportive services to enhance the network effects. It is difficult to compete with them. They have funding to promote the technology performance, using a new programming language and Ethereum has become a common term in the language when people talk about blockchain, along with Bitcoin.

DeFi, the second half of this book, is mainly built on Ethereum blockchain. This means crypto assets are able to speak to one another and the protocols are able to tap into each other and transfer data and information. That is why the DeFi space is more mature and saturated, as the crypto assets have more usability and utility in the ecosystem in general.

5.2. Signalling

What is signalling?

Signaling theory is like playing a game of charades. You let the other person guess your card without saying the words.

Talk is easy. The message becomes more credible when you show it using actions and other methods. Usually, that means putting money where your mouth is.

Dating and Marriage

Looking at the world of dating and marriage. How do we signal that someone is worthy of being a lifelong partner? This is signalled through society's definition of female beauty. We went from liking curvy ladies (signalling a wealthy family to be able to eat well) to slim ladies (signalling that they are educated to be consuming the right nutrients) to fit ladies (signalling they are able to manage themselves and time, and value their health).

Signalling in token space

Similarly, in the crypto space, it is easy to create a cryptocurrency. Fork $BTC or $LTC, change some aspects and you have a new coin. Anyone can just create a coin and flood the world. It is costless to create it. But how then, can you tell everyone that your coin is good? Every coin is unique, but how do you signal that yours is better? How do you increase the number of real active users?

Since it is cheap and easy for anyone to issue a new token, we have to make signalling more expensive. Otherwise, the market will be flooded with plenty of valueless tokens[3]. Signalling helps to increase the barrier to entry, to increase the quality of tokens in the market.

Examples of signals:

- Be innovative so that big publications pick up on your project. These are signals to the public that your company is so innovative that these big publishers are interested to report on them. That's how you can win the trust of the public.
- Pay money for your project/article to be published on Forbes, Techcrunch, Mashable, etc.
- Whitepapers that are peer-reviewed by academics.
- Frequently updated Github.
- Having a wide variety of experts with domain knowledge in your team (computer scientists, entrepreneurs, economists, academics).
- An active community of real and non-bot users on social platforms like Twitter, Telegram, Discord.
- (If MVP[4] is out) Total value locked in the protocol and ratio to the price of token.
- In addition to whitepapers, publish token economics papers, technical papers, yellow papers.

5.3. Monetary Policy

More details about monetary policy can be found in Box 3 in Chapter 10.

What is monetary policy

This is mainly applicable for digital currency and cryptocurrency, specifically, since they are a form of money. Some aspects <u>may</u> be able to apply to other token functions (utility, security), but let's just focus on currencies on this section.

Centralised Money

Things to consider in monetary economics:

- Fiscal policy: changing taxes, government spending, borrowing (aka managing money indirectly through governance mechanisms).
- Monetary policy: increasing/decreasing money supply, how to sustain demand of the currency through inflation targeting, stability of prices.
- Exchange rate regimes (if necessary):
    - Currency union (EU)
    - Managed floating (HKD-USD)
    - Freely floating (USD, GBP, CHF, JPY)
    - Pegs (Belize-USD)

Central banks control a country's currency. The Federal Reserve System (FED) in the USA controls how the USD is managed. The Bank of England controls how the GBP is managed. MAS controls how the the SGD is managed. Pretty much ~10^5 smart people in these organisations decide how the currency is managed and governed. That is very centralised.

Decentralised Money

The difference is that we want this to be decentralised. That means some core decisions are embedded in code and baked into the token ecosystem. Depending on the mechanism design, people in the network can vote to change certain systems. It gives more power to the people. In the crypto world, we have different ideas for the supply of token/digital money. Some like it capped, some like it uncapped. $BTC has a cap at 21 million, while others don't, like MakerDao.

There are also many other ways to design P2P digital currency with embedded monetary policy in code to reduce price volatility.

Ampleforth is a project that algorithmically rebalances the price of their money to achieve price stability in the long run. (We dive into more details in Chapter 10.)

5.4. Property Rights

What are property rights?

Property rights are socially enforced constructs to determine how a resource or good is used and owned.

Property rights is a huge topic on its own, since there are many ways to design the allocation of property rights. Here, I just want to focus on new ways to manage property rights for digital assets. Chapter 13 discusses more about property rights.

Regular property rights

If you own a share of Company XYZ, when they earn money you get a share of that too (via dividends). You are entitled to some rights for holding an asset.

That is just regular securities. We are now tokenising securities and putting them on blockchain, which gives you some form of rights to an asset. Similar to Indiegogo, you can fund a start-up. Different from Indiegogo, the tokens also allow you to own part of the project. You can benefit through dividends and profit sharing. That may not sound very revolutionary, but that is a first step in the right direction.

You could add other features in the tokens too, like interesting types of voting, other property rights, etc. Being on blockchain doesn't solve all the problems, but it does help to reduce inefficiency by being more transparent and making it easier to coordinate transactions.

New property rights

But here's the fun part: there are new types of property rights. We discuss more ideas in Chapter 13 and 25.

We have a new way of looking at property rights. Since goods are digital now, property rights are also evolving. We have to be creative to determine how to allocate these digital goods. This new way is inspired by Harberger's property taxation mechanism. Instead of determining a price and taxing it, the price is determined by the owner of the property itself.

You might be thinking, *alright, then I will price it as low as possible, so I pay less taxes.* Here's the catch. When you mention that price, anyone who wants to buy it at the price, can buy it from you. And you must sell it. So, you definitely want to price it at the right price, since if it is too low, someone else will buy it from you and you are not compensated the amount you value it for. If it is too high, then you will have to pay too much tax. This mechanism is the type of incentive compatibility we talked about before, which helps to align the objectives of all the parties concerned and create a self-governing system.

5.5. Lock-In

What is Lock-In?

Lock-in is a relatively new concept compared to the rest of traditional economics. This came with the evolution of information and technology, where we created information economics.

Lock-in is a way to get people to stay on your system. We essentially lock them in. There are many ways to do that:

- Make it difficult to leave the system (non-monetary ways).
- Keep upgrading the system so they have a reason to stay.
- Make it expensive to change the system.

We can create lock-in effects through three methods: product itself, complementary products (networks), tacit knowledge.

Features of digital information and lock in:

<u>Sunk cost: costs that you cannot recover</u>

Intangible information is hard to sell. Hence it increases lock-in with this intangible information, usually a type of knowledge. This information is also usually uniquely linked to the business ecosystem (branding, operating procedure, relationship in the supply chain).

E.g. a codified operating process is only very valuable to the company itself. It is also non-transferrable, since it is usually specific. This locks the knowledge worker into the ecosystem. The sunk cost is the development of the codified operating process and the training cost to upskill the knowledge worker.

<u>Spillovers</u>

Spillovers can strengthen lock-in effects through the sharing of ideas, marketing spillover, training spillover, ecosystem spillover.

E.g. the Uber ecosystem benefits from the spillover of more

people owning and using smartphones.

Synergies

Ideas and other ideas go well together and are worth more when combined. This creates strong incentives to work together. It also creates an alternative way for firms to protect their intangible investments against competition: by building synergistic clusters of networks, rather than protecting individual assets.

E.g. Ethereum's EEA[7] network and training more developers to code in Solidity than other smart contract languages.

WindowsXP

Did you know that 1.15%[8] of the world is still using Windows XP? Why does that happen, when there are better systems that Microsoft has created? Simple. It is expensive to upgrade to Windows 10.

Imagine how much it would cost to get the Windows 10 licensing fee for 100 people in your business. There are also other things like the enterprise systems that has been built on Windows XP, there is no real need to change the system to Windows 10 and the knowledge specific to that operating system.

Ethereum

Ethereum is working on becoming "the" Layer 1 platform for blockchain systems. You have the EEA and Consensys supporting participants and businesses in the network. Can you think of other ways that Ethereum can increase their lock-in effect?

The secret to lock-in lies in the smart contract programming language (solidity) and other tacit knowledge around this new technology stack. Ethereum also provides grants and supports many projects built on the Ethereum platform[9].

5.6. Principal-Agent Theory

What is Principal-Agent Theory

Simply put, it is to increase skin in the game for participants. This helps to align the incentives of all participants, as they will now have something to lose.

Utilities system

Your behaviour changes depending on whether the utility bills are included in the rent or excluded from the rent. When they are part of rent, you think less about your usage. When they are excluded from rent and you have to pay for the amount that you use, you are more likely to be conscious about your usage. Landlords are more likely to exclude utilities from rent to encourage tenants to be more mindful with the usage of utilities.

Bitcoin system

One example: paying for performance. You only get paid (transaction fee) when you can verify that work has happened (e.g. a block is validated). This is useful when the paying entity cannot specify the key aspects of the desired outcome in advance.

E.g. Bitcoin's transaction fees change based on demand and supply. It is not possible to create a complete contract, detailing all the possible outcomes. So, paying for performance is a good solution (transaction fees).

Bitcoin protocol does not specify the amount of computing power that each miner should contribute to ensure its successful validation. It would be difficult or impossible to measure it ahead of time.

The other alternative in contract theory is through direct compensation for delivering the services (block rewards). The miner gets to self-select on the input they want to contribute, based on the probability of them getting the block rewards. E.g. investing in better ASICs (self-selection) to contribute in the Bitcoin ecosystem.

We see both systems at play in Bitcoin (transaction fees + block rewards). It balances the two types of incentives:

1. The system is unsure of the value of the block being validated, hence the pay for performance system works as a percentage of the block value (transaction fee).

2. A block will be validated, no matter what. For this there is direct compensation and miners can self-select the resources (GPU, ASICs) used to get this direct compensation (block rewards) .

5.7. Schelling Point

What is the Schelling Point?

A natural point people tend towards when there is a lack of communication.

Making a choice

E.g. Here are four numbers. Which number will you choose? 584376, 230873, 10000, 238176. Probably "10000" because it is a natural comfortable number of people tend towards.

If I say we are all going to meet at New York's train station at 12pm, which train station comes to your mind? Probably Grand Central Station. Or, you are in a new city and you don't speak that language. There are two restaurants on the main street, one with a long queue and one with zero people inside. Which restaurant will you choose? Most probably the one with the longer queue.

Making a choice on blockchain

This is an important area in decentralised systems. Imagine that you have to coordinate activities amongst many individuals, with different incentives, different preferences, etc. How do you do that? The Schelling point is the natural way in which people will coordinate amongst themselves.

The easiest example is adding a block to the blockchain. Given two chains: 1 long chain (signalling many verified blocks) and 1 short chain (hard forked chain), which chain will you add your block to? Probably the long chain. (*This is how Ethereum consensus works too.*)

An example is SchellingCoin[10]. It is a decentralised data feed, a mechanism Ethereum built around financial contracts and derivatives. In simple terms, it allows users to submit truthful values and those who submitted the truthful values will be rewarded and those that did not (the rest) will be punished.

Why does this work? The truth is arguably the most powerful Schelling point out there. Everyone wants to provide the correct answer because everyone expects that everyone else will provide the correct answer and the protocol encourages everyone to provide what everyone else provides.

Notes

1. This is not an exhaustive list of economic concepts. I just chose seven, because it makes a nice title.

2. Conspiracy theories is a funny one. Remember in summer 2020, the World Health Organisation had to write a report to say that 5G does not cause coronavirus? Conspiracy theories has a network effect on the social acceptance and conversation around such theories. 2020 is a weird year.

3. As a matter of fact, John Maynard Keynes once predicted that in the future, everyone will have their own currency and the world will be flooded with valueless currencies. Fascinating how these ideas always existed, the world just did not have the right technology to experiment with these economic concepts.

4. MVP means minimum viable product. It is the product in its simplest basic form that still serves the objective it was meant to create. Another concept is MVE, minimum viable economics. That is the most basic economics in place, to build these token models.

5. It really depends on how the central bank is structured. In the US, the FED has 12 regional Federal Reserve Banks. Nationally, monetary policies are approved by the board of 12 people, seven board members and the 12 presidents of the regional reserve bank. When it comes to voting, only five of the 12 presidents vote at a time. In the UK, the Bank of England is governed by the bank's Monetary Policy Committee of nine people.

6. Harberger, A. (1964). Taxation, resource allocation, and welfare. In The role of direct and indirect taxes in the Federal Reserve System (pp. 25-80). Princeton University Press.

7. EEA is the Ethereum Enterprise Association. The goal is to help organisations adopt and use Ethereum in their technology architecture stack. Find out more at https://entethalliance.org.

8. That is a lot for a defunct operating system. Windows XP was launched in 2001. Microsoft officially stopped any updates and technical updates for XP on 14 April 2014. Yet, in Q4 2020, there are more people using Windows XP than Windows 8 (0.54%) and Windows Vista (0.11%)! Data retrieved on 25 Nov 2020 at https://www.netmarketshare.com/operating-system-market-share.aspx.

9. Think of this as Apple giving grants to iOS developers to develop apps. Ethereum foundation is Apple, Ethereum blockchain platform is iOS and the projects are the various apps you can find in the App store.

10. SchellingCoin was first discussed in 2014 by Vitalik Buterin at https://blog.ethereum.org/2014/03/28/schellingcoin-a-minimal-trust-universal-data-feed/.

Chapter 6: Market Design

There are three pillars in the design of token economics ecosystems.

6.1 Market Design 101 – Introduction

Market design is the design of the environment in which the participants can interact and transact with each other. In the physical world, market design is used in the design of kidney transplants[1], job markets for economists[2] or allocation of primary school choices[3].

Here, we're not talking about that. We are talking about market design in decentralised digital ecosystems instead – token-based ecosystems.

Market design is a form of microeconomic engineering[4]. It uses science (economics) and art (design).

How is it science? It applies tools and concepts from game theory and mechanism design.

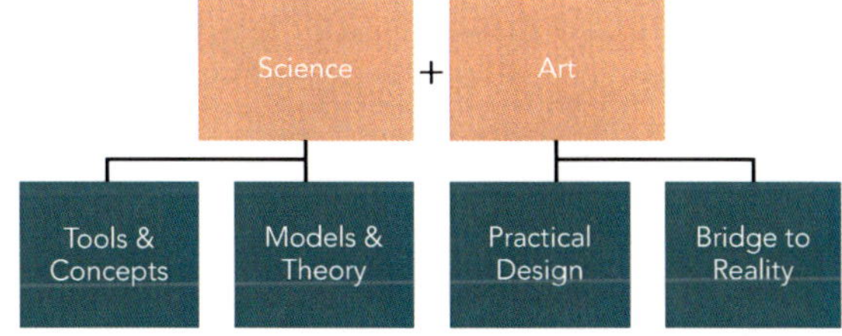

How is it art?
It uses practical design for decision making that is beyond theory. Remember how I said that people are the most irrational beings? In science, we usually assume that people are rational and they behave perfectly. But in reality, that is not the case. This is where design and art come in, to practically apply the science to reality.

6.2 How is Market Design Important to my Token Ecosystem?

There are a few problems in markets, but these are two main ones.

1. Markets are not stable and that leads to inefficiency. And we don't like inefficiency.
2. Markets promote certain outcomes (objectives we talked about in the last lesson), and we want to achieve them.

So, market design comes in to resolve the problems.

1. Make sure that markets are stable and safe, so that people will transact within the marketplace and ecosystem instead of outside.

Think about trading your cryptokitties (or digital art) on a marketplace. If people feel that the market is unsafe, their kitties (or art) will be lost in code or just disappear. Instead, they download the kitties (or art) into a thumbdrive and physically meet up to trade that thumbdrive with USD cash.

2. Add rules and constraints so that we can encourage specific behaviours and promote cooperative actions within the marketplace.

Ultimately, it is important to the token ecosystem. It helps us to encourage good behaviours to achieve the objective of the token ecosystem. For example, stability of currency, supply chain tracking, etc. It also allows us to understand how the market can fail and mitigate that risk. Good market design encourages participation in the network, increasing the value of the token ecosystem.

6.3 Market Design 102 – What is Market Design

Concepts	Explanation
What	Form of economic engineering
How	Formal rules to govern interactions
Why	Participants are naturally noncooperative

Let's begin formally. What is market design?

What? As mentioned, it is a form of economic engineering.

How? We include formal rules to govern the interactions of participants within the market. Like in a token ecosystem, we define what participants can, cannot, should, should not do.

Why? Participants are naturally noncooperative in nature. Unless there is an incentive to cooperate, we are usually selfish in our actions.

How to solve that?

We analyse the situation using noncooperative game theory. Then, as economic designers, we focus on the incentives for **individual** behaviours. We do this by looking at the environment (ecosystem) and consequences of actions.

6.3.1 What does market design include?

- Solving problems in existing marketplaces through **incentives**
- Making individual strategic decisions through interactions (behaviours)
- Organising and understanding markets through **rules**
- Considering behavioural economics in the interactions of users (behaviours)

6.4 Market Design 103 – Why Study Market Design

In general, economists look at situations and make predictions of behaviours and outcomes.

However, in market design, we take a more proactive approach. Instead of observing how markets behave, we can design how markets **should** behave.

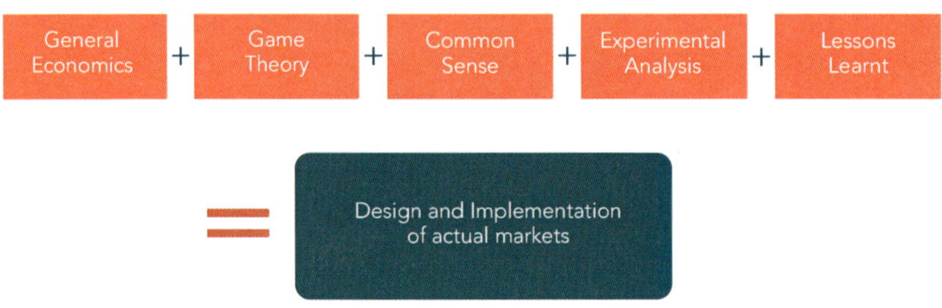

> *General economics + game theory + common sense + experimental analysis + lessons learnt = design and implementation of actual markets.*

6.4.1 New Digital Markets

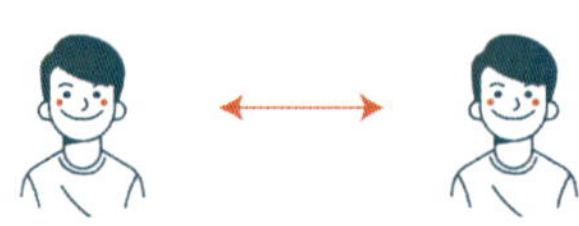

Thanks to technology, we can create "smart markets". These markets take in complex inputs and variables to determine the best outcome possible.

For example, platforms like Amazon allow for many options to buy a single item, including reviews from other buyers and Amazon suggests related products for you to purchase. These markets help us to make smarter decisions or the algorithms are smarter to deliver the best outcome. That is, for you to end up buying the best product, given your interest.

6.4.2. Market Failures

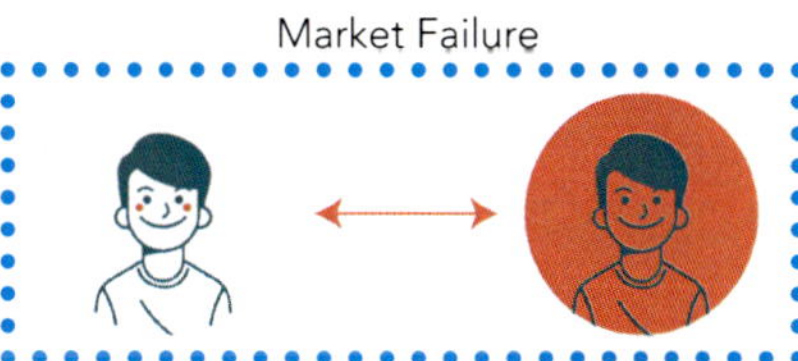

Another reason to study market design is because markets fail. They can fail in the market institution (token ecosystem) or the general tasks the markets perform (transactions). The design factors are usually the root cause of market failures.

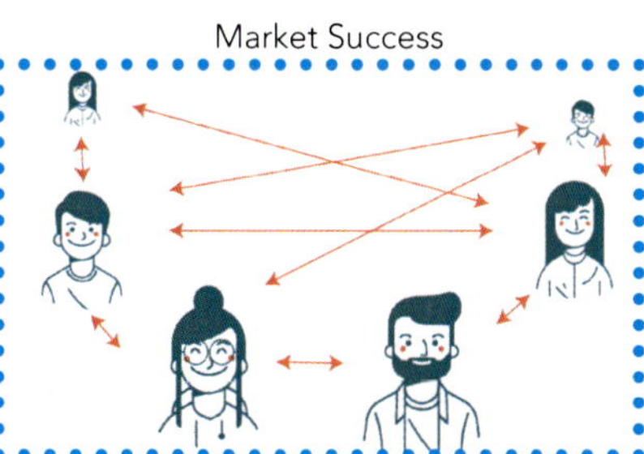

In new digital markets, we are usually talking about 2-sided markets. 2-sided markets are where you have to attract both the buyers and the sellers. You are the platform that allows transactions to happen.

In this case, we want to encourage behaviours of transacting on the platform or marketplace itself, and not outside of the marketplace. Otherwise, this can lead to inefficient results (aka market failures).

6.4.3. Good Market Design

Good market design allows trust to develop within the token ecosystem. And that is trust beyond the technology itself.

This is a type of trust where participants are able to communicate their honest preferences easily. We talked about this in Chapter 3 – dominant strategy incentive compatibility and Bayesian incentive compatibility.

If participants **reasonably believe** and trust that other participants (other users, users with authority, partners in the ecosystem) are equally honest, then they will believe that they are as likely to achieve their objectives as any of the other participants.

E.g. you and your partner are hosting a dinner party. Either of you can cook dinner or prepare the house. You can reasonably believe that your partner will cook as nice a dinner as you could because you both have the objective of impressing your dinner party guests and ensuring that they have a good time.

Successful market design encourages users to participate in the network, increasing the value of the token ecosystem.

So, we have to design markets better. How do we do that? Let's look at factors in market design.

6.5 Factors in Market Design

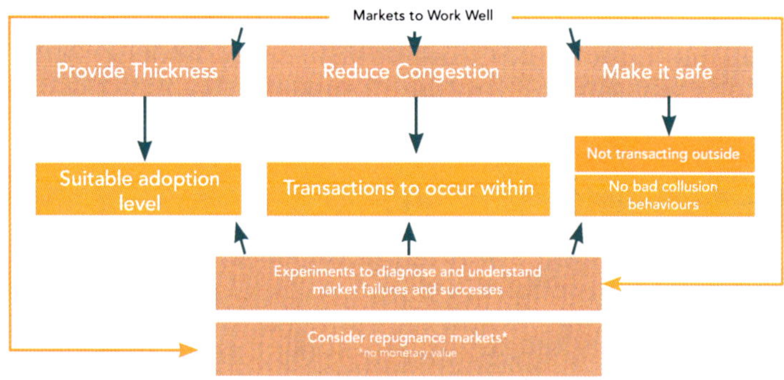

To work well, marketplaces need to[5]:

1. Provide **thickness** – Markets have to attract enough participants to reach a suitable adoption level. It does not make sense if you only have 5 participants. Then, these people can come together to transact or interact
2. Overcome **congestion** – thickness can cause many transactions to occur. We need to make transactions fast enough & provide sufficient time to consider all alternative options
3. Make it **safe** to participate in the market – for example, convey relevant information (e.g. eBay needs to share information about sellers and products)
    - As opposed to transacting outside the marketplace
    - As opposed to engaging in strategic behaviour that reduces overall welfare
4. Consider repugnance – these are special markets that generally do not include monetary value to them (e.g. assassin market, organ donation, adoption). Sometimes, some ecosystems view money as a taboo. More details in Section 6.9.4.
5. 5. Run experiments to diagnose and understand market failures and successes by testing new designs and communicating results to decision makers.

It is also important to consider opportunities and behaviours **outside of the marketplace or token ecosystem**. We do not model them, but they are important factors when designing the market.

Market Design Factors

FACTORS	EXPLANATION	REAL WORLD	CRYPTO WORLD
THICKNESS	Many participants and options	Airbnb apartment options	Distributions Partnerships Bonuses
NO CONGESTION	Time and resource to consider	Resources and time to consider	Govern transactions Charge fees Validators
SAFETY	Transact in ecosystem Easy to use	Payment Gateway 24h Customer Service	Transparency Staking Privacy Cryptography Peer-review

6.6 Thickness

A market provides thickness when it makes many potential transactions available at the same time. Relevant offers can be compared. The main issue with thickness lies in the network externalities and other economies of scope.

For example, Airbnb and options for apartments or rooms, cities nearby, etc.

6.7 Reduced Congestion

A market is congested if there is insufficient time or information to fully evaluate all the potentially available transactions.

Congestion is a problem of markets with many different options. E.g. Airbnb has many similar options and it is difficult to choose. What makes it easier is the superhost status and star-reviews.

6.8 Safety & Ease of Use

If it is risky to participate in the market, individual participants may try to manage their risk in ways that damage the market as a whole, or otherwise try to prevent their trading counterparties from being able to receive other offers.

Sometimes, even when there is thickness, people may not behave in the way we like, so they start transacting outside of the marketplace. This reduces the options available, because they are being transacted outside (off-chain).

E.g. Airbnb's guests can apply directly to hosts via the chat function. They get to skip cleaning fees and Airbnb service fees. They are transacting outside of the marketplace. Instead, Airbnb adds security features for hosts like insurance of their property, to encourage transactions to occur inside its marketplace.

In the environment of token ecosystems where safety can be measured in code, an additional layer of safety for participants can be included, like privacy features, cryptographic agility and peer-reviewed algorithmic codes.

6.9 Market Design and Token Economics

That being said, all markets are **different.** Various factors form the foundational building blocks to design markets, but the design solutions can vary based on the ecosystems.

6.9.1. Thickness (size of network)

Bring all the relevant parties who want to transact together. Make sure to consider the timing of transactions like when should offers be made and how long the transaction period can be left open.

For example, voting period or transaction validation period.

1. Mining (Relevance to proof of work [PoW])
   - Incentivise participation in the network through block rewards (e.g. $BTC)
   - More block rewards at first to increase early adopters (i.e. reward their risk-taking action with more block rewards)
2. Partnerships
   - Partner with related companies to drive early adoption and bootstrap network effect (e.g. Ethereum Enterprise Alliance)
   - Tokens to entice network partnership between companies and users (Business 2 Peer)
3. Bonuses
   - Extra token if someone joins the network through referral (Peer 2 Peer)
   - Airdrop

6.9.2. Reduced Congestion

Ensure that there is sufficient time to consider the options. Otherwise, there are too many offers and no time to consider them (aka congestion). Resolve this issue by having the protocol to help people make better choices.

An example is Yearn Finance. It uses onchain data to determine the best returns of interest rates and deposit funds there.

1. Govern Transaction
   - Grade transactions and remove low-quality transactions[6] to ease congestion
   - Meter bandwidth
2. Charge Fees
   - Access fees
   - Congestion fees (like road fees during peak hours)

3. Governing validators
   - Fixed set of validators for consensus (E.g. multi- sig wallet holders)
   - Randomly select groups of nodes for consensus
   - Specifying super-nodes with authority for consensus (E.g. MakerDao)
   - Proof of Authority Notary notes (mainly used within enterprise-level applications)

6.9.3.Safety & Ease of Use

Make it easy for people to join and safe for them to transact.

1. Resolving asymmetric information
   - Increase transparency for participants (e.g. share more details about counterparties before transacting)

2. Staking
   - Safety deposits that can be activated during a dispute
   - Skin in the game so everyone is less likely to be a bad actor (e.g. Synthetix and staking programs)

3. Privacy features
   - Privacy mechanisms like zero-knowledge proofs (e.g. zCash)
   - Ring signatures (e.g. Monero)

4. Cryptographic agility
   - Post-quantum security (e.g. QRLedger, IOTA, Corda)
   - Compatibility with secure hardware models and better key management

5. Peer-reviewed white papers
   - Fundamental algorithmic issues (e.g. algorithms and code that produce skewed results, creating non-random outcomes, collisions and forgery)

6.9.4.Additional consideration: Repugnance

Sometimes, repugnance trades can be resolved with efficient market design. Repugnance refers to the social constraints preventing exchange from taking place at positive prices.

In general, these markets exist because the use of money in these trades can be considered a taboo. These transactions are also generally outside of the usual market transactions like buying eggs and milk. Sometimes, these trades can be considered immoral. Example of repugnant markets:

- Adoption of children
- Surrogacy
- Sexuality
- Military service
- Voting buying[7]
- Pollution
- Organ transplant
- Friendship
- Admission to schools
- Nobel prize
- Genes and living tissues

Thus, market design becomes crucial in the economics design of these systems.

For example, BitTorrent. Uploaders seed the data while downloaders download the information. These transactions do not use money to trade, since the philosophies of the uploaders and downloaders do not always appreciate the use of money in trade. Instead, there can be new ways to manage the uploaders and downloaders to prevent free riding.

Notes

1. Tayfun Sönmez and M Utku U''nver. Market design for kidney exchange. The Handbook of Market Design, pages 93–137, 2013.

2. Peter Coles, John Cawley, Phillip B Levine, Muriel Niederle, Alvin E Roth, and John J Siegfried. The job market for new economists: A market design perspective april 6, 2010 forthcoming in journal of economic perspectives, summer 2010. 2010.

3. Atila Abdulkadiro `glu and Tayfun Sönmez. School choice: A mechanism design approach. American economic review, 93(3):729–747, 2003.

4. Alvin E Roth. The economist as engineer: Game theory, experimentation, and computation as tools for design economics. Econometrica, 70(4):1341– 1378, 2002.

5. Alvin E Roth. What have we learned from market design? Innovation policy and the economy, 9(1):79–112, 2009.

6. This can be helpful to combat front running of trade.

7. Schaffer, F. C., & Schedler, A. (2005). What is vote buying? The limits of the market model.

Chapter 7: {Case Study} Nexus Mutual

Nexus Mutual is the top insurance protocol by market capitalisation.

7.1. What is Nexus Mutual

Nexus Mutual is a decentralised insurance protocol based on the Ethereum platform. As of Q4 2020, it only covers the smart contract risks on the Ethereum platform.

The token $NXM is used to align incentives of the various users in the system. $NXM is used for staking in the system in terms of buying insurance cover, participating in work to be done, or voting in the governance capacity.

The $NXM token price is determined by two main things – total $ETH in the capital pool and minimum capital requirement (MCR). This is determined via a bonding curve function.

7.2. Getting Involved with $NXM

a. Directly

If you want to participate directly, you have to join Nexus Mutual and pay a membership fee. Once you are a member, there are different ways to participate, e.g., buying insurance cover, staking, or participating in governance.

When buying insurance cover on Nexus Mutual, users (you) choose three things:

1. Choose the asset that you want to get insurance for
2. Choose how long you want to cover it for
3. Choose how much you want to cover for

b. Indirectly

The indirect way is to buy a wrapped NXM. $NXM is the token that is used in Nexus Mutual and you can buy it indirectly with this thing called wrapped NXM or wNXM.

Now it's a concept similar to $BTC and $wBTC. A custodian keeps $BTC to mint $wBTC that can interact with smart contracts. Similar to this idea, $wNXM can be bought instead of $NXM itself. This is to skip the KYC process and membership fee payment.

Technically you can redeem one actual NXM for each $wNMX owned. $wNXM allows people to trade it on exchanges like Uniswap, whereas an $NXM token itself is not tradable on the secondary market. This is due to the KYC process for each $NXM holder. $NXM can only be owned by individuals who have completed the KYC process and have membership access.

7.3. How does Nexus Mutual Work?

Nexus Mutual includes three types of participants:

1. **Insurance Cover Buyers**: People who have paid for membership and can purchase insurance cover with $NXM

2. **Risk Assessor**: Checks the code, and general information on a project.They verify that the smart contract is well coded without any bugs.
3. **Claims Assessors**: Votes to accept or reject claims to pay the buyers, if something happens.

> Nexus Mutual *is a platform that aggregates all these three participants together, aggregates the insurance covers, and aggregates the funds available to facilitate the insurance.*

Let's say I'm a member and I buy cover from Nexus Mutual. Nexus Mutual has some funds available to cover my insurance cover for lending and borrowing on Aave.

Now for example let's say insurance coverage price is 0.5 ETH and I want to cover 300,000 ETH. That is the amount I am adding on Aave.

These are just arbitrary numbers but just imagine 300,000 for borrowing and lending on Aave and the cost for insurance is 0.5.

That 0.5 ETH goes into Nexus Mutual, which is a big pot of funds. Part of the funds will be used to reward the risk and claim assessors.

7.3.1. How do the Risk and Claim Assessors Work?

Risk assessors will look at all the different protocols in DeFi.

Back to our example:

Risk assessors own $NXM. They can either hold the $NXM and wait for price appreciation or use the $NXM in the Nexus platform.

How can risk assessors use $NXM?

Risk assessors use $NXM to provide insurance coverage for users to buy. Instead of pooling USD from everyone to provide the coverage, they use $NXM instead.

What are the steps required?

1. They do a technical dive in Aave. They check the smart contract code for bugs.
2. The code is secure and has no bugs.
3. Risk assessors put $NXM that they own in the Aave insurance coverage fund.
4. This fund is then used to provide the insurance coverage, if anyone wants insurance for their Aave transactions.

How do they know that there are bugs?

Usually, these risk assessors are experts in this technical field. Think of white hat hackers[1]. Instead of being cybersecurity experts, they are smart contract experts.

Why will they stake $NXM?

They stake $NXM because they can profit from their expert knowledge. They assess the code and find that there are no bugs. It's not possible to make profits from that information.

Instead, Nexus provides a platform to do that. They stake $NXM (that they already own) in an insurance pool. This pool now becomes the capital to pay out the losses, if a bug exists.

For everyone else, they can now pay a small fee to insure their transactions. Should a bug exist, there is insurance to cover the loss.

Because these experts have audited the smart contract and they know that there are no bugs, the insurance paid by everyone else will not be profits for the risk assessors.

7.3.2.How do the Claim Assessors Work?

Claims assessors, as you can imagine, assess the claim.

They look at the claim as reported by you and they will come up with a verdict which is either yes or no. That is their job — to say yes or no to the claim.

Claim Assessors have to stake $NXM to assess claims. They stake $NXM with their vote, either yes or no to the claim. Since there is no objective "right" answer, the answer is determined by the majority claim assessors' votes.

The majority outcome is either yes, "this is an error and Nexus Mutual needs to pay out" or "no, this is not something that Nexus Mutual covers".

- Claim assessors who vote differently from the majority outcome will have their tokens locked up for a period.
- Claim assessors who vote with the majority outcome will get their stake back, together with some additional $NXM.

7.4 Applying Market Design to Nexus Mutual

Just a quick recap: market design defines the environment in which users and tokens co-exist so that markets can operate and be governed efficiently. We talked about network effects before, pointing out that market design is a prerequisite to achieve network effects. Successful market design (aka good ecosystem environment) will encourage more users to participate and increase the value of the ecosystem.

Quick recap, market design looks at three factors:

- Thickness of market
- Reduced congestion
- Making it safe and easy to use

FACTORS	EXPLANATION	NEXUS MUTUAL	OTHER EXAMPLES
THICKNESS	Many participants and a variety of options to choose from or where to use the tokens at	B2B market B2C market	Distribution Partnerships Bonuses
NO CONGESTION	Time and resources to consider	Cooling off period for stakers	Govern transactions Charge fees Reward validators
SAFETY	Transact in the ecosystem in a safe and easy way	Tokens signal risk Token price determination includes long-run and short-run signals Know-Your-Customer (KYC) of members Ease of purchasing insurance	Transparency Staking Privacy Cryptography

7.5. Thickness of Market

Thickness is the level of adoption of the market. Now the thing about DeFi insurance is that it's very related to the adoption of DeFi in general. First, you have adoption of crypto. Then you have adoption of DeFi. Lastly, adoption of insurance in DeFi.

It's like a chicken and egg problem – if you don't have the market maturity or market adoption for DeFi then it's going to be very difficult to scale Nexus Mutual. Crypto insurance it's really dependent on the market size of DeFi. When we look at creating market thickness, we look at how we increase the participants or increase the network of users in the system.

7.5.1. B2B Market

Nexus Mutual provides insurance and sometimes this insurance is not enough to provide insurance just for users, but other protocols could also tap into this thing, so currently we have two systems that kind of white label Nexus' insurance to resell it in a different way to its users.

The first one is **Yinsure** finance who take the insurance cover that's provided by Nexus Mutual and then white label it and sell it in their ecosystem.

The other one is **Cover** protocol. They are trying to do a peer-to-peer coverage market. They also white label their insurance model, i.e. the insurance cover is provided by Nexus Mutual and they resell it to their market.

7.5.2. B2C Market

B2C is figuring out how to increase the different users by having them participate in various roles. There are four basic functions of using an NXM token: you have the member being able to buy cover, then you can be a risk assessor, you can be a claims assessor, and you can participate in governance. You want to increase users' participation with other users or members because you want them to be purchasing more insurance covers.

As DeFi continues to grow and as new people are coming into the system, that's how you get new users. As you have more protocols in place and you have more of assessors assessing the different smart contract risks and for governance, there's a lot of improvement proposals that come through so that's where the governance role kicks in and people will be voting (time-weighted or stake weighted votes) and that's how you increase purchase participation from a B2C level, so it's more like a peer-to-peer level.

7.6. Reduce Congestion

Nexus Mutual creates an environment in which participants can easily participate. Participants can choose from various positions, choosing whatever suits them best, with no barriers to participation.

To prevent bad actions by stakers and users, there's a 12-hour cooling off period for claim assessors.

If I'm assessing the claim for Aave's protocol, I can't assess another protocol's claim for 12 hours. This is quite important because you don't want people to be assessing claims for a lot of different protocols at once and then they keep saying yes to everyone and they try to exploit the system, so there's a 12-hour break between finishing the assessment of one contract and starting assessment of the next smart contract.

7.7. Safety & Ease of Use

7.7.1 Safety via Design

The token design of Nexus Mutual, $NXM, signals risks.

How?

As an **insurance cover buyer**, you can only purchase insurance cover when there are enough risk assessors staking their tokens to signal that the protocol is safe.

This brings us to **risk assessors**. These people audit the codes. When they determine that the code is safe, they put their money where their research is. They stake $NXM in the protocol. This becomes capital to provide coverage for buyers to purchase.

> *Having coverage to buy insurance signals that the protocol is audited by a third party. Thus, it is safe to use.*

Lastly, when a claim is submitted, a different set of users, **claim assessors**, are deployed to determine the validity of the claim to award a pay-out. A minimum vote (70%) is required before the voting passes. Otherwise, the vote will be extended to the entire platform and the decision will be crowdsourced.

7.7.2 Price Determination

The price of $NXM is defined by the math in the bonding curve. This reduces speculation.

Not only so, the bonding curve embeds two main factors in the curve, the long term and short-term variables. Investors can view $NXM prices as a proxy to evaluate the short-term and long-term forecasts. This is done via the Total Capital and MCR variables.

7.7.3 KYC and Membership

Nexus Mutual chose to follow the UK regulations of setting up a mutual company. Users purchasing $NXM have to go through a KYC process and pay a small membership fee. This reduces the risk of the company being shut down by the government.

7.7.4. Ease of Use

UIUX aside, members can purchase insurance coverage very easily on the system. The member dashboard also helps users to visually understand the network status in the system.

Notes

1. White hat hackers are ethical hackers. They are cybersecurity specialists who test a system's security. They do not hack the system to exploit and gain benefits. They have the permission to hack the system and test how secure it is.

Chapter 8: Mechanism Design

This is the second of three pillars in the design of token economics ecosystems.

8.1. Mechanism Design 101

Mechanism design defines the rules[1] of the ecosystem.

These rules exist to govern the actions of participants. These rules can be embedded in code (e.g. smart contracts) or a behavioural rule (voting, consensus).

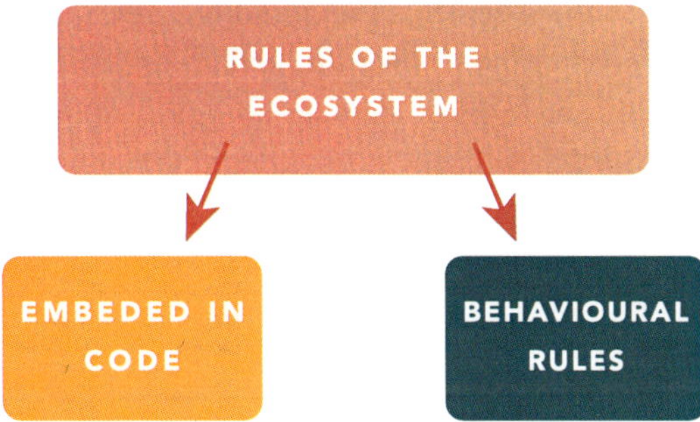

8.2. Why do we Need Mechanism Design?

In the first pillar, we learnt that market design is to design the environment for participants to interact and transact with each other. This second pillar is to define the rules of the behaviours within the environment.

This is more than just decentralised digital ecosystems. This can be applied to any institution, market, ecosystem, company, or any environment that can benefit from rules[2]. Mechanism design puts rules in place and figures out how the rules and game form can achieve the objectives of the ecosystem.

Think of mechanism design as one of the instruments in the toolkit as an economics designer. While there is no abstract generalised mechanism design formula, we will look at this design pillar through the various factors to consider.

8.3. How is it Important to my Ecosystem?

Good mechanism design affects the long-term sustainability of decentralised token ecosystems. It acts as one form of governance for the decentralised ecosystem.

Mechanism design is important because it affects the actions and behaviours of people in the network. It also seeks to account for changes or preferences within the ecosystem, which are important contributing factors to efficient mechanism design.

We also use mechanism design to understand which mechanisms are optimal for different participants. In Chapter 3, we discussed how different participants have different incentives and objectives, particularly in Section 3.5.4. Mechanism design seeks to understand which mechanisms are best for which type of participant. And how do we find the most adequate mechanisms to respond to the various participants' incentives.

8.4. Market Design 102 — What is Mechanism Design?

What? Mechanism design is the rules of the ecosystem.

How? It provides a framework to analyse the ecosystem, market or institutions. It seeks to understand the problems associated with incentives and private information (assumptions, expectations).

Why? There are many types of participants in an ecosystem, with different objectives and incentive mechanisms. We want to align them with rules or incentives, so that no one benefits at the expense of the other (e.g. Amy does not gain extra by Bobby losing something).

We are focused on incentives and the behaviours of participants because incentives and private information determine the behaviour of participants.

8.4.1. What does mechanism design include?

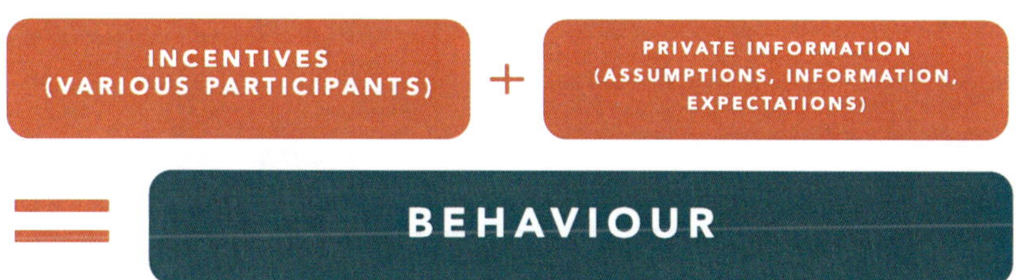

- Aligning various objectives of different types of participants through incentives
- Revealing private information
- Affecting behaviours of users

8.5 Why Study Mechanism Design

We need rules to govern the games we play and the actions we take. The goal is to align the incentives of the various participants. It is not easy in the centralised world, even tougher in the decentralised world.

In the centralised real world, a central entity can get together and deal with any situation that does not achieve the objectives (e.g. government, central banks, board of directors).

But in the decentralised world, there needs to be more rules in place to govern bad behaviour and negative outcomes.

For example, Facebook is a central entity. If you post something terrible, they have the authority to terminate and remove your account.

What about in a decentralised ecosystem? Who has the right and the authority to have the final say and remove your account? How do we weed out the bad actors? How do we encourage the good actors to keep participating?

This is why we have some mechanisms (aka rules) in place to manage such situations.

8.5.1. What are we doing with mechanism design?

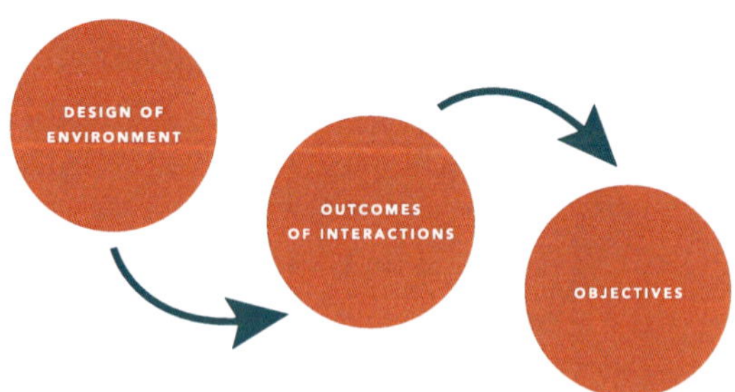

We are looking at the (1) the design of institutions, markets, ecosystems (e.g. environment) and (2) to understand how these affect the outcomes of interactions of the institutions (e.g. behaviours) to (3) attain the objectives (e.g. outcomes).

8.5.2.Assumptions Made (For Now)

Although people are not perfect and they are irrational, we generally assume that people will act on their best behaviour, given the private information they have. This is a strong assumption.

Through the gamified systems design that we talked about in Chapter 2, we can strengthen this assumption. But for this economics design layer, let's stick to this assumption.

8.5.3. Social Choice Function

We will be speaking a lot about social choice functions. As discussed earlier, social choice function is an analysis of many factors to reach a collective decision or outcome. This could be maximising utility, minimising costs, reducing time spent, increasing happiness, ensuring equality of individuals, etc.

In the real world, we are governed by a set of laws under a constitution.

Why is social choice function important? Because ultimately in an ecosystem, we want to make a collective decision to achieve a social goal that is good for everyone (social choice). We can analyse how good our decision or mechanism design is, with the social choice function.

8.5.4. Good Mechanism Design

The desired outcomes in good mechanism design depend on the objectives you want to achieve. It can include :

- Pareto efficiency[3]
- Strategy-proof mechanisms[4]
- Fairness[5]
- Or more general goals represented by a Bergson-Samuelson social welfare function[6] which allow trade-offs between efficiency and equality.

As mentioned before, there is no fixed rule or formula to design the mechanisms. However, we can look at the factors to get started with the first steps.

8.6 To get started

1. Define the problem that needs to be solved
2. Determine the social goal that needs to be achieved
3. Understand the constraints involved

We have discussed these in Chapter 4, with objectives and constraints. When designing the mechanisms, sometimes we dive deeper into objectives and constraints to specify goals and constraints. It is also possible to put them into a mathematical formula, if necessary.

How do we do that? Let's look at factors in mechanism design.

8.7 Factors in Mechanism Design

Mechanism design is complex. It covers classical general equilibrium theory to non-classical environments. Sometimes, it is also used to create general normative theory of economic policy.

Mechanism Design Foundational Principles

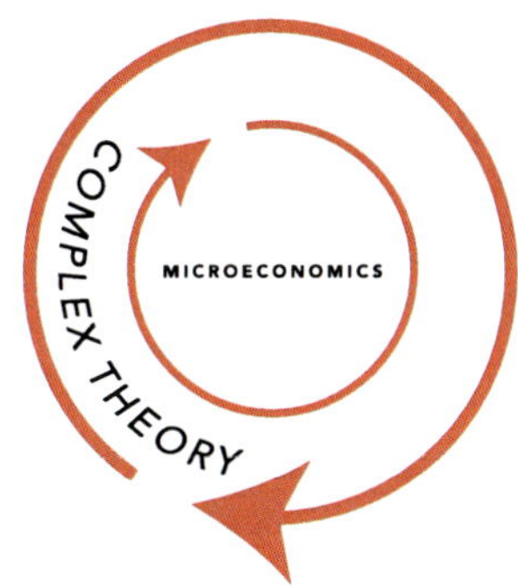

However, let's start simple.

The token economics model has many factors that are worth pondering upon when designing the mechanisms. However, it is important to remember that not all factors are equally relevant to your decentralised ecosystem. Some are more important than others. It all depends on your token function, token use-case, business model and more.

The three main factors of mechanism design are:

1. Governance
2. Non-financial incentives
3. Structure

8.7.1. Governance

Governance looks at how decisions are made and how problems are to be resolved. Back to the topic of incomplete contracts, there are many unforeseen issues that might happen but are not stated in the "rules of the ecosystem" (aka mechanism design). Hence, governance is part of the mechanism model to make decisions and resolve issues.

How decisions are made is the **consensus protocol**. This is usually non-automated.

How problems are being resolved is the **resolution mechanism**. This is usually automated with smart contracts.

8.7.2. Non-Financial Incentives

Token economics is all about incentives. Beyond financial incentives like financial rewards, non-financial incentives play an important role in mechanism design. This includes how voting on issues is done (the mechanism of voting) and how the ecosystem allocates resources.

How voting is done is the **voting protocol**. This is usually non-automated.

How the ecosystem allocates resources is the **allocation mechanism**. This is usually automated with smart contracts.

8.7.3 Structure

Structure of the mechanism looks at how participants transact with each other and how the ecosystem collects information in a decentralised and fair manner, to connect the off-chain with the on-chain world.

How participants transact with each other is the **bargaining protocol**. This is usually non-automated.

How the ecosystem is connected to the off-chain world is the **community information**. This is usually automated with smart contracts.

Mechanism Design

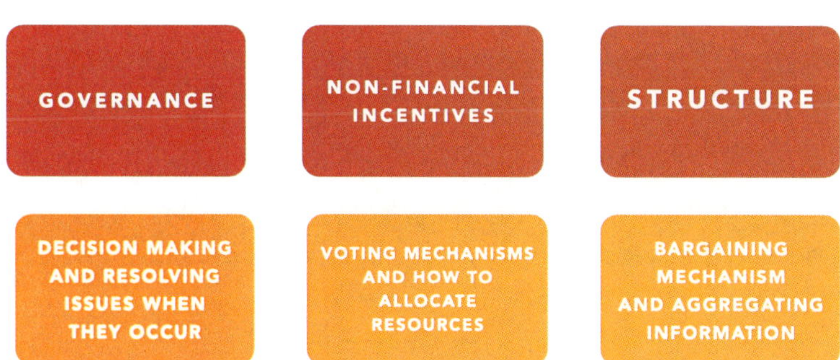

In the context of token ecosystems, mechanism design needs to:

1. Provide adequate **governance** – In the decentralised ecosystem, governance becomes of utmost importance to govern actions of participants in the ecosystem.

2. Include **non-financial incentives** – Financial incentives are discussed in the next pillar, token design. Other incentives need to be considered to account for preferences and asymmetric information.

3. Design **structure** of the mechanism – The mechanism is best to be Pareto efficient to protect the ecosystem, considering the main objective of the token ecosystem.

8.8 Governance

Ecosystems and markets exist to coordinate activities between participants in the market. It is much easier in centralised ecosystems because the central authority has the final say.

> *The debate around centralisation vs decentralisation lies around the fact that some level of centralisation is useful. In the September 2020 KuCoin hack, the hacker took funds out of the centralised exchange and swapped them for other assets. Core developers of some protocols decided to fork the code to retrieve the tokens, like Ocean Protocol (somewhat centralised) while some protocols decided to move on, like Synthetix (decentralised).*

However, it does not work like that in decentralised ecosystems, where there is no centralised 'final say'. Hence, governance becomes a crucial factor.

Governance can help to facilitate the transactions and activities within the ecosystem, making it safe for participation and preventing congestion when issues arise. This can take various forms, including the legislation and design of (smart) contracts.

Governance constrains the ecosystem differently, depending on token function, use-case and objective function. There are concerns with a high degree of centralisation, inflexible smart contracts, consensus protocols and the regulations and laws of the various judiciaries. It is also not limited to just smart contracts, but can also include various resolution mechanisms, consensus protocols and other layers of governance.

Real world example
Governance is highly related to the decision making process.

- How countries are being governed
- How companies make decisions (like board of directors decide that this year, the focus is to increase 20% in sales and 4 new projects from the research department and 10% reduction in cost)

8.9 Non-Financial Incentives

Depending on how attractively financial incentives are designed, non-financial incentives may also be considered as part of the mechanism strategies. This helps to further strengthen the incentive-compatible mechanisms to achieve the objectives.

Here, we are looking at aligning the other incentives to reduce information asymmetry or strengthen the desired strategy in the incentive design. Non-financial incentives can reach an optimal outcome through understanding the mechanisms involved and observing the outcome of choices.

Reputation is also a noteworthy variable to reduce information asymmetry, incentivise participants to report their true information, and so reduce the hidden information (moral hazards) when transacting within the ecosystem.

An important reason why non-financial incentives are important is because of the inevitable incompleteness of contracts. Most ecosystems are continuous and dynamic. Hence, some situations are difficult to foresee or describe in advance. And even if they are, it can be a challenge to incorporate them into the design of the mechanism.

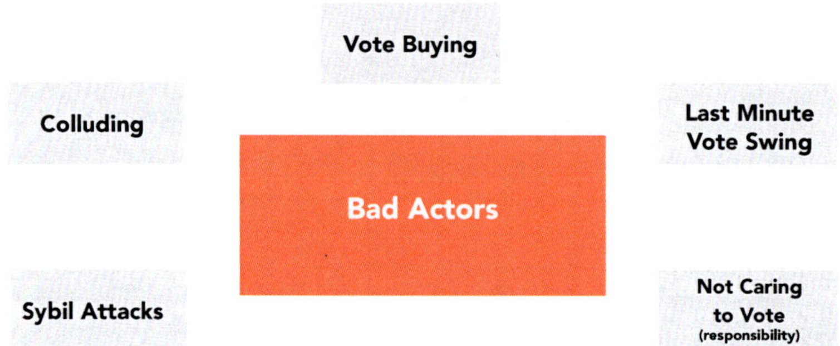

While we want to ensure that participants are incentivised to be part of the ecosystem, we also want to use this mechanism to disincentivise bad actors. Typical bad behaviours include vote buying, plutocracy, last-minute vote swings, participants simply not caring enough to cast their votes.

Hence, other principles from economics and some principles of complexity theory in engineering, will also be used in this area. The foundational principles stem from microeconomics mechanisms, which seek to understand why people behave the way they do. Complexity theory seeks to understand how decentralised systems work in nature. Token ecosystems are continuously evolving and adapting to new information. Therefore, instead of a steady state where mechanisms can be fixed, or statistical mathematics can be applied to analyse equilibriums, we have to look at how decentralised participants will adapt to the dynamic ecosystem by observing previous actions and possible future outcomes.

Real world example

- Superhost status on Airbnb to incentivise users to book their homes, good reviews through providing good service and clean accommodation to the guests, quality pictures to reduce information asymmetry when the guest has to decide to stay at the place based on a few pictures.

- NFI doesn't directly affect the participants now, but affects them in the long-run, especially when interactions are repeated.

8.10 Structure

The structure of the mechanism helps us to design how the various pieces of information relate to one another in the ecosystem. This way, it is easier to coordinate transactions and trade in the ecosystem and mitigate issues when problems arise. Ideally, we want to design a mechanism that is efficient.

Since we need to understand how information or data relate to each other (on-chain to on-chain, off-chain to on-chain, or on-chain to off-chain), it is important to consider the factors like how often participants will transact with each other, the possibility of large influential participants (aka "whale" participants), arbitrage, or bargaining in the ecosystem.

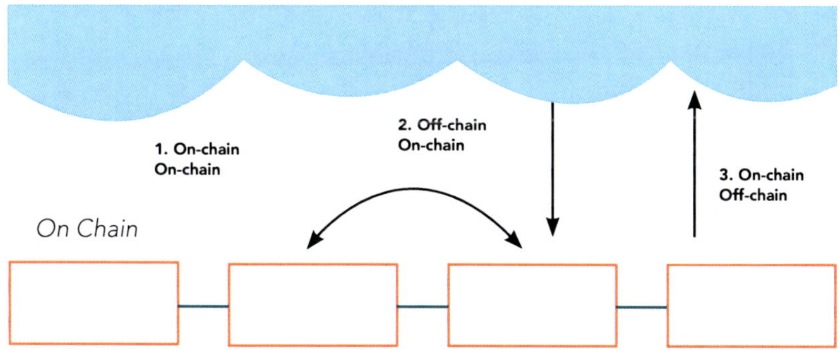

A problem in mechanism structure lies in ecosystems with opposing outcome functions (e.g. investors'/speculators' vs users' objectives). It is unclear how useful traditional mechanism design theory will be in these contexts, e.g., whether approaches based on analysis of specific mechanisms will be more useful than the attempt to characterise optimal mechanisms. Nevertheless, it is precisely by exploiting the special features of many important economic contexts that this approach has generated significant new insights.

Real world example

Structure really depends on the industry, use-case and objectives. The structural design can vary drastically on a case-by-case basis.

Legal sector of class action lawsuits

In the legal sector, one issue is class action lawsuits. These are lawsuits raised by a group of people, usually a group of people that have been wronged. They hire a lawyer to fight for their case against someone, usually a company.

The lawyer is paid by the effort they put in. Depending on if one can observe the lawyer's efforts, the structure to compensate for the lawyer's effort differs. It can be Lodestar Method (billed hourly or by some observable matrix) or menu of percentage fee when we cannot observe the efforts.

On one hand, it is easier to implement the Lodestar Method although with high admin costs. But on the other hand, it is easier to cheat.

So the solution really depends on the objective and factors to decide which structure is the best solution.

Once again, this is just a small case study that is particular to the legal industry. Structure is highly dependent on many variables. The next section has some simple examples and suggestions to get you started.

8.11 Mechanism Design and Token Economics

All ecosystems are **different.** These factors form the basic blocks to design the mechanisms.

Ecosystems come in two layers:
(1) automated mechanisms in code (e.g. smart contracts or algorithms) and (2) dynamic mechanisms which require the input of the ecosystem participants.

8.11.1 Governance (Rules and Strategies)

To govern actions within the token ecosystem in a decentralised manner, should something arise, there must be a balance between automation and human inputs.

1. Decision-making protocol (participants can have a say)
   a. Various decentralised layers of governance, in case of external faults, with different objectives (e.g. having enough votes staked on a proposal before it gets promoted to be voted upon in the governance vote)
   b. Honest interaction between participants
      i. CR mechanism to reveal true value
      ii. Layered TCR
      iii. Design details
   c. DAO, a decentralised autonomous organisation

2. Resolution mechanisms (automated mechanism)
   a. Smart contracts: Hardcoded into the system (e.g. money will automatically be paid when actions are done/ goals are met)
   b. Schelling point

Box 1: DAO, The Future of Decentralised Governance

As the world moves towards digitisation, many things are changing. That includes governance. Economics is really about organising and coordinating resources in our economy. Governance in the economics sense looks at organising and coordinating decision making in our economy. Introducing DAO, a new way of organisation in our increasingly changing economy.

Short-Fall of Traditional Governance

However, there are many short falls to centralised governance. Inefficient execution, incentive misalignment, smaller voices for the minority. What is the solution? Decentralised with autonomy in decision making, with automation and execution by machines, when possible.

That is DAO — decentralised autonomous organisations.

Note: While we mainly talk about blockchain, DAO can exist on both blockchain and non-blockchain technological stacks. It can also work in any digital ecosystem, platform or ledger.

A DAO is mainly a new way of governance and decision making. It could also combine with automated execution via smart contracts.

Importance of DAO

DAO is an organisation-wide decision making. Everyone that is part owner of this organisation also gets to vote on decisions. Decisions can vary — how to allocate funds, which projects to support, what to do with funds.

DAOs are:

1. Not centralised, so no one person can interfere with decision making
2. Transparent and auditable
3. Cannot be shut down by any one

Economics of DAO

Economics is more than just supply and demand. In DAOs, we will discuss these three economics:

- Economics of trust: we want to be able to trust the parties we are interacting with. This is done through smart contracts and skin in the game. Example: PieDAO
- Economics of coordination: decision making with a small group of shareholders is tough. Decision making with a decentralised group is even harder. DAO helps with this coordination. Example: MolochDAO, MakerDAO

- Economics of allocation: like how the government collects tax revenue and decides where to allocate it, the DAO also gets to decide on the governance structure of the ecosystem. Example: KyberDAO, Dash, LAO

Ultimately, DAO is a new way of organisation as our economies continue to evolve. It can use tokens or not. However, it is still part of the economics design since it is a way of decentralised governance. If you go deeper into details of the various DAO mechanisms, you will realise that the mechanisms are not the same.

Chapter 22 goes into more details about DAO.

8.11.2 Non-Financial Incentives (Other incentives to strengthen strategy)

Ensure that incentives account for financial and non-financial variables to strengthen the strategy desired in the mechanism design.

Voting Protocol Solutions (1/2)

PROBLEMS	SOLUTION	REMARKS
EASIEST VOTING PROTOCOL	TRADITIONAL VOTING	ETHEREUM INTEROPERABILITY MARKETPLACE FOR SMALL GAMES PARTNERS
HOW TO LOCK IN VOTING CHOICES	COMMIT REVEAL	INFRASTRUCTURE READY INCREASE SPEED DPOS CONSENSUS SOLVE LIQUIDITY WITH BINANCE DEX
HOW TO INCLUDE INTENSITY	QUADRATIC VOTING	COST TO CAST AN EXTRA VOTE INCREASES MARGINALLY
RULE-BASED VOTING	QUORUM VOTING	MINIMUM NUMBER OF PEOPLE NEEDED TO VALIDATE THE VOTE. POSSIBLE TO MIX WITH OTHER PROTOCOLS

1. Voting Protocol (Participants can have a say in this process)

    a. Traditional voting: each person can vote based on the amount of tokens they have, although this can lead to plutocracy and other attacks (Example: governance tokens)
    b. Commit-reveal: Imagine you shout out your choice to everyone in the network. Then you reveal that choice, and everyone can verify if it is what you committed to. (Example: Ethereum smart contract.)
    c. Quadratic Voting: Instead of 1 person 1 vote, you can now place as many votes as you want on the issue. It shows the intensity of your preference. The cost of the votes are related to the number of votes you cast. The cost of influence is in the units of votes. (Example: Gitcoin grant.)
    d. Quorum voting: minimum number of people to validate the vote (Example: Balancer using Snapshot in its governance process by having enough votes staked on a proposal before it gets promoted to be voted upon in the governance vote)

e. Delegated voting: users delegate votes to others, who can represent better democracy. (Example: Tezos)
f. Partial-lock commit-reveal voting: token-weighted voting. Voters can participate in multiple polls simultaneously and tokens are not staked. (Example Token Curated Registries)
g. Politeia voting: tracking proposals to vote on (Example: Dcred, Politeia)
h. Conviction voting: continuous voting process where voters continuously stake their votes and for a time period till the minimum threshold passes to approve of the proposal. (Example: Giveth)

Allocation Mechanism Solutions

PROBLEMS	SOLUTION	REMARKS
HOW TO ENSURE FAIRNESS	DEFINE IT MATHEMATICALLY WITH EGALITARIAN CURVE	• BY DEFININING ROI BASED ON INVESTED CAPITAL • CHECK OUT "CRYPTOCURRENCY EGALITARIANISM: A QUANTITATIVE APPROACH" PAPER • DEPENDS ON TOKEN FUNCTION
HOW TO REDUCE POWER OF BIG PLAYERS	ALLOW SMALL PLAYERS TO HAVE DISPROPROTIONATE ADVANTAGE	• IS THAT FAIR TO BIG PLAYERS? • WILL THIS WORK? • WHAT ABOUT RISKS OF SYBIL ATTACKS? • ARE SMALL PLAYERS INCENTIVISED TO MAKING RIGHT DECISIONS
NO SKIN IN THE GAME	INTRODUCE STAKING	• MOST EGALITARIAN COINS INVOLVE STAKES AS A DETERRENT FOR BAD ACTIONS • STAKING GIVES AN INCENTIVE BY HAVING SKIN IN THE GAME • WHAT ABOUT OPPORTUNITY COST OF STAKING?

2. Allocation mechanisms (Automated mechanism)

a. Reputation: to mitigate the moral hazard problems when transacting
b. Egalitarian mechanism models: each participant in the ecosystem enjoys the returns in terms of transaction fee, be it online or offline nodes (Example: Algorand.)

8.11.3.Structure (Incentives, Strategies and Efficient Trade)

Ensure that the underlying mechanism that allows the ecosystem to run is efficient. Strategy needs to prevent bad actors from colluding.

1. Bargaining Protocols (Participants can have a say in this process)
   a. Auction mechanisms: multi-attribute auctions, payment mechanisms, pace of auctions as solutions to congestion and safety issues.
   b. Bargaining payment mechanism (within the ecosystem)
      i. Fixed price: Price set by the system/project creator. Take it or leave it. (Example: Prices of tokens on crypto-exchanges)
      ii. Highest bidder/price: The person who bids the highest amount will be accepted. (Example: Bitcoin transaction fee)
      iii. Second highest price: The highest bidder will get the item. But instead of paying the price he bid, he will pay the second highest price instead. (Example: ENS domain)
      iv. Vickrey-Clarke-Groves auction[7]: The person whose bid maximises the total social good of the network is chosen. (Example: Celer Network)
      v. Reverse dutch auction: Price drops as time goes. (Example: Gnosis, Algorand)
      vi. All-pay: Everyone who participates has to pay. (Example: Augur)
      vii. Dynamic pricing: Price set by the smart contract, depending on the liquidity of the pool (Example: Automated market markets like Uniswap and Bancor)

2. Community information: Oracles (Automated mechanism) Oracles to aggregate the flow of information and data off-chain to on-chain within the token ecosystem
   a. Software oracles: handle information available online. (Example: Chainlink)
   b. Hardware oracles: Information available offline, via a client (i.e. RFID sensors, IoT devices). (Examples: VeChain, Weeve.)
   c. Inbound oracles: Provide smart contract with data from the external world (i.e. trade when ETH is worth £X). (Example: Oraclize.)
   d. Outbound oracles: Send data to the external world. Payment made on the blockchain can activate services in the external world (i.e. unlocking the bike by scanning the QR code, which is approved after payment on blockchain is received). (Example: Airbie.)
   e. Consensus-based oracles: Individuals provide input to the oracle system to inform/update the smart contract. (Examples: Augur, SchellingCoin, Witnet.)

Notes

1. Dilip Mookherjee. The 2007 nobel memorial prize in mechanism design theory. Scandinavian Journal of Economics, 110(2):237–260, 2008.

2. Nobel Prize Committee et al. Leonid hurwicz, eric s. maskin and roger b. myerson: Mechanism design theory. Nobel Prize in Economics documents, 2, 2007.

3. Ross, S. A. (1973). The economic theory of agency: The principal's problem. The American economic review, 63(2), 134-139.

4. Samuelson, P. A. (1977). Reaffirming the existence of "reasonable" bergson-samuelson social welfare functions. Economica, 81-88.

5. Fairness is a short word, but it carries a heavy weight. Here's the thing that is quite difficult to manage: what is fairness. What is fair to one is not fair to another. Fairness by "AI" is also dependent on who built it and what data is given to it. Thus, fairness in this context is really an evolving term. Fairness can change depending on the users and participants in the ecosystem. It's important to note who decides what is fair and who defines that. This is where a governance token comes in handy, to capture value the decision of "fairness" in a token.

6. Samuelson, P. A. (1977). Reaffirming the existence of" reasonable" Bergson-Samuelson social welfare functions. Economica, 81-88.

7. MacKie-Mason, J. K., & Varian, H. R. (1994). Generalized Vickrey auctions.

Chapter 9: {Case Study} MakerDAO

9.1 DAO-Based Platform

MakerDAO is a DAO based platform that contains $MKR and $DAI. $MKR and $DAI are two types of tokens in the ecosystem, where $MKR is the governance token and $DAI is the currency token. $MKR (and its holders) govern $DAI and its stability.

> *$DAI is soft pegged to the USD. 1 $DAI is about 1 $USD. This value is maintained by the collaterals and $MKR token holders.*

A DAO is a decentralised autonomous organisation where no central entity owns the ecosystem, nor governs it. It is governed in a decentralised way, both with machine (automation) and humans (non-automation).

In general, MakerDAO is a smart contract platform built on Ethereum. The smart contract creates $DAI tokens using collaterals. These collaterals are digital assets on blockchain, e.g. $ETH, $BAT, $REP, $YFI.

9.1.1 Objectives of MakerDAO

The objective of MakerDAO is to be a global currency that is governed in a decentralised way through autonomous feedback mechanisms and incentive mechanisms.

As of Q4 2020, $DAI has been one of the key enablers in the decentralised finance (DeFi) ecosystem. One issue with the current financial market is that it is opaque and limited in terms of access. With MakerDAO and DeFi, it is possible to increase the efficiency of financial markets through a decentralised and transparent currency, yet at the same time allow a relative stability of token value to facilitate trade.

More on how MakerDAO enables DeFi can be found in Chapter 13.

9.1.2 How It Works

Firstly, how does MakerDAO work?

To understand the mechanism design behind MakerDAO, let's first understand how the system works.

The smart contract currently uses ethereum, through a collateralised debt positions (CDP)[1], to create DAI tokens. These $DAI are thus backed by these on-chain collaterals ($ETH, $BAT). In MakerDAO, the ecosystem is always over-collateralised, so the value of the collateral is always greater than the debt.

MakerDAO, the system, enables anyone to leverage digital assets (e.g. $ETH) to generate $DAI, the output. Then, like any other currencies, $DAI can be freely spent.

Another way to look at it is that new $DAI tokens are minted when a user stakes their digital assets ($ETH, $LINK, $USDC, $YFI) with MakerDAO's smart contract. By staking digital assets, they can create $DAI.

9.1.2.1 Collateral Types in MakerDAO

What are the collateral types in MakerDAO? MakerDAO started with a single collateral, only accepting $ETH. On 18 Nov 2019[2], the Maker foundation moved from single collateral $DAI to multi-collateral $DAI.

This is to hedge against massive fluctuation in any single digital asset. This uses a similar concept to "basket of goods" which is used to measure a country's purchasing power, "basket of reserve currency" to back a country's national currency, or "basket of companies" in a financial portfolio. The goal is to reduce the risk of any sudden movement in a specific variable.

That being said, it is a challenge to design the token economics of the ecosystem and launch a close-to-perfect model. Hence, the goal is to include more digital assets in the collaterals as MakerDAO ecosystem continues to grow and the ecosystem is tested in the real market.

9.1.3 Tokens in MakerDAO

MakerDAO uses a 2-token model in its ecosystem. This is because each token has a specific objective and function.

$DAI is the token with a money function, and it acts as a form of currency. It is a form of payment (via DeFi), store of value (1 $DAI = 1 USD) and unit of account (1 $DAI = 1 USD).

$DAI is also known as a "stable coin" because it is soft pegged to 1 USD. The value is backed by collaterals on-chain via CDP. It is completely decentralised; anyone who wants to own $DAI can buy it on exchange or stake $ETH for $DAI.

$MKR is a token with a utility function, and it acts as a form of governance in the MakerDAO ecosystem. $MKR holders are part of the decentralised governance for $DAI. They are responsible in the decision-making process. They can vote and have a say on issues and proposals in the ecosystem. $MKR tokens are created or destroyed in accordance with price fluctuations of the $DAI coin in order to keep it as close to $1 USD as possible. $MKR has a value, and the value is determined by market forces, e.g. demand and supply of $MKR tokens.

	$DAI	$MKR
TOKEN FUNCTION	MONEY	UTILITY
PURPOSE	STABLECOIN USERS CAN USE THEM IN A P2P PAYMENT OR USE THEM IN THE DEFI ECOSYSTEM.	GOVERNANCE HOLDERS ARE RESPONSIBLE IN DECISION MAKING PROCESS AND CAN VOTE ON ISSUES OR PROPOSALS IN THE ECOSYSTEM
HOW IS VALUE DERIVED	ON-CHAIN COLLATERAL BACKED, E.G. DIGITAL ASSETS (FOR EXAMPLE, ETH)	MARKET FORCES THROUGH DEMAND AND SUPPLY OF MKR TOKENS VIA EXCHANGES
HOW IS SUPPLY CREATED	WHEN SOMEONE CREATES NEW DAI THROUGH CDP OR BURNS DAI THROUGH WITHDRAWING CDP	CREATED OR DESTROYED IN ACCORDANCE WITH PRICE FLUCTUATIONS OF THE DAI, TO KEEP IT AS CLOSE TO $1 USD

9.1.4. MakerDAO in DeFi

DeFi is decentralised finance. DeFi hopes to transform the financial landscape by bringing transparency, speed and accessibility to the industry. It is not about a radical change, but to introduce new use-cases, new products and improve efficiency using new technology.

There are two main ways to enter the DeFi space. Either through a lending protocol or an exchange:

- Lending is where you use your assets as collaterals (e.g. $ETH) to generate a DeFi asset (e.g. $DAI). Interest is payable for this service.
- Exchange is where you give up your assets (e.g. $ETH) for a DeFi asset (e.g. $DAI). You pay a small transaction fee for this service.

> *$DAI plays the role as a lending solution in the DeFi space.*

9.1.4.1. Who uses MakerDAO in DeFi?

To understand the effectiveness of incentive mechanisms, it is important to acknowledge the main participants and users of the system.

MakerDAO remains one of the most used protocols due to the demand of stable pegged USD, like $DAI.

- Lending protocols like Aave, Compound, Celsius. They use $DAI as $DAI has less volatility in pricing and allows for more stable lending and borrowing.
- Decentralised exchanges like Uniswap, Curve, Balancer. $DAI is a common token pegged to USD, which allows for easy trade and demand.
- Derivative platforms like Chai use MakerDAO's $DAI Saving Rates (DSR) to represent a claim on deposit in the DSR. And Opyn to long or short $DAI.

9.2. Applying Mechanism Design to MakerDAO

> *Quick recap: Mechanism design defines the rules of the ecosystem. These rules exist in two forms:*
> - *Automated via smart contracts, code or algorithms*
> - *Non-automated, which require a level of human intervention and participation*

9.3. Governance

In the 2-token model of MakerDAO, governance is clearer as MakerDAO has a governance token[3], $MKR. That being said, the mechanism of making decisions and resolving issues is not as easy as simply holding on to $MKR tokens with hopes that their value will appreciate.

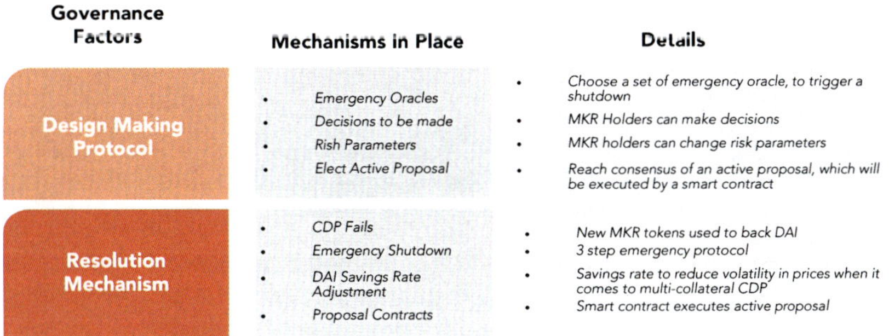

9.3.1 Decision Making Protocol

9.3.1.1 Emergency Oracles

The governance process chooses a set of emergency oracles who have the ability to trigger an emergency shutdown. The emergency oracle is part of the emergency shutdown mechanism. It allows the platform to survive against issues like run on a bank, sudden instant devaluation of the collateral, etc. Maker has its own oracle solution with information from within the DeFi space and other areas.

9.3.1.2. Decisions to be Made

MKR holders can make decisions on issues such as:

- Trigger an emergency shutdown
- Add new CDP type
- Modify existing CDP type
- Modify $DAI saving rate
- Choose a set of price oracles
- Choose a set of emergency oracles

9.3.1.3. Risk Parameters

The following risk parameters are governed by $MKR holders:

- Debt ceiling
- Liquidity ratio
- Savings rate
- Liquidation penalty
- Auction duration
- Auction step size

9.1.3.4 Elect Active Proposal

Linked to the resolution mechanism, $MKR holders can reach consensus on an active proposal. The proposal is then empowered by a smart contract to modify internal variables on the platform.

9.3.2. Resolution Mechanisms

What happens when things do not go as planned? MakerDAO has some solutions and resolution mechanisms in place.

9.3.2.1. CDP Fails

If CDP fails, new $MKR tokens will be used to back $DAI. There will be a total of 1 million $MKR tokens in existence.

9.3.2.2. Emergency Shutdown

This directly enforces a target price on holders of $DAI and CDPs. A 3-step emergency protocol is created:

1. The emergency shutdown is triggered by $MKR voters or the emergency oracle selected by Maker governance. If this happens, CDP users will want to withdraw their collaterals. What happens? (1) Stop CDP creation and manipulation. (2) Freeze price feeds at a fixed value that is then used to process proportional claims for all users. (3) CDP users are able to immediately withdraw the net value of collateral in their CDP.
2. Post-emergency shutdown auction processing. A timer is needed to allow pre-existing collateral auctions to finish. The auction processing period is set by the maker governance to be longer than the longest collateral auction duration.
3. $DAI holders can claim remaining collateral with their $DAI directly, at a fixed rate. There is no time limit for when final claims can be made. In the multi-collateral model, $DAI holders can get proportional claims to collateral types according to the collateral portfolio.

Crypto Black Thursday

On 12 March 2020, a collapse happened in traditional financial markets. This also caused a sudden collapse in the crypto market that triggered an emergency shutdown of these markets.

What Happened? Why was there a collapse?

Two things happened. (1) Coronavirus, a global pandemic, caused great panic in the capital market. (2) There was an oil price war in February 2020 which affected the capital market.

As much as we want the capital market and crypto market to be independent from each other, they are connected. The collapse in the capital market caused a massive collapse in the crypto market. 50% of value was removed from the crypto market.

What happened on crypto?

Crypto is a technology stack. That means data and transactions are flowing from A to B. Imagine an expressway with cars. The expressway size is fixed.

Because value is dropping, people are moving their crypto due to margin calls, moving to liquidate, or purchasing digital assets. This means more cars on the expressway.

The increase in transactions caused network congestion. How is network congestion resolved? As we discussed in Market Design (Chapter 6), gas fees are to be paid. This is the toll for driving the car on the expressway.

During this period, two things happened:

1. The value of collaterals dropped. That means CDP was under-collateralised. That meant people had to either
   a. Add more collaterals OR
   b. Have their collaterals auctioned off to pay for the debt (as seen in the section above)
2. To add collaterals to your CDP, a high gas fee has to be paid.

And the result?

As a result, many people could not add to the collaterals in time. The emergency shutdown was executed as planned and many of the CDPs were auctioned off.

The good: The system worked as it was planned.
The bad: Everyone was too busy with transactions and collaterals. Some of the CDP were auctioned off at $0. That means some people managed to get a lot of $ETH for free, minus the debt owed. That amounted to about 5.4M $DAI.

For a more detailed explanation, Maker documented their experience online[4].

9.3.2.3. $DAI Savings Rate Adjustment

Prices deviate in the short run. To deal with this, the $DAI savings rate changes to reduce price instability. The $DAI savings rate is a global system parameter that affects how much $DAI holders can earn in return on their holding over time, and base borrowing costs for generating $DAI from CDPs.

9.3.2.4. Proposal Contracts

$MKR token holders will cast votes to elect a proposal as active. Proposals are executed once they have gained approval by $MKR voters. The changes are applied immediately to the internal governance variables, then the proposal contract wipes logic and is not re-used. Modifications are delayed for 24h until the proposal contract takes effect. This is to protect the platform against malicious governance proposals that harm the system.

9.3.2.5. Malicious Hacking

Malicious hacking can be against smart contract infrastructure. In the worst-case scenario, all the collaterals are stolen. Smart contract security is in place in MakerDAO and undergoes security audits. The smart contract also requires formal verification to prevent hacks from happening because a smart contract can be subject to internal technical hacks. This means bugs in the code, not an external technical exploit or governance token hacking.

9.3.2.6. Black Swan Event

One issue is the risk of black swan events. These are rare but significant events that impact the ecosystem negatively. CDP collateral has a debt ceiling that is allowed to grow over time, and the ecosystem is always over-collateralised.

9.3.2.7. Pricing Errors

Since information comes from oracles and there can be technical issues such as mispricing error or market factors that affect the value of $DAI, this can impact the MakerDAO ecosystem and internal variables. The Maker community has a large capital pool to act as Keepers of the market to maximise rationality and market efficiency so as to allow $DAI to work despite market errors.

Keepers[5] are incentivised by profit opportunities to contribute to a decentralised system. They also trade $DAI around target prices.

9.4 Non-Financial Incentives

MakerDAO has various incentives to align the incentives of all participants to ensure that $DAI is stable with respect to USD. Since $MKR tokens are part of the governance mechanisms, there are more considerations to designing them as incentives.

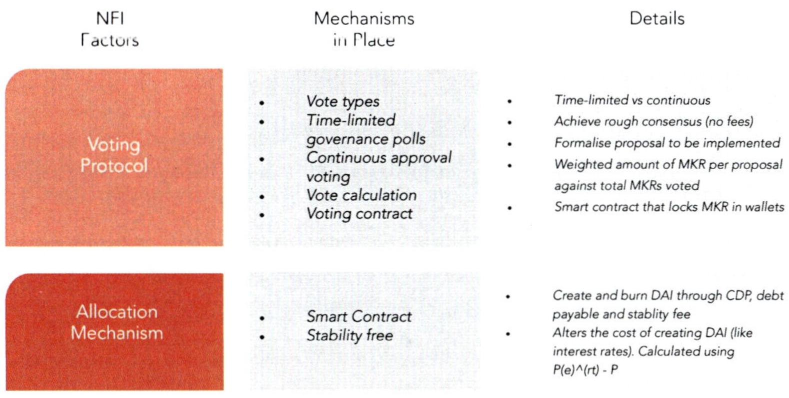

9.4.1. Voting Protocol

How voting is done, what is the purpose of voting, what types of voting are there?

MKR tokens are used to vote on issues. 1 $MKR token = 1 vote. These issues include determining the $DAI savings rate.

9.4.1.1.Vote Types

There are 2 types of votes available:

- Time-limited poll. Governance polls: a signal vote to establish soft consensus on important matters and gauge the sentiment of potential risk parameters
- Continuous approval voting. Executive vote: execute "hard" and definite changes to the system

9.4.1.2. Time Limited Governance Polls

A governance poll is used to achieve a rough consensus in the governance community before votes are cast, since votes have the cost of gas fees. Thus, the outcome of voting is already known. The voting process itself is not decision making, but a way to securely implement decisions that are made into the system.

9.4.1.3. Continuous Approval Voting

MKR holders have to maintain the health of the MakerDAO ecosystem, stability of peg and defend against bad proposals. $MKR tokens are used to vote for proposals that are beneficial and will be implemented into the ecosystem.

The policy of staked votes continuously challenges and reinforces the status quo of the system. Proposals are compared to the majority vote between the new desired proposal and the most recent successful proposal. Old proposals are deleted and wiped away, so changes to old successful proposals need to be submitted with changes. The system is continuously active, which requires continuous governance. New proposals can be submitted at any time by any $MKR token holder.

9.4.1.4. Votes Calculation

How are votes calculated? Votes are weighted by the amount of $MKR that votes for a proposal. For example, 50 stakeholders hold 600 $MKR and vote proposal A. 100 stakeholders hold 400 tokens and vote proposal B. A wins by 60% since 60% of the total votes have gone to proposal A (600 / [600+400] = 60%).

9.4.1.5. Voting Contract

The voting contract uses a simple smart contract mechanism. It locks up $MKR and is controlled through hot or cold wallets to ensure the safety of the staked $MKR. The cost involved is the gas payable when a vote is cast.

A proxy contract can also be created to provide additional security benefits. For instance, proposals can be voted with $MKR from a cold wallet through a hot wallet to gauge the sentiment on an issue. Then, the $MKR will be returned to the cold wallet and no fees are required.

9.4.2.Allocation Mechanism

9.4.2.1 Smart Contract

The smart contract that governs the creating and burning of DAI creates an autonomous feedback mechanism through:

- Generate DAI from collateralised CDP
- Deposit collateral
- Pay debt and stability fee
- Withdraw collateral and close CDP

The smart contract holds collateral assets ($ETH) and allows the user to generate $DAI. The user can exchange their collateral asset back after repaying the debt accrued and the equivalent amount of $DAI.

9.4.2.2 Stability Fee

The stability fee alters the cost of creating $DAI. It is a variable like interest rates on a loan.

The Maker smart contract collects a fee calculated against $DAI withdrawn against the collateral held in a CDP. People get to vote on the savings rate.

Users pay the stability fee when they want to pay the debt by returning $DAI to CDP. Think of this as interest on a loan. The rate is proportional to the amount of $DAI returned. The amount can be paid in $DAI or $MKR.

This risk parameter is used to manage supply and demand for $DAI during negative growth periods. When the demand for $DAI decreases, the savings rate associated with minting new $DAI increases. More users will want to repay the CDP (debt) and $DAI is burned. This reduces the $DAI available and increases the prices of $DAI. When the fees increase, it is also more expensive to create new $DAI, which increases the prices of $DAI once again.

The fee is calculated on a continuous basis using a continuous compound formula: $P(e)^{rt} - P$. The collected fees are then burned.

9.5 Structure

MakerDAO focuses on transparency and decentralisation. Hence, the structure of the economics mechanism needs to be clear and easily understood. This is especially important as part of the governance token, $MKR.

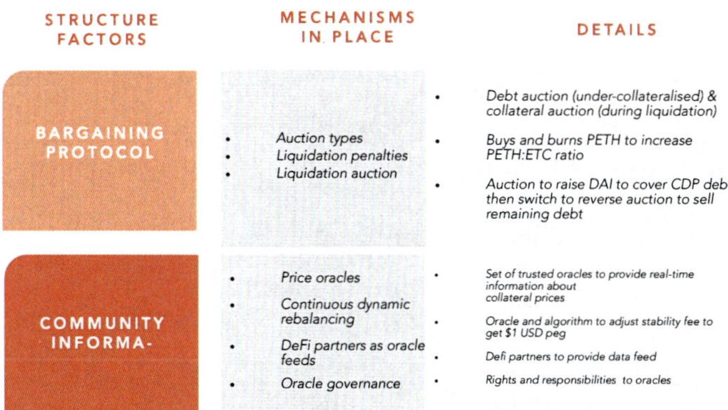

9.5.1 Bargaining Protocol

9.5.1.1 Auction Types

There are two types of auctions in MakerDAO when undergoing an emergency shutdown and liquidation:

- Debt auction: when CDP becomes under-collateralised, a reverse auction is created to sell $MKR for $DAI.
- Collateral auction: collateral from CDP is sold through an auction during liquidation. This is to ensure that the debt owned by the CDP is covered and to give the CDP owner the best price for their excess collateral refund.

9.5.1.2 Liquidation Penalty

The liquidation penalty determines the maximum DAI raised from a collateral auction. This is used to buy MKR and remove it from the supply. The excess collateral is returned to the CDP owner. Think of this as a stock buyback in a company, to reduce the stock available and increase the prices of stock.

9.5.1.3 Liquidation Penalty (Single Collateral DAI)

Note: this system is no longer in use. But it is useful to understand how it works before it gets more complicated with the multi-collateral $DAI system.

In a single-collateral DAI model, the liquidation penalty buys and burns PETH to increase the PETH to ETH ratio.

The protocol for liquidation is as follows:

1. Defaulted CDP is closed by a Keeper. CDP assets are sent to a smart contract (LPC) and the CDP assets are for sale.
2. Liquidation penalty AND stability fee are applied to the $DAI-dominated loan.
3. LPC removes PETH collateral to satisfy the outstanding debt.
4. CDP owners can remove their remaining collateral. They receive the value of the leftover collateral minus debt, stability fee and liquidation fee.
5. The seized PETH is for sale.
6. The $DAI earned from PETH sale is burned and removed from the supply.
7. If there is insufficient $DAI from the sale, PETH is drawn from the pool and offered for sale. But this negatively impacts the ETH:PETH ratio.

9.5.1.4. Liquidation Auction (Multi Collateral DAI)

A liquidation auction will be used when MakerDAO moves to multi-collateral $DAI.

9.5.1.4.1 High-Level Understanding

High-level understanding: let's say the CDP is valued at 500 $DAI. MakerDAO buys the collateral of the CDP and sells it via an automatic auction.

An auction is used to raise 500 $DAI. Each bid increases the CDP by 10 $DAI. The bid reaches 500 $DAI. This is to have enough $DAI to cover the CDP debt.

Now, it switches the auction mechanism to reverse auction. CDP is auctioned by dropping the price. CDP starts at 500 $DAI and in each time period it decreases the CDP by 10 $DAI. It stops when someone decides to buy it.

9.5.1.4.2. Technical Explanation

MakerDAO will buy collateral of a CDP and sell it in an automatic auction. The auction will determine the price of the CDP by market forces, since prices are unknown. The system will raise enough $DAI to cover the CDP debt. This is done by diluting the supply of $MKR tokens and sell it to bidders in an auction format.

Collateral of the CDP is sold, where proceeds up to the CDP debt amount plus liquidation penalty will be used to buy $MKR and remove it from the supply. This counteracts the $MKR dilution in the previous stage.

When enough $DAI is raised via the auction to cover the CDP debt and penalty, the auction switches to reverse auction to sell as little collateral as possible. Leftover collaterals will be returned to the original owners.

9.5.2 Community information

How does MakerDAO gather decentralised information from the community? What does it do with it and how does it affect the closed-loop token ecosystem?

9.5.2.1 Price Oracles

A set of trusted price oracles are chosen by $MKR voters. These provide real-time information about the prices of collateral assets.

Maker's oracle uses two feeds, Light Feed and Dark Feed . Light Feed comes from raw data from DeFi protocols. Dark Feed are anonymous individuals. The goal is to have a 1:1 ratio. Any protocol can apply to be a Light Feed to provide information to the Maker system. The governance then provides Data Models and tooling to calculate prices of digital assets.

9.5.2.2. Continuous Dynamic Rebalancing

With multi-collateral $DAI, oracles and algorithms are used to adjust the stability fee to get the $1 USD peg. A smart contract is triggered and affects the stability fee when $DAI is trading above or below $1 USD. This works in a semi-automatic manner so $MKR token holders can also have a say on the stability fee.

9.5.2.3 DeFi Partners as Oracle Feeds

Feeds are bots run by individuals to publish prices of assets in real time. Using DeFi partners as oracle feeds, it provides both pseudonymous feeds, but the reputation of the partners are also being staked, reducing the risk of false information.

As of Q4 2020, the DeFi partners are dYdX, 0x, TokenSets, Gnosis, Kybe[7], Infura, Etherscan, Gitcoin, and Argent[8]. These are the Light Feed oracles.

9.5.2.4 Oracle Governance

An oracle governance[9] framework is a proposal to define the rights and responsibilities of the governance mechanism. It includes:

- Defining criteria for selecting new feeds
- Defining criteria for selecting new oracles
- Adding and removing feeds
- Adding and removing oracles
- Identifying performance metrics for feeds and oracles
- Selecting the oracle price sensitivity parameters
- Selecting the Oracle Security Module (OSM) delay parameter

9.6 Conclusion

Although the MakerDAO ecosystem is known as a stable coin that is pegged to the USD, it is ultimately a decentralised monetary platform that is transparent. It might seem to stick to the USD in terms of valuation, but the ecosystem in place is robust with both automated and non-automated mechanisms.

This is just Layer 1 of possible enhancements to the financial industry moving forward. There are plenty of use-cases of $DAI in DeFi applications that can really unlock constraints in the fintech industry.

9.7 MakerDAO References

- *MakerDao whitepaper: https://makerdao.com/en/whitepaper#overview-of-the-$DAI-stablecoin-system*
- *Blog: https://blog.makerdao.com*

Notes

1. CDP: A digital asset that is added into the MakerDAO ecosystem. It holds collateral assets deposited by the user and permits the user to generate $DAI. Generating $DAI accrues debt. This debt can be paid anytime or when the owner wants to withdraw their collateral (CDP).

2. https://blog.makerdao.com/multi-collateral-$DAI-is-live/

3. In Q2 2020, governance tokens became one of the most popular token functions for native tokens. They serve the philosophy of a decentralised ecosystem, governed and owned by the community. Whilst the narrative is important, it is important to add the incentive mechanism and governance function into the design of the token. For example, how decisions are determined, how votes are evaluated, how to ensure a level of governance that is deemed to be "decentralised" enough.

4. The event allowed Maker to test their system in times of massive price collapse, while also testing for robustness in the system. As a result of this event, improvements were made to the governance mechanism. Specifically, a diverse collateral portfolio, structured governance process (machines) with versatile response (humans), and to improvement of the Keeper role in the governance system. https://blog.makerdao.com/the-market-collapse-of-march-12-2020-how-it-impacted-makerdao/

5. The crisis of 12 March 2020 highlighted some limitations of the Keeper ecosystem. During the market collapse, Keeper bots had trouble accessing funds for liquidity purposes and some could not participate in auctions.

6. For more information, check https://forum.makerdao.com/c/oracles/13.

7. Kyber, Infura, Etherscan and Gitcoin are the newest Light Feed oracles as of 9 July 2020, https://blog.makerdao.com/makerdao-approves-4-new-light-feeds-for-oracles/.

8. Argent is approved as a Light Feed oracle on 20 July 2020, https://blog.makerdao.com/governance-polls-psm-implementation-appoint-argent-as-an-oracle-light-feed-and-more/.

9. MakerDAO Oracle Governance: https://blog.makerdao.com/introducing-oracles-v2-and-defi-feeds/

Chapter 10: Token Design

This is the last of the three pillars in the design of token economics ecosystems.

10.1 Token Design 101

Tokens are the incentives of the ecosystem. Hence, we can directly affect behaviours of participants through the design of these incentives. Token design applies to the design of tokens, specifically related to their core function: security, utility, money, pegged token (aka stable token). Tokens can also be fungible or non-fungible in nature.

Token design is everything that involves the token, for example, how are the tokens used to incentivise specific behaviour, token supply in the market, and token policy. Token policy is how the token is governed and managed.

10.2 Why do we Need Token Design?

In the first pillar (Chapter 6), we learnt that market design is to design the environment for participants to interact and transact with each other. The second pillar, mechanism design (Chapter 8), is to define the rules of the behaviours within the environment. This last pillar is to design the incentive itself: the token.

As the token can have various functions, the factors to consider in the design of tokens can vary vastly. It also depends on the objective of the ecosystem, whether it is to encourage users to save the tokens, to use the tokens, or encourage specific behaviours like increase brand exposure. The token is a medium to achieve the objective(s) of the ecosystem.

10.3 How is it Important to my Ecosystem?

Depending on the permissioned or permission-less distributed ledger technology (DLT) system, some of the factors in token design may not be relevant. Some permissioned DLT systems also may not require tokens. However, rules are still required (aka mechanism design), hence mechanism design and token design are two separate pillars.

10.4 Token Design 102 - What is Token Design

Concepts	Explanation
What	Token engineering of tokens, the main incentive of the ecosystem
How	Rules are coded or embedded into the token E.g How tokens will be managed and goverened, the functions and rights
Why	Influences the behaviours of participants E.g change the relative costs and benefits of choices made

What? Token design is the engineering of tokens, the main incentive of the ecosystem

How? It seeks to design how tokens will be managed and governed, and the functions and rights they can hold. (Mechanism design, on the other hand, seeks to design how the ***system*** is managed and governed.)

Why? These token designs are rules that are coded or embedded into the tokens, that influence the behaviours of participants. A change can affect the relative costs and benefits of choices that participants make.

10.4.1. What Does Token Design Include?

Since token design is the engineering of the token as a core incentive, a significant factor that affects the design is the function of the token. It could be a security, utility, currency or pegged token (e.g. stable token). Depending on the functions, the design can differ greatly under the various economic domains, e.g. monetary economics, financial economics, property rights.

Token Design Includes:

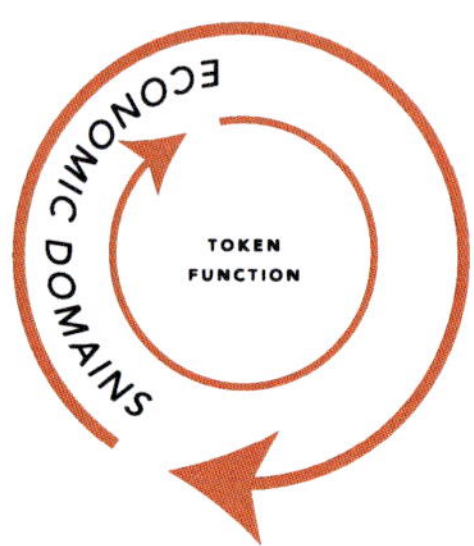

- Incentivise specific behaviours (demand)
- Supply of tokens
- Prices level of tokens
- Token governance

10.5 Token Design 103 - Why Study Token Design?

These token design rules are coded or embedded into the decentralised system, sometimes with a smart contract, i.e., the smart contract can contain a mathematical function that governs the exchange rate of the token instead of exposing the exchange rates to factors outside of the ecosystem. That could affect the stability of the value of tokens.

Token design is important to ensure that the tokens, the incentive of the ecosystem, follow the rules of the tokenised economy. Since token economies are decentralised, it is important to establish certain rules of the tokens into the programmable code to ensure a level of coordination and governance.

10.6 Factors in Token Design

To work well, tokens need to:

- Define the **token policy**.
- Reward with **financial incentives** to encourage specific behaviours outlined in Mechanism Design.
- Design **proper architecture** of the token bearing in mind various aspects of the tokens including property rights, identity, payoffs.
- Mathematical **proofs or models** for necessary valuation, supply, etc.

10.6.1 Token Policy

Token policy is adapted from traditional monetary economics and monetary policy. It seeks to design how tokens will be managed and governed. This is unlike mechanism design, where mechanism design seeks to design how the system mechanism is governed and managed.

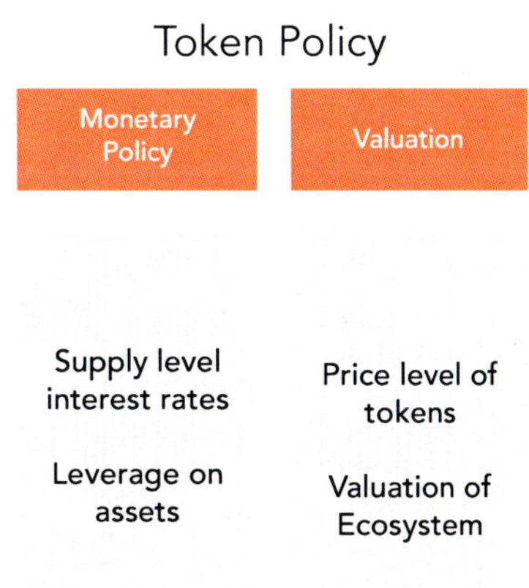

Token policy includes monetary policy and valuation of the tokens.

Traditional monetary policy[1] includes open market operations, discount rates, required reserves and quantitative easing. The equivalent in token policy is to open the market by listing on exchanges or secondary market transactions. Although discount rates are not as applicable in the decentralised market, the relevant application can be through leverage of collateralised assets or through the savings function of the token policy.

The incentives for token holders to save is a function of the expected growth in demand of the platform and expected growth in money supply[2]. The required reserves can be achieved through saving choices as the ICO design stage, bonded in a token bonding curve[3] or as a leverage on the collateral in the smart contract[4].

Token policy constrains markets differently, based on the objectives of the token ecosystems, such as ensuring price stability (pegged tokens), fairness through active participation, leverage on collaterals, etc.

Unlike monetary policy, token policy can extend to use-cases beyond the function of money. Token policy also considers expansionary or contractionary policy[5], such as minting or burning tokens available in the network when necessary.

10.6.1.1 Token Valuation

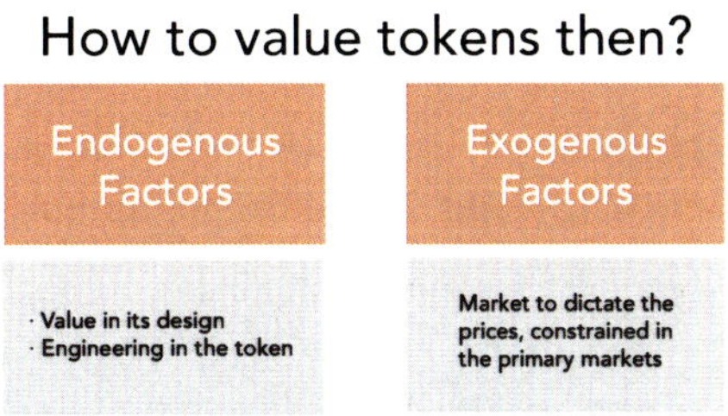

Valuation is a factor that is more relevant to token functions like securities and money. The tokens should derive their values from factors within the ecosystem like platform activities, growth of the platform, dynamic price equilibrium, etc. The monetary policy also plays a role in determining the valuation of the tokens. Two valuation models for utility tokens use dynamic price equilibrium and dynamic adoption[6].

How to value tokens then?

Endogenous Factors	Exogenous Factors
· Value in its design · Engineering in the token	Market to dictate the prices, constrained in the primary markets

Real World Example

Exchange Rate Regimes

Types	Fixed Exchange	Intermediate Exchange	Floating Exchange
Explanation	Pegged to something (gold, USD, EUR) at a specific rate	Exchange Rate us within a specific range of values	Exchange Rate fluctuates in a wide range
Real World	· Currency union (EUR) · Panama pegs to USD · SGD and BND	· CHF to Euros · HKD to USD · Currency Basket (SGD)	Major Currencies · USD · GBP · JPY
On- Chain World	· Tether, USDC, USDT pegs to USD · Bancor's smart tokens · Gold-backed crypto	· MakerDAO DAI pegs to USD	· BTC · LTC · ETH

The central bank of the US, the Federal Reserve System (FED), controls how the USD is managed. The Bank of England controls how the GBP is managed. The MAS controls how SGD is managed. Pretty much a handful of smart people in the institutions decide how the currency will be managed. This is a centralised approach.

The difference in the crypto world is that it is mostly decentralised. This means that the main decisions are embedded in code and baked into the token ecosystem. Depending on the mechanism design, people in the network can vote to change certain systems. This approach gives more power to the people.

For example, Bitcoin increases the supply of bitcoin algorithmically by halving the block rewards every four years. It also has a limit on the total amount of $BTC available. On the other hand, MakerDAO increases the supply of $DAI with collaterals. $MKR tokens get to vote on the stability fee that the collaterals generate. There is no limit on the total amount of $DAI available.

10.6.2 Financial Incentives

Financial Incentives
Rewards for Participating

Returns on
Equity Owned

It is important to balance introducing too much incentives at the beginning to encourage adoption.

The ecosystem can reach mass adoption much easier with financial incentives to encourage participation. Financial incentives include participating in platform activities and returns to investment. Some aspects stem from fiscal policy, in terms of taxes (transaction fees) and savings or investments (via the foundation).

10.6.3 Platform Activities

Sometimes this involves financial rewards for joining (e.g. airdrops), and it can also involve potential returns to equity owned, or arbitrage on the exchange rates of the token price in dollars in two periods. Financial incentives become an important constraint to achieving network effects in the ecosystem. However, it is also important to balance introducing too many incentives at the beginning to encourage adoption, which might lead to issues of pump and dump schemes.

10.6.3.1 Utility Token Inflation

In general, platform activities are when native tokens are used as a reward when the transaction activity is not related to the native token. Examples are:

- Compound rewards lenders and borrowers with $COMP. Lenders and borrowers need not only trade in $COMP.
- Uniswap rewards liquidity providers with $UNI for staking tokens in their decentralised exchange. Traders are free to trade in any token, not only $UNI.

10.6.4. Returns to Stake

Returns of investment of returns to stake is another financial incentive to consider. There are many ways protocols are rewarding stakers as an incentive mechanism.

10.6.4.1 Token Inflation with Staking

Unlike the utility token inflation model, this token inflation is a result of staking. Users have to stake native tokens and be rewarded with native tokens. E.g. Kyber rewards $KNC to stakers via the governance voting allocation.

This becomes an interesting play between tokens locked up in stake and inflation rate of the ecosystem.

10.6.4.2 Token Curated Registries

TCR (token curated registries) were very popular in 2018/19. We mentioned TCRs back in mechanism design (8.11.1). Instead of staking as a collateral, decentralised liquidity provider or as part of governance, TCR uses staking as a signal to rank preferences. Users are then rewarded for their participation via native tokens. Ocean Protocol uses a Layered TCR[7] to allow users to rank the datasets and earn OCEAN.

More details of token curated registries can be found in Chapter 13.5.

10.6.4.3 Financial Security Function

For security tokens, the tokens could be an alternative to traditional financial assets and there is an opportunity cost to holding them. This is where financial economics is used. Returns on investment is also a huge factor for projects in the decentralised finance (DeFi) movement.

> *In DeFi, this "returns to stake" mechanism is paired with a governance utility function to add to the value accrual of the native token. As a result, it mixes two asset classes in traditional finance: equities and fixed income.*

10.6.4.4 Non-Fungible Tokens (NFT)

In Q3 2020, we saw a cross between two categories in crypto, finance (DeFi) and art (eSports, crypto-art, collectibles). Aavegotchi was one of the projects that combined both. Aavegotchi allows users to stake their \$aDAI, interest generating \$DAI from Aave, to generate non-fungible tokens and access the Aavegotchi platform.

It is such composability that allows the various protocols to interact and build upon each other. Like Lego blocks, tokens are embedded with rules like bricks, which can be built upon other token Lego blocks to create new structures.

10.6.5 Architecture

Architecture
Design of Token Structure

Property Rights	Distribution Structure	Algorithm, Math and Code

Tokens can help to govern actions through property rights and establish trust through proper structure.

The architecture of the token reflects the components that make up the token, including factors like property rights (defining rights that the tokens hold, payoffs based on the rights) and identity features.

Property Rights

Property rights include bargaining power, ownership, identity and property rights. Other than the rights to own the token, it can also include the rights to stake, the rights to participate in governance mechanisms, the rights to own part of the project or underlying asset, etc. Combining this with interest rates (token policy), the tokens can be designed in new creative ways to incentivise users.

Identity is another variable of consideration. The role of blockchain is enabling the property rights inherent in the concept of self-identity. This is due to traceability of ownership over self-identity without a third-party.

10.6.5.1 Token Design of Non-Fungible Tokens (NFT)

When designing tokens, it is also important to remember the other types of tokens available. The current token designs discussed are mainly fungible tokens. The class of non-fungible tokens represent real world assets, digital unique assets or rights like intellectual property rights will open a new dimension to the design richness in the architecture of tokens.

Box 2: A Case Study on Digital Currencies

One key area in gaining mass adoption is to extend the function of tokens to outside the ecosystem, instead of just allowing them to be transacted within the ecosystem. Hence, this box is on digital currencies.

Money has 3 functions

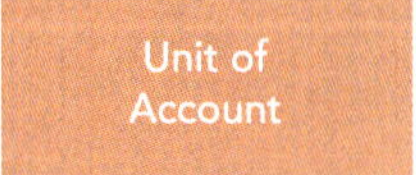

Medium of Exchange

Store of Value

Digital currency is a category of currency that exists electronically. Currencies are a form of money with 3 main functions: a unit of account, medium of exchange and store of value. They are digital representations of currency, instead of physical representation like coins and dollar bills.

Added advantages that digital currencies has over physical currencies include, but are not limited to:

- Instantaneous transactions
- Automatic update of accounting ledger
- Cross-border transfer of ownership

Digital currencies are not new. What is new is the technological infrastructure that digital currencies are built upon. Digital currencies can exist on any digital ledger, and today, new forms of digital ledgers exist, like decentralised ledger technology.

Types of Digital Currencies

Digital Currencies

STATUS	LEGAL TENDER			NOT LEGAL TENDER
NAMES	Current Bank Issued Digital Currency (CBDC)		Cryptocurrency	Virtual Currency · Everything else that is a digital form of money
UNDERLYING TECHNOLOGICAL INFRASTRUCTURE	Built on DLT	Built on private, non-distributed ledgers	Built on DLT Encrypted with cryptography	Built on digital ledgers · Private, non-private · Distributed, non-distributed
VALUATION	· Central bank monetary policies · Government fiscal policies		· Currency back by fiat and 1:1 peg (Tether) · Pegged to a basket of goods / currencies (Libra) · Market forces to determine value (bitcoin)	· Self-determined peg (1 QQ token = 1 RMB) · Self-determined valuation (world of warcraft money) · Market forces (Liden dollars in second life)

Legal Tender

Central Bank Issued Digital Currency

Central bank digital currency (CBDC) is a digital form of fiat money issued by a central bank. Fiat money is money established through government regulation or law. Other terminologies include digital fiat currency or digital base money.

Base money is money in the economy. That includes money held by commercial bank reserves, total money circulating in the public and cash that is held in the central bank's vault. It is money that is liquid, meaning you can change them into other assets without difficulty.

It can be built on distributed ledger technology or private, non-distributed digital ledgers.

Not Legal Tender

Digital currencies that are not legal tender includes privately-issued cryptocurrency and virtual currency.

Privately Issued Cryptocurrency

Private issued cryptocurrency is a digital currency issued on DLT and secured with cryptography. Hence the term, "crypto" and "currency".

By being issued privately, it means that it is issued by a private institution, foundation or consortium. This is opposed to currency issued by a legal established institution like central bank or credit institution or e-money institution.

That being said, the premise of cryptocurrency being built on DLT is that it is distributed, at least to a certain extent.

Privately Issued Virtual Currency

Virtual currency is a type of digital money that is unregulated and accepted among a specific digital ecosystem or community. It has similar characteristics as traditional fiat money, except that it is not legal tender and not issued by a central bank.

Virtual currencies may not be universally accepted, but it is accepted within a specific community. For example, in the gaming community like World of Warcraft or an ecosystem of commercial ecosystems, e.g. QQ coins in Tencent's ecosystem.

Monetary Policies that can be Implemented

Monetary Policies

STATUS	LEGAL TENDER		NOT LEGAL TENDER
NAMES	Monetary Policies	1:1 Pegged Exchanged Rates	Self-determined Rates or Market Forces
EXPANSIONARY (INCREASE SUPPLY)	· Increase inflation · Reduce interest rates (ELB) · Reduce require reserves · Reduce discount rates (LiBOR) · Sell more gov. bonds · Print more money	Can't do anything (No indenpendent monetary policy)	· Reduce interest rates (ELB) · Reduce collateralised assets · Create more native currency · Increase leverage on collaterals
CONTRACTIONARY (REDUCE SUPPLY)	· Reduce inflation · Increase interest rates (ELB) · Increase required reserves · Increase discount rates (LiBOR) · Buy gov. bonds	Can't do anything (No indenpendent monetary policy)	· Increase interest rates · Reduce supply of money (burn) · Reduce collateralised assets · Reduce leverage on collateral · Increase savings function

Since digital currencies are a form of money, to govern the digital currency, monetary policies are used. Monetary policy manages and governs money, be it physical fiat or digital currency. More specifically, monetary policy affects the money supply. Money demand is affected by market forces.

Whoever that governs the money supply can implement various types of monetary policy:

- Expansionary policy (increase money supply)
- Contractionary policy (reduce money supply)

Legal Tender

Central Bank Issued Digital Currency

Like physical fiat, the central bank implements various monetary policy to affect the money supply. Typical tools by the central bank includes, affecting the

- Inflation rates
- Interest rates
- Required reserves
- Inter-bank lending rates
- Open-market operations: Buying or selling government bonds
- Printing more money

Not Legal Tender

There are 2 types of non legal tender money:

1. Money that is a fixed 1:1 exchange rate
2. Money with an independent monetary policy

Monetary policy can be a pegged exchange rate or a self-determining exchange rate

Fixed Exchange Rate

For digital currencies with a fixed exchange rate[9], they do not have an independent money policy. They have to follow the monetary policy of the said fixed currency, e.g. monetary policy by the central bank in USD (Federal Reserve).

Independent Monetary Policy

The other types of digital currencies have an independent monetary policy. The policies implemented are similar to the central bank's monetary policy.

- Interest rates
- Collateralised assets (underlying assets backing the valuation of native currency)
- Creating or burning native currency
- Leverage on collateralised assets: as opposed to reserve ratios mandated by central banks to commercial banks, the monetary policy can alter the leverage given on the collateralised asset
- Savings function: savings function can be affected through interest rates, which affects the returns of the asset (native currency). This can create a substitution effect against other types of assets.

Digital currencies are not new, including the monetary policies to affect the supply of currency. However, there could be new tools with more efficient implementation of monetary policies moving forward.

10.7 Token Design and Token Economics

All tokens are **different**, especially since they can have different functions. These factors here form the basic blocks to design the mechanisms. They may or may not be relevant.

10.7.1 Token Policy (Attributes of a Token)

At the design stage token policy can be defined then coded into the token ecosystem.

1. Monetary policy
   a. Supply of tokens, expected growth of money supply
   b. Inflationary, dis-inflationary or deflationary tokens
   c. Distribution of token allocation
   d. Velocity: how often tokens change hands (if necessary)
   e. Exchange rate regime: fixed-exchange (pegged), intermediate-exchange, floating-exchange
   f. Zero-lower bound (ZLB) or effective-lower bound (ELB)
   g. Negative interest rates or currency with an expiry date
   h. Reserve ratio or leverage given on collaterals

2. Token valuation: variables that can allow tokens to have endogenous value

a. Endogenous Factor
   i. Backed by off-chain assets: fiat currency, gold assets, even the possibility of government bonds
   ii. Bonding curve (discussed further in Chapter 11)
   iii. Net present value
   iv. Expected value of funds
   v. Dynamic price equilibrium
   vi. Demand growth of platform or demand of tokens
   vii. Savings function: Savings function depends on the:

- Growth rate of tokens
   a. [Automated] Fixed token inflation increases tokens every specific time period
   b. [Not automated] Token inflation with respect to tokens staked or locked-up

- Expectations of future price level (or utility) of tokens
    c. E.g. holding the token longer increases the ranking of the token compared to newly minted tokens. This could result in shorter withdrawal times when the token is used to stake
    d. E.g. the exchange rate of native tokens increases over time due to growth of the ecosystem, which means that the token-dominated price of products decreases.

    So there is an incentive to save the native token, since the expected future prices of products is lower

Savings function

Growth Rate of Tokens	[Automated] E.g. BTC increases tokens every 10 mins due to block validation [Not Automated] E.g. Tokens released from holding by investors or others due to lock-up periods
Expectations of Tokens	E.g. Old tokens increases the ranking of the token compared to newly minted tokens. This could result in shorter withdrawal times when staking. E.g Exchange rate of native token increases over time due to growth of the ecosystem, which means that the token-dominated price of products decreases.

viii. Heterogeneity of user base: different risk appetites resulting in different demands of the token at different times, to smooth out the demand of tokens

ix. Platform productivity: expectation of platform's growth demand, efficiency at coordinating participants and achieving objectives

b. Market to dictate

   i. Dutch auction: Dutch auction works in a similar way as Vickrey-Clarke-Groves auction, where this method generates the greatest social welfare. This works for similar goods and goods are priced by the market. E.g. government bonds or the launch of a new token.
   ii. Exchange rate of tokens to dollars reflect buyer's willingness to buy in both a centralised order book way and a decentralised market maker method.
   iii. Scarcity of tokens affecting pricing choices causes buyer

competition that reveals consumer values

iv. Rational expectations of exchange rate in next period
v. Value to users: the ecosystem or network effects that add value to users
vi. vi. Automated market maker using each token pool to dictate market prices, facilitated by arbitrage traders to achieve price equilibrium in various exchanges

10.7.2 Financial Incentives (Incentive Features)

Rewards for participating in the token economy to further strengthen the incentive-compatible mechanism to achieve the objectives.

- Platform activities
    a. Transaction fees
    b. Rewards for joining the network
    c. Discount tokens (discussed in Chapter 14)
    d. Referral links
    e. Reward policies beyond mining

- Returns on investment
    a. Expected returns to tokens owned: via staking or changes in value of underlying asset
    b. Arbitrage on exchange rates of token prices
    c. Price level volatility of the tokens
    d. Liquidity mechanisms: exchanges, liquidity function
    e. Riskiness of token

10.7.3 Architecture (Design of Token Structure)

Tokens can help to govern actions through property rights and establish trust through scale economies.

1. Property rights
    a. Economics of property rights: claim rights, ownership rights, rights to participate in governance decision making process
    b. Harberger taxation
    c. Representation of an identity and the rights of the identity (i.e. person, art, digital representation of something in physical form)
2. Distribution
    a. Allocation and lock-up of tokens in various time periods
    b. Conviction staked inflation funding: distribution of newly minted tokens as a function of number of tokens staked and duration of staking period
3. Peer-reviewed Algorithm and Code for the token

Box 3: A Crash Course on Traditional Monetary Policy

Central Bank

Monetary policy is how money is managed and governed. It is usually managed and governed by the country's central bank.

The purpose of managing and governing money is in 2 folds:

- Ensure price stability (by managing the supply of money against the real demand of money)
- Ensure general trust in the currency

There are two basic types of monetary policy: expansionary (more money in the system) and contractionary (less money in the system). Depending on the economy, which defines the real *demand of money*, one of the two monetary policies will be implemented (increase or decrease the supply of money).

Monetary Policy Typical Tools

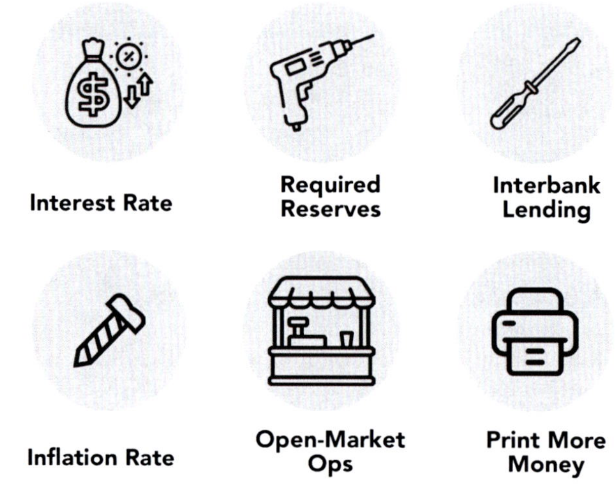

Money supply is changed by affecting the interest rates of money.

- Open market operations: sell/buy government bonds.

That means borrowing money from its citizens and the rest of the world, with a promise to return the full amount with interest and some form of dividends (coupon rate) per period. These government bonds can also be traded in a secondary market.

- Discount rate: change interest rate from central banks to commercial banks.

That means the commercial bank can have more (or less) money to lend out to people. This is because commercial banks can borrow money from the central banks at a lower (or higher) interest rate. E.g. HSBC can borrow more money from the Bank of England (BoE) because the discount rate has dropped. That means it is cheaper to borrow money. They will borrow money and lent it out to people like you and me at a lower rate than before. We use the money to buy a house or as business loans to buy new machinery.

Usually, a drop in the discount rate translates to a drop in the interest rates of commercial banks, i.e., if it is cheaper for the HSBC to borrow money from the BoE, it is also cheaper for me to borrow money from HSBC.

- Required reserves: amount of money commercial banks must hold in the bank vaults

Central banks dictate this amount. This is to ensure that banks have enough money when people withdraw physical cash from the ATM. This also affects the amount of money commercial banks can lend to people like you and me.

E.g. In September 2019[9], the People's Bank of China (PBoC), China's central bank, cut the required reserves to 13% for big banks and to 11% for small banks. This was part of the move by the central bank to increase the supply of money into the economy and stimulate economic activities.

- Quantitative easing (QE): printing more money

Central banks do this by buying back government bonds or financial assets and adding more dollar bills (money supply) into the economy. This is a new form of expansionary policy and used when typical expansionary policy is ineffective. E.g. The Bank of Japan (BoJ) used QE on 19 March 2001 to promote private lending in the Japanese economy.

Impossible Trinity

The impossible trinity is three factors that affect the currency. Central banks have to choose two out of three of them.

- Fixed exchange rate: exchange rate is pegged to another country's currency (hence, the other currency's monetary policy will affect native country's monetary policy).
- Free capital flow: Money can flow in and out of the country easily. This is affected by interest rates and exchange rates of both the native country and another country.
    - This is because there is an opportunity cost to place money in a specific country. If the interest rate is better in another country, it might be wiser to put the money in the other country. That means reducing the demand for the native currency.
- Sovereign monetary policy: independent monetary policy, where central banks can change and affect the interest rates.

Monetary Economics

Monetary policy is one aspect of the big umbrella of monetary economics. There are other things to consider that affect money in the country. This may be managed by the central bank or by the government (the state).

- Fiscal policy: changing taxes, government spending, borrowing.
  - Managing money supply indirectly
- Nominal anchors: variable, to pin down expectations of private agents about the nominal price level
  - Long-run methods to achieve price stability and general trust in a currency
  - Exchange rate regimes
  - Currency union (EU)
  - Managed floating (HKD-USD)
  - Freely floating (USD, GBP, CHF, JPY)
  - Pegs (Panama-USD)
- Exchange rate regimes
  - Currency union (EU)
  - Managed floating (HKD-USD)
  - Freely floating (USD, GBP, CHF, JPY)
  - Pegs (Panama-USD)

Notes

1. Read Box 3: A Crash Course on Traditional Monetary Policy

2. Christian Catalini and Joshua S Gans. Initial coin offerings and the value of crypto tokens. Technical report, National Bureau of Economic Research, 2018.

3. Bancor: https://www.economicsdesign.com/portfolio/bancor/

4. MakerDao: https://www.economicsdesign.com/portfolio/makerdao/

5. Read Box 1: A Case Study on Digital Currency's section on monetary policy

6. These are models created and analysed by two different papers [Catalini and Gans (2018) and Cong et al. (2018)], which sheds light on the value of utility tokens.

7. Trent McConaghy uses a multi-layered TCR system to gradually increase the rights and responsibilities of users as they add more stake. This adds to a more diverse layer in governance (mechanism design) with regards to decision making, access control, reputation and resolution. Read more at https://blog.oceanprotocol.com/the-layered-tcr-56cc5b4cdc45

8. Fixed exchange rates need not be a 1:1 peg. It can be a 1:0.725 peg, depending on the institution governing the monetary policy.

9. The move was effective from September 16, where the PBoC cut its reserve requirement ratio by 50 basis points, adding 900 billion yuan ($126.35 billion) of liquidity into the Chinese economy. (China's PBOC cuts reserve ratio for banks as economy stalls, CNBC, Sept 2019)

Chapter 11: Bonding Curves

Bonding curves are a method to link 2[1] variables together. The method is most commonly used in decentralised exchanges (DEX) and fundraising.

11.1 What is a Bonding Curve?

A bonding curve is a curve (equation) that connects two variables. For example, token prices change when the token supply changes. This is determined by math, coded in a smart contract. This is not determined by other factors like trading in the secondary market.

11.1.1 Use Case 1: Decentralised Exchange via Autonomous Market Maker

Specific math and examples can be found in Chapter 13.

A bonding curve is a smart contract execution that creates its own market for tokens without order books. It is also known as an automated market maker. The two key differences compared to traditional exchanges are:

1. Matching orders with math instead of a central limit order book (CLOB)
2. Crowdsourcing market makers instead of specialised market making firms

To start with, a pool is created, known as a liquidity pool. Anyone can add assets to this liquidity pool. To incentivise people to add assets to the pool, they earn some transaction fees when trade occurs and earn the native tokens of the protocol.

Example: The liquidity pool only has two types of tokens, $ETH and $TOKEN. As a liquidity provider, you add the same value of $ETH and $TOKEN into the pool. Let's say you contribute 10% of the $ETH and $TOKEN in the pool. When a trade occurs, you receive 10% of the transaction fees.

When someone trades, they add a token (Token A) in exchange for the other token (Token B). How much Token B does the person receive? Traditionally, it depends on the order in the order book. Now, the orders are matched with math and executed with smart contracts.

Example: Jamie adds $ETH into the pool and gets $TOKEN out. The amount of $TOKEN Jamie receives depends on the amount of $ETH and $TOKEN in the liquidity pool. Prices are not fixed so are always fluctuating.

11.1.2 Use Case 2: Bonding Curve for Fundraising

Fundraising use-cases use a specific immutable smart contract. The smart contract implements a bonding curve contract to automatically mint, burn and distribute tokens.

The amount to mint, burn and distribute is defined by a mathematical formula

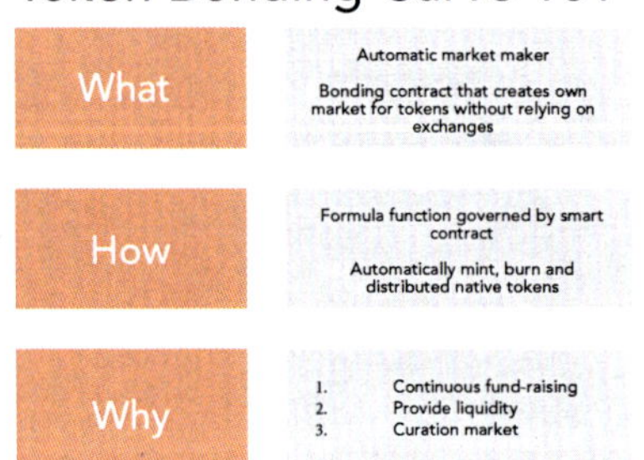

This is used in three use-cases:

1. *Raising funds using a buy and sell function (e.g. Aragon fundraising function)*
2. *Determining price in a closed economy (e.g. Nexus Mutual $NXM pricing)*
3. *Curation market using tokens as a signal (e.g. this book)*

When fundraising, this incentivises adopters to purchase tokens early as it is cheaper in the early stages as the system grows.

11.1.3 Use Case 3: Curation Market

The curation market uses tokens as a signal to reduce information asymmetry (e.g. Ocean protocol). This use case is still relatively new, and this book seeks to be an experiment on this use-case (See Chapter 25).

A curation market is more evident when we cross non-fungible tokens (NFT) with DeFi. Users can stake tokens, governed by a bonding curve, in exchange for an NFT. It mixes both DEX mechanisms (use-case 1) with fundraising mechanisms (use-case 2), depending on the use-case. The permutations are endless, and this could be a critical piece in the future technological stack.

11.2 Four Properties of a Bonding Curve

1. Always liquid and always continuous

Tokens can be minted or exchanged at any time (continuously) according to the prices set by the function and governed by a smart contract. Tokens can be burned or exchanged at any time (continuously) to the smart contract, which entitles the user a proportion of the reserve pool (collateral) or assets. The smart contract becomes the market maker.

2. Prices are hard coded according to some mathematical curve.

In general, token prices increase as more tokens are in circulation. The mathematical curve[2] can be defined in variables that affect the objectives of the ecosystem.

3. Smart contracts govern the system.

In use-case 1: Smart contracts help to execute the trade with the liquidity pool by being the aggregate market maker. The price of exchange depends on the depth of the pool, not on external exchange prices.

In use-case 2: Collaterals are kept in smart contracts as reserve pools. A smart contract executes a mathematical formula, sometimes by solving some function.

4. It allows for claims on future cash-flow, governed by smart contracts.

For it to not be a Ponzi scheme, the tokens should allow users to claim on future cash-flow by the ecosystem. This could be earning via transaction fees or earning via future profits from the ecosystem.

11.3 Considerations of Token Bonding Curves

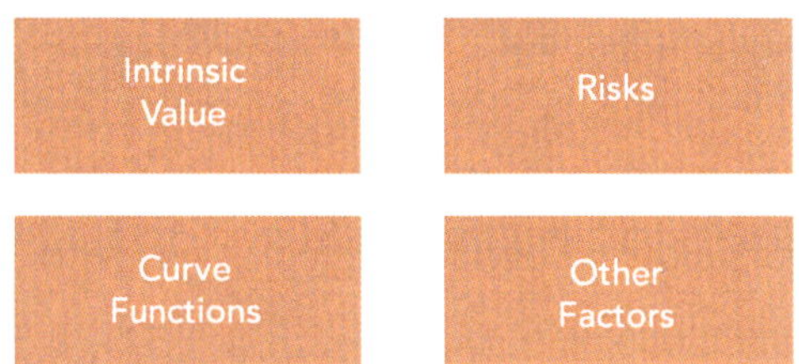

11.3.1. Intrinsic Value

The intrinsic value is different, depending on the use-cases.

11.3.1.1. Decentralised Exchange

Value comes from the ease of liquidity, availability of liquidity and network of other tokens to interact and trade with.

11.3.1.2 Fundraising

Value comes from the entitlement to future cash flow. Other than value increasing from more participants joining the ecosystem, the value can also increase from revenue generated from the ecosystem. Depending on the system, it is possible for tokens to be seen as a form of financial security by regulators.

11.3.1.3 Curation Market

Value comes from the entitlement to future cash flow or accurately signal market sentiments.

For curated products in the intellectual property domain, a non-fungible token (NFT) can be issued and traded via token bonding curves to trade the intellectual property (IP). The IP is attached to NFT and the NFT allows for the transfer of ownership. The NFT is transferred under a bonding curve, and the buyer sends collaterals to the smart contract and receives the NFT. The prices of NFT will increase as more people demand it (tokenised signal for curation).

11.3.2. Mitigating Risks

11.3.2.1 Decentralised Exchange

Risks: transaction is validated before someone buys a large amount by paying more gas fees.

Solutions: have a maximum limit on transaction fees for each transaction, or a percentage-base fee for transactions.

11.3.2.2. Fundraising

Risks: Ponzi scheme, pyramid scams, pump and dump

Solutions: This can be done by ensuring that the fund is not immediately in profit in the short-term. The curve can reduce short-term speculation and encourage people to participate long-term. This changes the behaviour of users to keep tokens for certain periods to ensure profit. Also, ensure that the curve is supported by a proportion of the revenue from the ecosystem.

- Time-lock for selling tokens
- Premium for selling tokens
- Disallow sell function (except on secondary market)
- Proportion of the revenue supports the curve

11.3.2.3 Curation Market

Risks: manipulation of data by someone with many tokens, defining payout for the curated product

Solutions: the contract can include a continuous staking and curation mechanism to increase the cost of manipulating data.

11.3.3 Curve Functions

There is no one "perfect" curve function for the bonding curve. It depends on the objectives of the ecosystem and the use-case. There are some functions available, linear function ($y=mx + c$), power function ($y = x^a$), exponential function ($y = a^x$), logarithm function ($y = a\log(x) + b$) and variation function (e.g. $y = m(1 + a)^{\log x} + b$).

> *Play with the various functions and parameters:*
> *http://bit.ly/bondingcurve*

It is also worth considering the use of 3D curves. The z-axis adds another dimension that can affect the token prices. This could be platform productivity level, technology adoption curve, users in the system, active users as a fraction of total users, etc.

11.3.3.3.1 Linear Functions

Price and supply are related linearly, but it can be an issue when the project increases in demand and size. In linear functions, the first few token holders are rewarded too much in comparison to the rest of the token holders. It also does not give much to design with, only changing m and c in the equation.

11.3.3.2. Exponential Functions

Exponential functions are good as they increase prices slowly initially, which encourages the holding of tokens. However, the function accelerates aggressively in the last 20%. This makes it volatile as it opens the market to speculation and the growth rate can be unmanageable.

Logarithm functions work in the opposite way, where the prices at the start increases rapidly, which creates speculation and volatility.

11.3.3.3. Other Factors to consider

- Incentivise early adopters
- Price stabilisation at the end
- Cost appreciation based on some factor of supply increasing (or productivity of platform or token)
- Prevention of abuse or arbitrage

- Growth of underlying product (s-curve, as a function z-axis)
- Returns appropriately attractive across reasonable range or to focus more on early adopters

11.4 Practical Questions to get Started

- What function is the bonding curve used for? Decentralised exchange (instant liquidity), fundraising, curation market or something else?
- How many users can the project attract and sustain? (At the introduction stage, at the maturity state)
- Are both early and late adopters adequately incentivised to participate? Do you want them to be equally incentivised?
- Can I attract the amount of capital needed to take the project to an adequate level of adoption?

11.5 Two Variations to Bonding Curves

11.5.1. Augmented Bonding Curve (ABC)

This is based on complex system research. It is a design for a new incentive mechanism. The objective is to create a new funding model, governed by participants in a continuous organisation.

The problem with the general bonding curve is that it is subjected to manipulation in pursuit of speculative returns. Tokens can also be burned anytime or after an arbitrary deadline.

As such, ABC uses conversation principles[3] and mechanisms to create a robust and controlled environment to manage speculation and to align incentives to generate returns. Tokens minted in period 1 will be locked up in period 1. This is to affect the stability of reserve flow.

ABC combines the general bonding curve with a funding pool, lock-up mechanism and inter-system feedback loops[5].

11.5.2. Dynamic Bonding Curve (DBC)

The objective is to incentivise early adopters, punish freeloaders and encourage active participation in the ecosystem.

The problem with the general bonding curve is that it can be manipulated with a large token holder transacting and increasing unfair volatility.

As such, DBC adds a feature, where prices of tokens are determined by the proportion of token owned[5]. This encourages users to continuously participate, which is an objective in the ecosystem.

Notes

1. It can be more than 2 variables, but we stick to a simple 2-variable model as it is possible to graph it out in a 2D graph. The more variables to add, the more dimensions are created. A 3-variable bonding curve requires a 3D graph to visualise.

2. While most people think of a bonding curve as a 2D function, bonding curves can be a 3D function. They can also be used to facilitate trade without money, e.g., using a bonding curve to determine the relationship between upload volume and download volume. In an open-source content market, it can facilitate the exchange of information volume without money.

3. The conservation principle is a physics principle, where energy conservation equation is subjected to a constant invariant function.

4. For more information, check out https://medium.com/giveth/deep-dive-augmented-bonding-curves-3f1f7c1fa751 for the system design, flow and background mathematics.

5. For more information, check out https://tokeneconomy.co/dynamic-token-bonding-curves-41d36e43befa for a case study and mathematical function.

Chapter 12: {Case Study} Bancor

Bancor is part of the decentralised finance (DeFi) movement as it acts as an automatic market maker. To be an automatic market maker, Bancor allows for instant and continuous liquidity of less traded tokens that exist in the Bancor ecosystem. The prices and supply of the token is defined mathematically, governed by a smart contract.

There are two types of tokens in the ecosystem, a liquid token (utility function) that provides liquidity in the ecosystem and a relay or array token that represents the reserve pool.

Bancor System

Concepts	Explanation
What	*Solutions to illiquid tokens* Provides continuous liquidity, governed by an algorithm in a smart contract
How	*Smart contract and math and common network token*
Why	*Continuous liquidity for tokens with low demand*

> *What is Bancor*
> *Bancor is a solution to tokens with liquidity problems. Bancor provides continuous liquidity*[1] *and the liquidity is governed by an algorithm in a smart contract*[2].

12.1 Introduction to Bancor

Continuous Liquidity Bancor does not require exchanges or oracles to provide prices of tokens, exchange rates and liquidity function. It uses an autonomous liquidity mechanism that provides automatic price determination of the tokens. Refer to bonding curve use-case 1 in Chapter 11.

Governed by Smart Contracts The liquidity is executed and governed by smart contracts using a common denominator[3] token that exists in the Bancor ecosystem. They are called network tokens, more commonly known as liquid tokens[4]. In the rest of this article, the term "liquid token" will be used to refer to the common denominator token.

Smart contracts hold balances of other tokens and provide instant liquidity between the tokens available in the Bancor ecosystem.

12.1.1. Simple Introduction (ELI5[5])

Imagine a cookie shop with various cookie jars. Each cookie jar is a set of cookie pairs: chocolate chip cookie and another cookie flavour.

You can trade peanut butter cookies for chocolate chip cookies using the cookie jars. Since each cookie jar has chocolate chip cookies, you can trade peanut butter cookies for chocolate chip cookies in Jar 1. Then use that chocolate chip cookie to trade for macadamia nut cookies in Jar 2.

In the same way, Bancor's token, $BNT, helps to facilitate trade between the various tokens in the cookie jar. Instead of a cookie jar, there are liquidity pools. Instead of peanut butter and macadamia nut cookies, there are tokens from various protocol projects.

12.1.2 Technical Introduction

Bancor is a non-custodial exchange that uses pooled liquidity to facilitate trade. It does not require order books nor third party intermediaries.

Instead of matching buyers with sellers, a market-matching algorithmic mechanism provides liquidity through smart contracts. The ratio between the reserve collateral in the smart contract and liquid token is fixed and embedded in the algorithmic mechanism.

Other than liquidity between two tokens on the same blockchain platform, Bancor also allows liquidity across different blockchains[6].

A liquidity network exists when there are various tokens that exist in the ecosystem, and they are each connected to a common denominator token, the liquid token (chocolate chip cookie). If peanut butter cookies and macadamia nut cookies both trade with the liquid token (chocolate chip cookie), then by transitive property[7], you can easily liquidate peanut butter cookies for macadamia nut cookies (via chocolate chip cookies).

Think of the US dollar (USD) as the common denominator for the global currency. Most central banks around the world have USD in their reserves. Hong Kong wants to change some Hong Kong dollars (HKD) to Swiss Francs (CHF). But Switzerland is not too interested in HKD. What can Hong Kong do? Hong Kong can change HKD to USD. And give Switzerland some USD to get their CHF. USD enables the trade to happen because both countries have USD and accepts USD.

In the same vein, USD is the liquid token in the Bancor ecosystem. It allows for trade to happen easily, because every type of cryptocurrency (e.g. country) have the liquid token and accepts the liquid token.

12.2 Objectives of Bancor

The main objective of the Bancor protocol is to provide liquidity by being an automatic market maker[8]. The purpose is to enable privately issued tokens to have liquidity, even if the token is new, only used by a niche community of users, or has low demand in general.

12.2.1 Problems with Liquidity

Double coincidence of wants Traditionally, liquidity happens when there is a match between buyers and sellers. Both users have to want the *same quantity at the same time* and same place to execute an exchange. The challenge today is to find a match between buyer and seller. This can be difficult when the demand for the item is very low.

Reliability of exchange Liquidity problems can be solved with exchanges. However, unless the token is a significant trade volume to be an efficient marketplace to find marketmakers, it is not a reliable exchange. The top 10% of tokens are traded actively on exchanges. The rest of the 90% have low demand and low frequency, hence low reliability that trade can occur[9].

Long-tail problem The barrier to entry for a person to release a privately issued cryptocurrency is very low. Thus, we see a boom in many cryptocurrencies. However, only the top 10% tokens are actively traded (representing more than 95% of trading volume). This means that there are a lot of tokens (90% of tokens) that are in the market with low trade volume, hence the lack of liquidity. This is the long tail problem, where the tail includes many small tokens with low trade volume, which represents 90% of the trade. This can be due to a niche token with a small community or new tokens with low initial adoption rate.

12.2.2 Solutions for Liquidity

Manual Market Maker The traditional solution in the financial market today is to have market makers. Market makers always buy and sell any financial products, which solves the liquidity problem. They are typically large financial institutions with significant reserve capital. They gain profits because they can hold bigger risks and earn from the spread. The crypto market is very volatile and risky, so we do not see as many market makers in the market as the traditional financial market.

Automated Market Maker The other solution is to create decentralised liquidity via a token. This token has a liquidity mechanism built in, hence a liquid token. It will always be bought and sold through smart contracts. Prices are determined algorithmically via a formula and governed by a smart contract. This allows for continuous buying and selling of tokens. It is linked to more than one other token in the network, as the base denominator that enables trade between the token pairs.

12.3. Tokens in Bancor

Bancor uses a two-tier token model in its ecosystem: liquid token and relay token[10].

> Note: As Bancor is the platform that allows for other tokens to be liquidated, the other tokens present as known as reserve tokens. They are ERC20 or EOS-compatible tokens like $ETH, $BAT, $DAI, $EOS, $EMT, $DICE.

A liquid token in Bancor is a smart token with a single reserve that mints and destroys itself by sending or withdrawing the reserve token to or from its smart contract. In order to connect to the Bancor network, a liquid token must use $BNT or a derivative of $BNT as its reserve token. $BNT is itself a liquid token backed by $ETH. It serves as the network token that connects the Bancor network. This is because all liquidity pools have $BNT in their reserve.

Relay tokens are used to provide liquidity staking. The token holders are entitled to a fraction of the future cash flow. Relay tokens represent proportion of the value in the reserve pool (aka relay). This is further discussed in the financial incentives factor below.

12.3.1 Token Features in Bancor

There are three types of tokens that Bancor can create: (1) Liquid token, (2) Relay token, (3) Array token.

The table below shows the types of tokens native to Bancor, explanation and examples of those tokens in the ecosystem.

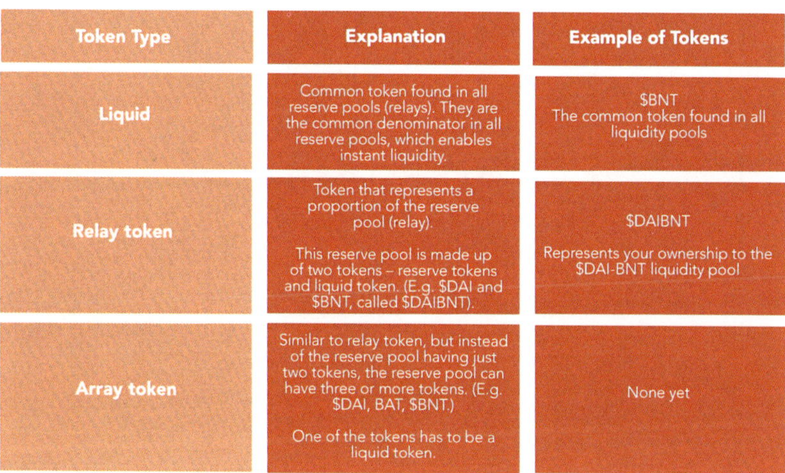

Token Type	Explanation	Example of Tokens
Liquid	Common token found in all reserve pools (relays). They are the common denominator in all reserve pools, which enables instant liquidity.	$BNT The common token found in all liquidity pools
Relay token	Token that represents a proportion of the reserve pool (relay). This reserve pool is made up of two tokens – reserve tokens and liquid token. (E.g. $DAI and $BNT, called $DAIBNT).	$DAIBNT Represents your ownership to the $DAI-BNT liquidity pool
Array token	Similar to relay token, but instead of the reserve pool having just two tokens, the reserve pool can have three or more tokens. (E.g. $DAI, BAT, $BNT.) One of the tokens has to be a liquid token.	None yet

12.3.2. Liquid Token

What: Liquid token is a utility token that enables conversion in the Bancor ecosystem. It enables instant convertibility to any number of other tokens in the network.

How: Liquid token is the common denominator token in all reserve pools (relays) in the Bancor ecosystem. It is like US dollars, the universal currency that is in most central bank's reserve. It also never faces liquidity risk, thanks to the built-n automatic market maker, governed by the smart contract.

Why: This makes it easy to transfer tokens within each reserve pool, using liquid tokens.

Anyone can purchase liquid tokens by transferring reserve tokens to the smart contract. In return, the person will receive newly minted liquid tokens.

Example: ERC20 token, $DAI and liquid token, $BNT.

1. You use $DAI to purchase $BNT.
2. Send $DAI to the smart contract, and it will calculate the amount of $BNT you will receive in return.
3. This is the amount of $BNT that is newly minted for you.
4. You can get $DAI back by sending $BNT tokens back to the smart contract. It will burn the $BNT and issue $DAI from the reserve pool, to you.

12.3.2.1 Price Calculation

Prices are determined by the amount of supply in the market and a fixed ratio. It is similar to a bonding curve[11]. This fixed ratio is the reserve ratio (RR)[12]. This ratio is fixed and set by the token issuer. This ratio is calculated using the value of the reserve pool against the value of the liquid token:

$$\textbf{\textit{Reserve Ration}} = \frac{\textbf{\textit{Value token pool}}}{\textbf{\textit{Value of liquid token}}}$$

This is used to maintain price stability of the liquid token.

12.3.2.2. Bancor Token (BNT)

BNT is a liquid token in the Bancor network. It is present in all reserve pools. Its value comes from its ability to trade between all token trading pairs in the ecosystem. There are no fees incurred from transacting $BNT, but it can result in a higher transaction fee (i.e. gas in Ethereum) because the smart contract requires more power.

Since Bancor is a utility token, its purpose is to access the Bancor ecosystem. Valuation comes from intrinsic factors like network effects (more reserve pools using $BNT) and usage volume and frequency of $BNT in the ecosystem. $BNT also has a limit on supply (total supply is 75,843,715), so the increase in minting and usage will drive the valuation up. This, however, adds value to the reserve pool, since the reserve pools are also made up of $BNT.

12.3.3. Relay Token

Relay tokens are used to own part of the reserve pool (relay). This allows for decentralised participation in the pools. Participants are incentivised to join as they will be rewarded with transaction fees when the reserve tokens are being transacted. Relay tokens can be bought on Bancor.

When someone buys a relay token, they are adding liquidity to the relay's reserves by increasing the reserves. The relay tokens they receive in return represent their contribution. A transaction fee is incurred when the reserve token or relay token is traded. The transaction fee is then added to the reserve pool. When relay tokens are burned, the token holders are entitled to their proportion in the reserve pool, which includes earnings from fees.

12.3.3.1 Price Calculation

Prices are determined by the tokens in the reserve pool. In relay tokens, two tokens are used in the reserve pool, governed by a smart contract. It typically maintains a fixed 50% reserve ratio between the two token reserves.

12.3.4. Tokens Summary Table

Table 2 shows the comparison between the two existing token types (native to the Bancor ecosystem) and the reserve token (not native to the Bancor ecosystem).

Token Types in Bancor

Variables	Liquid Token	Relay Token	Reserve Token
Other names	Network token, native token	Smart token, staking token	Base token, reserve currency, connector token
Example	$BNT	$DAIBNT	$DAI, $BAT, $EOS
Purpose	Enable liquidity, instant convertibility and access to any token in the network	Enable staking and reduce price slippage in the relay Access to future cash flow generated from transaction fees	This token is any token that joins the Bancor ecosystem to attain liquidity. It can be an ERC20 token or EOS-based token. They exist in their original forms in the Relays (aka reserve basket) of Bancor.
Reserves Needed	Single reserve token	50% reserve token & 50% BNT	Not applicable
How is value derived	$P = \frac{\text{Value of reserve pool}}{\text{Supply of Liquid Token x RR}}$ Algorithmically with a fixed ratio, governed by a smart contract.	Based on the value of the relay (aka money pot)	However, the individual token's policy specifies
How is supply created	Minted or burned when people send collaterals (reserves) to smart contract or smart token to retrieve connector balance.	The token issuer determines it	However, the individual token's policy specifies

12.4 Bancor in DeFi

DeFi is decentralised finance. DeFi hopes to transform the financial landscape by bringing transparency, speed and accessibility to the industry. It is not about a radical change, but to introduce new use-cases, new products and improve efficiency using new technology. An important aspect of the financial space is liquidity. When assets are liquid, it is easier to trade and move the asset around.

12.4.1 How is Bancor Involved in DeFi?

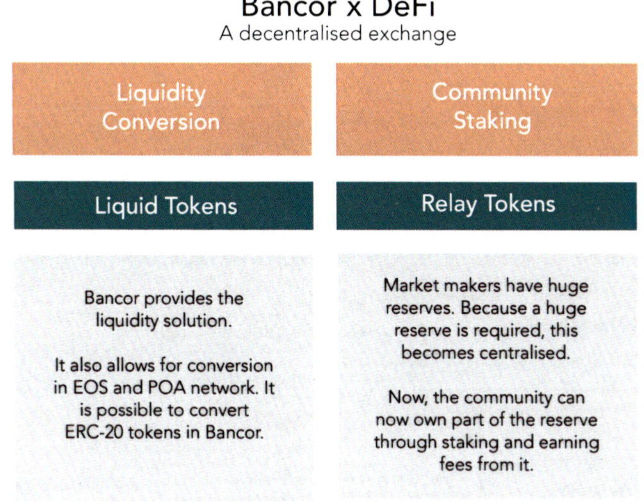

12.4.1.1. Liquidity

Bancor provides the liquidity solution in DeFi, under the DEX function. Other than just providing liquidity on Ethereum based tokens, it also allows for conversion in the EOS and POA network. It is possible to convert ERC20 tokens to EOS-based tokens in Bancor.

12.4.1.2. Community Staking

Traditionally, market makers have huge reserves, which allows them to be a market maker and take advantage of spreads. Because a huge reserve is required, this becomes centralised to a few institutions.

With DeFi, the community can now own part of the reserve through staking and earning fees from it. The community can do this via owning relay tokens.

12.5 Applying Token Design Bancor

Token design is the design and engineering of the token. It seeks to design how tokens will be managed and governed, and the functions and rights it could hold.

In this specific case study, we will discuss Bancor and its token design.

The three main factors of token design are:

1. Token policy
2. Financial incentives
3. Architecture

Token Policy

Token policy determines how tokens will be managed and governed. It may include a mix of automation through smart contracts and participants' inputs through governance mechanisms.

How tokens are governed is the **monetary policy**. This can be automated or a mix of automation and non-automation.

How tokens and/or ecosystem is being valued is the **valuation**.

Attributes of the token	Incentive Features	Design of Structure
E.g. Monetary policy & valuation	E.g. Platform activities & return to stake	E.g. Property rights, lock-up periods

Financial Incentives

Economics is all about incentives. The most direct incentive is financial incentive. This is to encourage specific behaviour to coordinate actions of participation towards a shared objective of the ecosystem. The key goal is the shared objective, not valuation on secondary markets.

How activities in the ecosystem incentivises behaviours is the **platform activities**.

How the ecosystem and token project enable returns is the **return on investment**. This is closely linked to the token policy implemented.

Architecture

As tokens can be embedded with programs, architecture defines the building blocks of the token and tokens as a whole. This can include technical aspects like underlying algorithmic formulas coded in the smart contract and property rights issued to the tokens or non-technical aspect like allocation, and distribution of the tokens as a whole.

What rights the token hold is the **property rights**.

How the tokens are distributed and allocated in the entire ecosystem is the **distribution**.

Coded governance of the token in terms of algorithm and mathematics is the **algorithm and code**.

12.6 Token Policy

Bancor has two types of tokens (liquid token, which is a utility token, and relay token). We will name the tokens in the section, where it is applicable.

12.6.1 Monetary Policy

Monetary policy determines how the supply of tokens is managed and governed. All the math is discussed in 12.8.3.

12.6.1.1.Supply & Price of Liquid Token

The supply and price is governed by a smart contract. In the smart contract, there is a mathematical formula that defines the supply and price. The smart contract executes the formula, hence managing the issuance and governance of liquid tokens.

Since the smart contract will always mint and burn tokens, it changes the supply and price of tokens in the Bancor ecosystem (primary market). The prices, when traded in a secondary market, are not governed by the monetary policy discussed here.

The effective price of the liquid tokens exchanged is:

$$\textit{effective price} = \frac{\textit{reserve tokens exchanged}}{\textit{liquid tokens exchanged}}$$

12.6.1.2. Connector Weight of Liquid Token

This is also known as reserve ratio, constant reserve ratio, fractional reserve, exchange rate. It is the fixed ratio between a token's value and the value of the reserve pool.

This means that the prices of liquid tokens (e.g. $BNT) change with respect to the reserve token. This price is constantly recalculated to maintain the fixed ratio.

For example: The price of HKD changes in terms of USD. Instead of changing the prices of HKD in terms of USD, we want it fixed. The supply and price of HKD will change, to ensure that the price of HKD in terms of USD remains fixed.

12.6.1.3. Initiating a New Relay

It is possible to create a new reserve pool with a new reserve token and $BNT. A liquidity provider[14] has to deposit an equal amount of $BNT and the new reserve token. The minimum total value of reserve is US$20,000, of which $10,000 worth of $BNT is needed.

12.6.2 Token Valuation

Token valuation is how the token is priced and valued.

12.6.2.1. Token Bonding Curve for Liquid Token (1 Reserve Token)

The price of liquid token is defined by the formula, $P = S^a e^A$

P is the price of the token
S is the supply
a is the function of the constant ratio
A is an arbitrary constant

The cost payable to purchase liquid tokens in the reserve token is defined by the formula,

$$E = Ro\,(\sqrt[F]{1 + \frac{T}{So}} - 1)$$

E is the amount payable in terms of reserve token, R_{oi} s the initial monetary value of reserve tokens, F is the constant ratio, T is the change in liquid token supply and S_o is the initial liquid token supply.

12.6.2.2.Token Bonding Curve for Liquid Token (Multiple Reserve Tokens)

Trade in one reserve token will affect the price of a liquid token in terms of the other currency. Since this is not implemented in the Bancor ecosystem yet, this paper will not go into details about the valuation but will provide the math formula.

Supply of liquid token (BNT), $S = So \prod_{i=1}^{M} (\frac{Ri}{Rio})^{F_i}$

12.6.2.3. Prices of Reserve Pool for Relay Token

Relay tokens are tokens that own a proportion of the relay. The price is derived from the value of the relay, with includes the reserve token and $BNT. The relay token can be calculated as a fraction of the sum of value of the reserve token and the value of $BNT in the reserve pool.

12.7 Financial Incentives

12.7.1. Platform Activities

12.7.1.1. Insurance for Impermanent Loss

One of the greatest risks in decentralised exchanges are impermanent losses. These are losses due to external trading activities when someone puts their tokens in the liquidity pool as opposed to keeping them in their wallet.

To combat this, Bancor provides insurance for impermanent loss incurred, if any. One change in Bancor V2.1 is to allow for single-sided liquidity provision. Bancor protocol will then mint the required $BNT to support the liquidity pool. As a result, the protocol is able to earn transaction fees. These fees can be used as the insurance fund to compensate for losses.

If there is a lack of fees in the insurance fund, Bancor will then mint $BNT tokens to compensate for the loss.

12.7.1.2. Price Slippage of Liquid Token ($BNT)

Price slippage refers to the change in the price of the liquid token. Price slippage occurs due to market depth (size of reserve pool), not from the difference in buy and ask price.

Relay tokens represent the relay (reserve pool), which holds the reserve tokens and the liquid tokens. The reserve mints and burns liquid tokens to fulfil the trade and determine prices. When a person sells $BNT to the relay to get the reserve token, it increases the supply of $BNT in the reserve and reduces the supply of reserve tokens. This changes the reserve ratio, so the price of $BNT will be changed to ensure that the reserve ratio is constant.

The larger the number of tokens exchanged relative to the size of the reserve, the larger the price slippage (changes in price). Technically, one does not need to hold $BNT to execute the trade. $BNT is the common denominator for all reserve tokens and acts as a medium of exchange.

12.7.1.3. Transaction Fees in Bancor

Although there is a spread in the exchange, transaction fees exist. They are like a commission fee payable to execute the conversion. This is to incentivise users to stake tokens in the reserve pool to reduce price slippage.

ELI5: If you want to exchange USD for GBP, you go to the money changer. Let's say, £1 GBP costs $1.25 USD. This is the amount you find on Google. At the money changer, they can charge you two types of fees, exchange rate fees and commission fee.

1. The exchange rate the money changer gives you can be something like £1:$1.30. This means that to buy £1, it costs $0.05 more. This is the profit the money changer earns. It is called exchange rate fee, or spread.
2. The money changer can also charge a commission to accept this conversion. This can be 5% of the total amount transacted. This is the commission fee he can earn.

Bancor is the money changer. It does not charge an exchange rate fee, because that is fixed. But it can charge a commission fee, which is the transaction fee. These fees will be awarded to the corresponding relay token holders.

12.7.1.4. Liquidity Mechanism

Smart contract governs the liquidity mechanism. It will constantly burn and mint tokens accordingly.

12.7.2 Return of Investment

12.7.2.1. Staking in Bancor: Transaction Fee in Relay Token

Every time there is a conversion in the reserve pool, a small fee is charged. It usually ranges between 0.1% and 0.3%. This fee is charged per conversion and is deposited into the reserve pool. The fees are an incentive for liquidity providers to stake their tokens to reduce price slippage. The larger the reserve, the lower the slippage.

Currently, the relay determines the transaction fees. In the future, the amount can be voted on by the relay token holders.

12.7.2.2.Arbitrage of Liquid Token Prices

BNT is a utility token within the Bancor ecosystem and used in all trading pairs. However, it is also traded on various exchanges (secondary markets). The prices on the secondary market can be different to prices in Bancor. This difference will not last for long, as it shows a clear arbitrage opportunity.

Arbitrage is when the same item has different prices. It is possible to buy the item in the market at a lower price and sell it in the market at a higher price. Traders will take this low-risk opportunity to earn profits (difference in prices). They will purchase $BNT until prices on exchanges are the same as prices in the Bancor ecosystem.

12.7.2.3. Liquid Token in Secondary Market

Since $BNT can be traded on a secondary market, how does it affect the price and supply in the Bancor ecosystem, the primary market? It is not affected at all. The price in the Bancor ecosystem is determined by supply of $BNT. Since $BNT can only be created in the Bancor ecosystem itself, the total supply does not change. The only thing that changes in the secondary market is ownership of $BNT. The supply remains the same.

Prices only change when interacting with $BNT directly, i.e. converting tokens via the reserve pools in Bancor.

12.8 Architecture

Since liquid tokens and relay tokens are different, they have different architecture and building blocks.

12.8.1 Property rights

There are no property rights in liquid token, other than to facilitate conversion. They act as a medium of exchange and access to Bancor ecosystem.

12.8.1.1. Property Rights of Relay Tokens

Relay tokens have the rights to be entitled to future cash flow, generated from the transaction fees incurred.

When a trade is executed in the relay, a transaction fee is incurred. The transaction fee is returned to the reserve pool. When a user burns the relay token, they are entitled to a proportion of the reserve pool, which includes their stake and earning from transaction fees.

For example, I own 10% of the $DAIBNT relay. When someone trades $DAI and increase or decrease $DAI in the pool, a transaction fee is incurred. I earn 10% of the transaction fee. When I burn my $DAIBNT tokens, I am entitled to 10% of the total value in the reserve pool. That includes my initial stake and transaction fees earned.

12.8.2. Distribution

12.8.2.1. Token Distribution of $BNT

Total supply of $BNT is 79,323,978[16].

12.8.2.1.1 Breakdown of Distribution

- 20% held by the ETH reserve pool of $BNT
- 40% to develop Bancor protocol and other technology (technological R&D)
- 12% is for marketing and developing the ecosystem (marketing)
- 10% is for setting up relay tokens, array tokens, proxy tokens for digital assets and cryptocurrencies (admin)
- 18% is for operational overhead and legal expenses (operations)

12.8.3 Algorithm and Code

Architecture: Algorithm

Mathematical Building Blocks of The Token

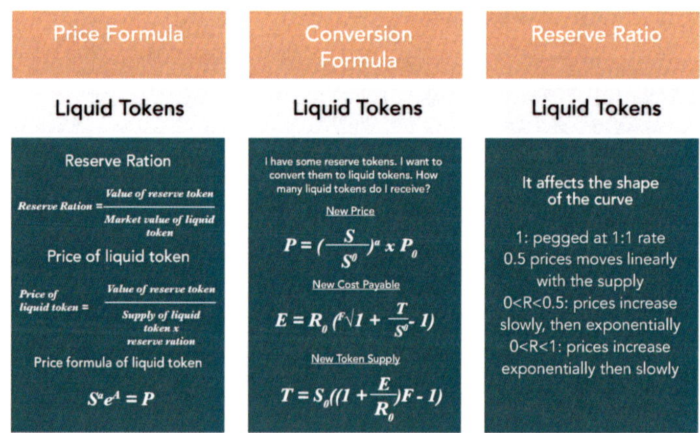

12.8.3.1. Price Formula for Liquid Token

There are 4 variables in the formula:

R is the value of the reserve token. E.g. if $ETH is $160 and I have 10 $ETH in the reserve pool, the value is $1600

S is the supply of liquid token

P is the price of liquid token

F is the (fractional) reserve ratio. It has a value between 0 and 1, hence the use of the term "fractional"

Reserve ratio is the ratio between the value of the reserve token and market value of liquid token.

$$\text{Reserve Ratio} = \frac{\text{Value of reserve token}}{\text{Market value of liquid token}}$$

This means that the value of the reserve token is a fraction of the value of liquid token.

$$\text{Value of reserve token} = (\text{Reserve Ratio}) \times (\text{Market value of liquid token})$$

Market value of liquid token is also known as the market cap.

$$\text{Market value of liquid token} = P_{\text{liquid token}} \times S_{\text{liquid token}}$$

Price of liquid token is then,

$$\text{Price of liquid token} = \frac{\text{Value of reserve token}}{\text{Supply of liquid token} \times \text{reserve ratio}}$$

Scenario: a tiny supply of liquid token is bought (dS).

1. The reserve pool changes. The person pays reserve tokens to buy the liquid tokens. $dR = P\,dS$
2. Since $R = FSP$, $dR = P\,dS$.
3. Combining it, we get $PdS = FsP$.
4. When supply changes, prices change too. But the reserve ratio remains the same and is not affected. Using chain rule, we get $P\,dS = F\,(S\,dp + P\,ds)$.
5. Bringing dS to one side, we get $P\,dS\,(1\text{-}F) = FSdP$.
6. Bringing F to one side, we get $P\,dS\,(1/F - 1) = S\,dP$
7. Let $a=(1\,/\,F - 1\,)$ *we get* $P\,dS\,a = S\,dP$
8. Bringing all the S to one side, we get $a\,dS\,/\,S = dP\,/\,P$
9. *Expanding that, we get* $a\,1\,/\,S\,dS = 1\,/\,P\,dP$
10. Using inverse differentiation of log function, *a* $d\,logS = d\,logP$
11. Since S and P are both variables, not a function. Integrating the equation gives us $a\,log\,S + A = log\,P$
12. Expanding that, $log\,S^a + log\,10^A = log\,P$
13. Simplifying that, *we get* $S^a\,e^A = P$

Where A is an arbitrary constant and e is the natural number. This is the price formula that the smart contracts hold.

12.8.3.2. Conversion Formula for Liquid Token

Now consider this scenario. I have some reserve tokens, E . I want to convert them to T -liquid tokens, so that I can use them later. How much liquid tokens do I receive?

The formula above cannot be used, since it does not have the variable of reserve tokens. We have to use a backward method to figure it out.

1. What is the new price in terms of new supply?
2. What is the cost payable to buy new tokens, given the change in supply?
3. What is the change in supply as a function of cost payable?

This formula can be used as the conversion formula[17].

1. New price, given the increase in supply is $P = (\frac{S}{S^0})^a x P_0$

2. New cost payable, in terms of reserve currency is the area under the curve. So

$$E = \int_{So}^{So+T} PDS.$$ Solving that we get $$E = Ro\,({}^F\sqrt{1 + T / So} - 1)$$

3. Rearranging the equation in terms of T, $T = S_0\,((1 + E / R0)^F - 1$ This is the amount of liquid tokens received when paying E reserve currency.

12.8.3.3. Impact of Reserve Ratio

Since the price formula is an exponential function, subjected to the reserve ratio, the shape of the curve changes, depending on the ratio. The reserve ratio[18] is a figure between 0 and 1.

12.8.3.3.1 Reserve Ratio = 1

When the reserve ratio is 1, the curve is a horizontal line. This means that prices do not change and are always constant. It is not responsive to the supply in the ecosystem. This is also known as a fixed peg, e.g. 1 Panama dollar is pegged to 1 USD.

12.8.3.3.2 Reserve Ratio = 0.5

When the ratio is 0.5, the curve is upward sloping and straight. This means that prices move linearly with the supply. Since it is not possible to gain profits with $BNT, a straight-line curve makes the most sense.

However, if it is possible for the liquid token to be earning transaction fees, where the transaction fees will increase the reserve base, a 0.5 reserve ratio might not be a good model. This is because the first few token holders are rewarded too much in comparison to the rest of the token holders.

12.8.3.3.3 0 < Reserve Ratio < 0.5

The curve is now an upward sloping exponential graph. The further the reserve ratio is to 0.5, the steeper the curve. This means the prices are more sensitive to the change in supply.

Exponential functions are good as they increase prices slowly initially, which encourages the holding of tokens. However, the function accelerates aggressively in the last 20%. This makes it volatile as it opens the market to speculation and the growth rate can be unmanageable.

12.8.3.3.4 0.5 < Reserve Ratio < 1

The curve is now an upward sloping exponential graph. The closer the reserve ratio is to 1, the higher the steeper the curve is at the start, where the prices at the start increase rapidly, which creates speculation and volatility.

Since Bancor uses this formula as part of the $BNT, which has no objectives other than to be the medium of exchange in the ecosystem. The best model for the reserve ratio is to be 0.5[19].

However, this could change when the liquid formula has other objectives.

12.9. Conclusion

Bancor provides liquidity in their network of tokens using a liquid token, $BNT. $BNT is used in all reserve pools, which enables instant conversion between tokens. The upgrade of the system also provides insurance for impermanent loss incurred while trading. These all align to allow more liquidity in the system, which reduces price slippage and increases the economic value accrued by the protocol.

12.10 Bancor References

- Economics Design and Engineering for Robust DLT Ecosystems: https://www.economicsdesign.com/portfolio/economics-engineering/
- Bancor whitepaper: https://storage.googleapis.com/website-bancor/2018/04/01ba8253-bancor_protocol_whitepaper_en.pdf

Notes

1. Continuous liquidity is where a token can be converted to another token all the time. It does not require someone else to buy or sell the token, it can be converted (liquidated) anytime.
2. A smart contract is a simple software program that, once committed to a blockchain, is guaranteed to run unchanged for as long as the underlying blockchain remains operational. Smart contracts have many of the same capabilities as regular blockchain uses, i.e., they can invoke other smart contracts and hold balances of tokens in escrow. A well-defined smart contract can be viewed as a reliable, incorruptible, and fully automated intermediary.
3. Common denominator is a common feature that exists in a network. For example, most central banks in the world have US dollars in their reserves. This makes the US dollar a common denominator between many central banks. Having a common denominator makes it easier to match between parties.
4. Network token: These are tokens in the network that facilitate liquidity. Any token in the network can be converted to the network token easily, which can easily be converted to another token in the network.
5. Explain like I'm 5. Simplified explanation to help you grasp the concept of Bancor.
6. Cross-chain liquidity is the act of converting a token based on one blockchain into a token based on a different blockchain. E.g. $DAI, which is an Ethereum-based token to LEO, which is an EOS-based token.
7. Transitive means if a is greater than b, and b is greater than c, it means that a is greater than c. E.g. if 10 is greater than 5 and 5 is greater than 1, it means that 10 is greater than 1.
8. An automatic market maker is a program that will continuously buy and sell tokens according to the algorithmic prices. It replaces order books with code.
9. Trade occurs when the marketplace (exchange) finds a buyer and seller, and they can engage in an exchange of goods (or tokens). This will be rare when there is a lack of buyer and seller of the specific goods (or tokens).
10. Relay tokens represent a proportion of the reserve pool.
11. Check out Chapter 11 to learn more about bonding curves.
12. Other terms include constant reserve ratio, fractional reserve ratio, connector weight.
13. DEX refers to decentralised exchange. An exchange that is decentralised and not owned by a central entity.
14. This can be an institution, foundation of the reserve token, group of people or an individual.
15. Accurate as of October 2020.
16. This is accurate as of Bancor's launch in 2017, https://www.coindesk.com/150-million-tim-draper-backed-bancor-completes-largest-ever-ico.
17. Details of the conversion formula can be found in https://drive.google.com/file/d/0B3HPNP-GDn7aRkVaV3dkVl9NS2M/view.
18. The flexibility in reserve ratio weights is useful as the system evolves. Especially when we fully integrate to Web 3.0.
19. The reserve ratio allows for flexibility to change the weightage of the exchange. This allows for the system to integrate prices of other secondary markets to determine the value of tokens and reduce impermanent loss. However, due to the time delay of systems, this allows for arbitrageurs to profit freely at the expense of liquidity providers. Thus, until we resolve that in Web 3.0, the weightage will remain at a 0.5 fixed weight.

Chapter 13: Other Economics Principles

13.1 Discount Tokens

Discount tokens are a form of digital asset. They have a utility function, with the right to receive a discount on purchases. This model is used for services, not products. The token is not used to price items, but to receive a discount on the pricing. Discount tokens are developed by Sweetbridge[1].

Discount Token

Concepts	Explanation
What	Right to receive a discount on purchases Utility Function
How	Tokens is not used to price items, but to receive a discount on price
Why	Continuous liquidity for tokens with low demand

Unlike gift cards or coupons, discount tokens are not burned or destroyed after they are used. They continue to remain in the possession of the holder. Like gift cards or coupons, the tokens allow a user to receive a discount. The maximum discount one can receive is 100%, which renders the service free.

The value of the discount token comes in two forms: the use value (gaining discount on items) and the resale value. This is similar to the NYC cab medallion model. The medallion has a value on its own, and you can resell it. It also gives you the right to drive a cab in NYC. This right gives you the economic opportunity to earn cash in addition to being a medallion owner.

13.1.1. Four General Criteria for Discount Tokens

4 General Criteria for Discount Token

No tokens activated = no discounts received

When the amout of tokens used is the amount where the service will be free, the discount received is 100%

When the fee of the service is increase, the more tokens are needed to get a discount

The maximum tokens used is where the discount is 100%. (The service is free)

1. $f(t,y;X)$ has property $f(0,y;X)$. That means when no tokens are activated, no discount is received.

2. The number of tokens needed to eliminate all fees (aka service is free) is $t_{free}(y;X)$, which satisfies $f(t_{free}(y;X), y;X) = 1$. That means when the amount of tokens used is the amount where the service will be free, the discount received is 100% (aka 1).

3. Discount tokens required to get 100% discount $(t_{free}(y;X))$ is strictly increasing in y. $\partial t / \partial y\ t_{free}(y;X) > 0$ *for all* X. That means when the fee of the service increases, the more tokens are needed to get a discount.

4. The maximum tokens that can be used is bounded by $t_{max}(y;X \leq t_{free}(y;X)$. This is where the discount is 100% and the user does not need to pay.

13.1.2. Functions of discount tokens

1. Cost of service is $\boldsymbol{C(t,y; X) = c \cdot y \cdot (1-f(t,y;X))}$
   - *Where $\boldsymbol{C(t,y;X)}$ is the cost function that includes t, tokens activated, $\boldsymbol{y}$, quantity purchases and $\boldsymbol{X}$, global network state*
   - *The discount function (given by the discount token) is $\boldsymbol{f(t,y;X)}$.*

2. Discount model

   The services can be purchased with tokens or without. Nonetheless, the prices are set by the service provider and determined by market demand.

   The amount of discount received per token, however, is dictated by the needs and utility of the network. In general, the discount size increases as the network grows. This is a method to determine the valuation of the token using endogenous variable network growth. It provides incentives for users and early supporters to purchase tokens, as they will receive more discounts as the network grows.

3. Network utilisation metrics
   - Discount function when 1^2 is $f(t{:}X) = t \cdot X_u / X_T$
   - The maximum discount one can get is 100% (aka 1), where the item is free. Hence, $t_{max}(x) = t_{free}(x) = X_T / X_U$

4. Sufficient operating revenue in the presence of discount tokens
   - The discount token reflects the overall usage of the network,

     $\boldsymbol{f(t, y;X) = t \,/\, tfree\ (y;X)}$
   - *The cost, given the discount token is now,*

     $\boldsymbol{C(t, y;X) = c \cdot (1 - t /(t_{free}\ (y;X))) = c \cdot (t_{free}(y;x) - t)/(t_{free}\ (y;x)),}$

     $\boldsymbol{valid\ for\ 0 \leq \ \leq t_{free}(y;x)}$

5. Effects of network growth

Early participants will have increasing discount as the network utility grows. This is because when tokens are purchased early, the network utilisation is still low. As the utility grows, the size of discounts per token will be reduced. That means the token required to get a discount is less. This means that the user needs less token and can sell the extra tokens and cash it out.

- $t_{free}(y; X) = \beta \cdot Xt / Xu$ where β is the operating fee or other system-level design parameter $(\beta > 0)$, X_T is the tokens activated by the token holder and X_U is the network utilisation. Network utilisation, X_U, increases with more active users.

6. Deriving Value from Utility

The utility value per token activated per unit of time is $U(X) = C / \beta \cdot XT / Xu$. This is calculated from by partial differentiating from the cost function.

Per unit of time is included, as we assume a time-based service. For example, a per-license-per-period utility. The value comes in two ways: (1) buy and use of discount token or (2) holding on to the token that provides a return, *r*. The fair value of the token is $U(X) = 1 / r$ $(U(X)) = cX_u / r\beta X_T$

This is calculated using the present value of perpetual annuity. For non-time *based, define* $\boldsymbol{y}$ *by the level of service per* activation period change. For example, rental of servicwes.

7. Operating Cost

Operating costs can come from transaction costs on blockchain and general maintenance and operating cost of the service. Discount tokens need to account for funds required for ongoing operations.

- *A constraint can be set,* $t_{max}(y;X) < t_{free}(y;X)$ *so that services will never be free.*
- *Add* $\beta > 1$ *in the cost function so users will receive* $1 / \beta$ *of revenue and* $1 - 1 / \beta$ *will be used for operating costs. Network revenue can be defined as* $\sum C(ti, yi, x = x \cdot (1 - 1/\beta)Eyi$ *.The cost is* $C(0, \sum yi; X) - \sum C(ti, yi, X) = 1/\beta\ C(0, \sum yi; X)$

8. Incentivise increased utility of discount token by making use of discount token strictly better off than just holding it. By using the token, the user gets to receive perpetual discounts. When the value of the token increases, the user can sell it off, making profits. If an investor only purchases the discount token to wait for the increase in value on the secondary market, the only economic benefits are the profits from selling the token. For a user, they will gain the economic benefits as well as the economic savings earned when using the tokens for discount on services.

13.2 Property Rights

Property rights are socially-enforced constructs to determine how resources or goods are used and owned.

13.2.1 Types of Property Rights

1. Open-access (e.g. stuff on GitHub. Or the ocean)
2. Public property (e.g. Ethereum. Or a park) – owned by all, but its access and use are controlled by state or community
3. Common property (e.g. permission DLT. Or board of directors) – owned by group of individuals
4. Private property (e.g. Your private key. The Coca Cola recipe)

Property rights is a huge topic on its own, since there are many ways to design the distribution of property rights. Here, we will focus on new ways to manage property rights for digital assets.

13.2.2. Harbarger Taxation

For example, we can do this with digital art.

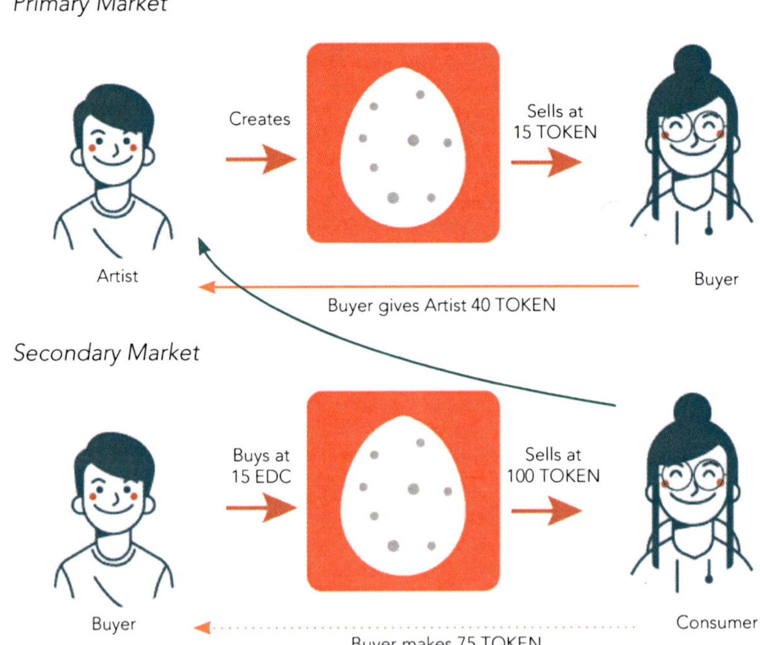

The desired goal is to ensure that the artist benefits from the art they created, as well as making sure that whoever owns the digital artwork doesn't keep it forever. More collectors at more fair valuations means more people can participate in digital art ownership and collecting.

For example:

1. The Artist (A) creates the art.
2. When A sells the art to Buyer (B), he gets the profit. (Straightforward)
3. (B) sells the art to Consumer (C).
4. (B) gets to keep the profit and the transaction fee (aka the "taxes") will be given to (A).
5. This can keep going on, and the transaction fee will always be given to A.
6. New buyers will not price too high, because the transaction fee is calculated based on the price. They also wouldn't sell it when the price is too low, since they cannot profit and rather keep the art in their possession instead.

13. 3 Conviction Staked Inflation Funding

Conviction Staked Inflation Funding

Concepts	*Explanation*
WHAT	DISTRIBUTE NEWLY MINTED TOKENS USING AMOUNT AND DURATION OF TOKENS STAKED
HOW	LOGARITHMIC-FUNCTION TO INCENTIVISE EARLY STAKERS
FOR	CONTUNUOUS FUNDING FOR OPEN-SOURCE PUBLIC PROJECT

This model is used for continuous funding for open source projects. The tokens staked are rewarded according to the number of tokens staked and time period the tokens have been staked for.

They are associated with a logarithmic function . The longer period of stake, the more (new) tokens are minted and distributed to that staked address.

The inflationary component represents new tokens minted or created. Part of the new tokens minted (e.g. 15%) will be distributed to the staking addresses. The proportion one receives of the new minted tokens is relative to the amount staked and duration of staking.

The more tokens staked, the more one receives new minted tokens. The longer one stakes the token, the more one receives new minted tokens. The two variables in the model are amount staked, $\boldsymbol{s}$, and time, $\boldsymbol{t}$.

The logarithmic function is used to ensure that one small token holder staking for six months will gain more benefits than one large token holder staking for one week. The logarithmic function is used to incentivise users to stake earlier. Small users can gain more rewards by staking early.

The opportunity cost also increases over time, because the gradient flattens out as time passes. This means that users would rather have their tokens in other places than participate, removing speculators. The remaining stakers are usually people who truly believe in the project, instead of being merely speculators.

This could also be a risk, being less incentivised to stake in the long run because the rewards are much less. The initial growth of rewards to the staked tokens are also quite high, which can introduce speculation. Hence, this model works better for public projects, where most users are more interested in social welfare than personal individual profits.

13.4 Contract Theory

Contracts are inherently incomplete. That means, they are only enforceable to the extent that events are verified by a third party.

E.g. The cost of health insurance to a person is determined by your health status. But that is impossible to figure out, so you use signals instead. Like how much do you eat on a day-to-day basis, how often you exercise, etc.

Herein lies the problem. Even if all relevant information is verified, you cannot write a contract that contains all possible issues that could arise. That will be costly and, anyway, some events cannot be specified in advance.

Why do we need contracts then, if it is not holistic enough? Back in the day, markets helped to facilitate spot contracting, meaning the buyer and seller trade at the same time. You can verify the product and pay physical money at the same time.

As the market evolved, things got more complicated. Verification could not always happen instantly. Transactions could not be executed immediately. This complication can be solved using contracts. Contacts ensure that trade is executed as agreed upon by the parties.

The ultimate aim is to turn a trade, which requires actions to be taken, into a sequential format, into a spot trade.

Back in the DLT space, the problems with contracts is not what is in them, it is what is not in them. When it comes to facilitating trade, the greatest gain in efficiency does not come from the ability to automatically execute previously veritable terms. This is already working in the system today with all sorts of sensors and IoT devices.

DLT focuses on improving the **quality of information** so that more factors can be used in contracts which makes them more complete. (Example: It is difficult to account for a driver's behaviour. Now with tech, we can extract, record and verify data, turning this into real efficiency gains.)

An example is to pay for performance, which is the proof of work consensus model. It can exist beyond Layer 1 protocols. The applications in DApp can be tokens in a liquidity pool to provide work, i.e. the work of facilitating the exchange of tokens. Rewards will be given, via transaction fees, when work can be verified as having happened. That exists when a user exchanges tokens in that decentralised exchange, after comparing the various risks involved in the other DEX options.

While the DEX protocol does not specify the key aspects of the desired outcome in advance, e.g. the ideal amount of liquidity in the pool, the users (liquidity providers and DEX users) are able to self-select the input they want to contribute and trade.

Income risk:

Expected income via transaction fees – expected risk of price slippage or impermanent loss.

This can be risky, as the desired behaviour (amount of liquidity provided) is not specified and agreed upon, thus the liquidity providers are unable to access their risks (e.g. price slippage and impermanent loss). Liquidity providers need to be compensated more for the same level of liquidity provided so that they will accept the income risk. Thus, a native token is usually provided to compensate for the risk and make it more attractive for liquidity providers to enter the ecosystem.

This specific contract is more efficient than using a pay for performance contract, which is to compensate.

13.5 Token Curated Registry (TCR)

Token curated registry (TCR) was introduced in Chapter 10 when we talked about token design.

TCRs are decentralised lists of things. They can be decentralised lists of pizza places in Milan or best lakes in Canada. To cast your vote in this list, you have to stake a number of tokens. People can challenge your vote and you can either win their tokens or lose your staked tokens. To create the effect of people coordinating and agreeing towards a single point, TCRs are a possible solution to do that. They are a form of communication in terms of the tokens staked.

Does this remind you of something we also discussed earlier? This is an example of Schelling point, the 7th wonder in Chapter 2! The goal is to find out the "right" answer from the community.

13.5.1 Application

Ranking Datasets

We discussed Ocean protocol using TCR to curate AI datasets and rank them. An external feedback loop is attached to bonding curves in terms of external verification. At the surface level, the bonding curve ranks databases. Tokens are staked to signal that the data will have future popularity.

Miners earn from serving up datasets and making them available when asked. Otherwise, they lose their stakes. By providing the datasets, they get to earn a fee from their staking amount too.

Rank Online Courses

Let's say, I have an online economics school for students with a number of different courses. A reputation token is used, $EREP[4].

Upon completion of a course, students can rate how good that course is. If they think the course is good, more people will join the course, and they will stake $EREP at the course. Slowly, it becomes a ranked list of how good people think particular courses are.

The bottom 20% of courses will lose their tokens and those tokens will be distributed proportionally to users in the other courses.

This gives the courses a reputational value and people will naturally tend towards the course with the highest stake. It also signals that the course is good, since many people voted on it and staked their tokens on it.

If the tokens have monetary value and are traded in the secondary market, it can greatly disincentivise people to participate. Instead, the token can be an internal utility token for reputation purposes and to reward the online course creators.

Notes

1. Check out https://sweetbridge.com to learn more about their project.
2. We look at y=1 in this case, because we assume that the service is a software service, and one user would just purchase the access. Hence, the purchase quantity is 1.
3. This model is still being discussed and explored. Follow the conversation here https://github.com/ethereum-funding/blockrewardsfunding/issues/39
4. This is not a real token. It is an example.

PART 2: DECENTRALISED FINANCE

Chapter 14: Economics of Decentralised Finance (DeFi)

Decentralised finance (DeFi) is the current trend in the token economics space. In general, the goal of DLT is to remove intermediaries. One of the sectors populated with many intermediaries is the financial sector. There are plenty of intermediaries in the space, from brokers to traders, relationship managers, and funds.

Tokenisation brings about the possibility of codifying the majority of the business logics and executing them with machines (aka smart contracts). This frees up the margin (aka money) rewarded to intermediaries which can then be distributed to reward users in the system.

Decentralised finance is important because it has the potential to revolutionise the traditional financial sector as we know it in the following ways:

- Perhaps money can be managed by codifying monetary policy in machines, algorithms and smart contracts. Money can then be neutral[1], without any political ties and agenda.

- Or allowing trade with assets (e.g. tokens) without having a counterparty orderbook, because machines will always be the counterparty, providing liquidity.

- Maybe it is a constant rebalancing of your financial portfolio based on the exposure you are interested in, and the machine rebalances it automatically without having to pay your portfolio manager the high management fees.

The possibilities are endless because there are huge inefficiencies in the market. As we bring the systems into a digital space, we are making the system more efficient – better, faster, quicker. Hence, it is important to understand the economics and design of these DeFi math and systems infrastructure that we are building. Applications like portfolio management, decentralised exchange and decentralised insurance can exist on a codified business logic form.

14.1 Introduction to DeFi

14.1.1. What is DeFi

DeFi is a movement that uses decentralised networks to transform the financial system as we know it, by removing the intermediaries.

This means taking the existing financial systems (like NASDAQ exchange, portfolio managers, hedge funds) and building them on new systems.

New governance, new incentives, new mechanisms. A whole new world.

Box 4: Comparing Traditional Finance with Decentralised Finance

Balance Sheet	Traditional Company	DeFi Protocol
Assets	Tangible assets (machinery) Intangible assets (algorithm, client, relationships)	Intangible assets (community network, smart contract algorithm)
Liabilities	Debt	Crowdsourced liquidity
Equities	Owner's equity Shareholder's equity	Token representing equity Token representing share of profits

Similar to traditional companies, a DeFi protocol also includes the usual Assets, Liabilities and Equities in the balance sheet. The difference is that instead of laws and regulations defined by the government the company is incorporated in, DeFi protocols define the rules that users and tokens have to follow.

The rules are everything we have discussed in the first half of the book. A DeFi protocol operates like a traditional company but is structured in a new and innovative way.

We discussed the difference between tangible and intangible assets in Section 2.2.3. That discussion is around economics.

This second half of the book is around DeFi. And that is what we will focus on. The innovative ways of crowdsourcing liquidity (debt) and distribute ownership of the protocol to the community (equity).

This is what DeFi is about. Removing intermediaries and distributing value-add to users of the system, instead of only to shareholders with sufficient capital to begin with.

The underlying principles of a traditional company exists in DeFi. The mechanism to apply the principles are different, primarily focusing on decentralisation.

14.1.2. Why DeFi?

Before we move into the details of "how the whole DeFi thing works", it is important to start with "Why". The existing financial system, infrastructure and products have been in place for years. Despite the various financial crises, the economy is still surviving. So, why do we need DeFi?

Simple. Because the existing system is inefficient, and incentives are not distributed equally. That means people at the top of the value-chain are earning so much, while others at the bottom are struggling to pay for their meals. Or that intermediaries (aka the intermediaries) are earning so much when we can codify this business logic with machines. Or that money is not neutral and tied to political agendas. This only hurts those at the bottom of the value-chain.

So, there are ways to increase efficiency in the system. And we can do this by building them on a decentralised finance infrastructure. How? On to the next point.

14.1.3 How does DeFi Work

1. **DeFi is about removing intermediaries**

The way to do it is to codify business logic.

For example, instead of having a centralised orderbook to match sellers and buyers on an exchange (e.g. New York Stock Exchange), you can use machines to be the counterparty to trade with. These machines will always follow the code, and the code is defined by math. In the exchange of an exchange, it uses the formula found in physics, the energy conservation theory.

In that sense, math is the underlying foundation that defines the infrastructure of DeFi. Code is the language that computers will be processing the math and information.

DeFi is like building a tall skyscraper. Math is the foundational pillars and bricks. Code is the cement.

2. **Distributing governance to peers.**

Removing intermediaries and executing business logic with machines is powerful. The next powerful thing is to solve, or reduce inefficiencies, in governance.

Governance and corporate governance are huge problems. Both in the "real" physical world and the online digital world. Coates (2018) highlighted that passive indexing, private equity and globalisation is reshaping the idea of ownership and governance. In the future, there is a strong likelihood that the world will be controlled by 12 individuals, owning the governance votes via passive indexing and funds.

This problem is still not solved. And by bringing the system to a digital space, we only intensify it. However, new technology also brings about new opportunities to solve this problem. Instead of giving the governance power to the 12 individuals, it is possible to distribute the governance to the users who use the system. It is also possible to delegate your governance vote to experts in the area.

The concept is that now we can distribute governance, and people using the system have an active voice in the governance moving forward. No doubt, there will be issues, but this is a positive baby step in the right direction.

3. **Incentivising behaviours.**

Freeing up the margins that would have gone to the intermediaries and intermediaries, we can now look at redirecting these incentives to encourage certain behaviours.

For example, instead of an expensive listing fee on NASDAQ, listing can be free or with low fees on a decentralised exchange. The fees will be allocated to encourage behaviours, like incentivising users to be liquidity providers and they will be rewarded with the appropriate amount of fees.

This last point is the largest game changer in DeFi. We can now explore new and innovative ways to encourage behaviours, as products and services are now common goods. Instead of the Tragedy of The Commons, we have these incentives in place to encourage Collaborative Commons.

14.1.4. Who is in DeFi

DeFi is about decentralisation right? You can imagine a very distributed segment of participants.

Back to the skyscraper model, this is how it works.

You need the **investors** to be funding your commercial skyscraper. You need the **architect** to design the skyscraper and the blueprint. You need the **machines** like cranes to be building them. You need the construction **engineers** to be using the machines and building the skyscraper according to the blueprint and design. You have the **companies** renting out an office space in the building (e.g. WeWork). You have **employees** in the companies using the office space (e.g. members of WeWork).

The value is returned to everyone in the system. Investors with their returns from rental. Architects, engineers and builders with salaries and wages. Companies and employees with a space to work, a network to connect to, and a community to transact with.

In the DeFi model, this is how it works.

Instead of a skyscraper, it is a community with a protocol.

You have **investors** to fund the idea of building this. They can be VCs, funds or anyone with capital. You have the **architect** to design the business logic, incentives and blueprint of how the community, protocol and system works, e.g. Economics Design. You need the **machines** to enable this to work. That is the protocol itself, aka code. Instead of construction engineers to build the skyscrapers, there are **computer science engineers** turning the blueprint and design into code. The special part here is that the **companies** and **employees** can be the same. The companies are retail investors; people with some funds, wanting to invest. The users can also be investors, to be part of the system and use the protocol available.

Summary Table

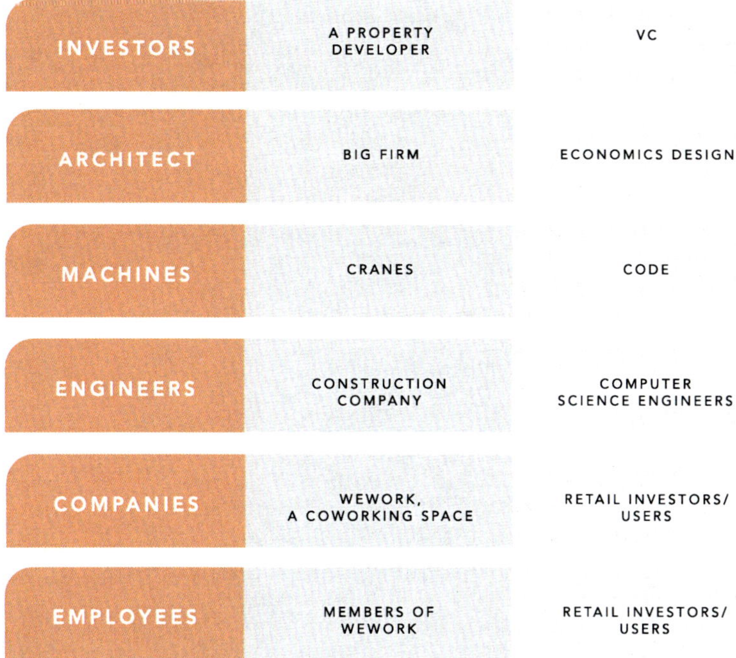

INVESTORS	A PROPERTY DEVELOPER	VC
ARCHITECT	BIG FIRM	ECONOMICS DESIGN
MACHINES	CRANES	CODE
ENGINEERS	CONSTRUCTION COMPANY	COMPUTER SCIENCE ENGINEERS
COMPANIES	WEWORK, A COWORKING SPACE	RETAIL INVESTORS/ USERS
EMPLOYEES	MEMBERS OF WEWORK	RETAIL INVESTORS/ USERS

14.1.5. Where is DeFi

DeFi exists digitally, online. Thus, the key consideration is what the jurisdiction is of the various participants (see above).

Regulation is very important, and the regulators are figuring out ways to regulate the space, while the space is innovating with new concepts every single day. It is a very exciting time to be alive.

14.1.6 When DeFi Started

You can trace DeFi all the way back to Bitcoin.

Ten years ago, we saw the creation of Bitcoin – a decentralised money. Building upon this asset (decentralised money), we are now at the stage of decentralised finance. Think of your phone and apps. DeFi is the operating system itself (e.g. Android, iOS), and the apps are the various financial protocols that exist on the phone.

The entire system is a huge Lego building block to stack on top of each other. That's where the fun begins.

14.2 Nine DeFi 101 FAQ

1. Why is decentralisation important?

Because users like you and me can now take control of the money we use, instead of relying on banks and intermediaries. They are taking a lot of mark-up in this process. We redistribute these mark-ups to users like you and me.

2. What "power" does DeFi bring?

It gives people the ability to create and move money across the world at any given time. It also tries to solve the problem of the unbanked and create more equal access opportunities to users around the world.

3. What's the difference between DeFi and bitcoin?

Bitcoin is money. It's programmable money. DeFi is the operating system of money. Bitcoin is like the Facebook app, and DeFi is the iOS that your iPhone runs on.

4. Is DeFi a scam?

DeFi is a sub-category in finance. Is finance a scam? It could be and it could not be. It's difficult to generalise the entire industry into a scam or not. In general, there are real projects working on DeFi and looking to disrupt the existing systems in place. At the same time, there are bad actors cheating money using the system.

5. Why is DeFi important?

As mentioned earlier, decentralisation is the crux of the future. Others are likely to share about financial inclusion and digitisation, so here is the economics perspective instead.

In economics, we have two resources, Labour (L) and Capital (K). In the past (physical and centralised ledger that we covered in Chapter 2), we priced goods based on the hours of labour used to produce them. That is all good, equal and easy.

As we evolved, we started to use machines to enable the completion of tasks. Suddenly, pricing of goods is not just the cost of labour, but the cost of machines. Machines are capital. People who own the machines are capital owners. People with capital are now reaping the profits. People providing the labour are not receiving as much of the profits.

If anything, the world of tomorrow is inching closer towards benefiting capital (K) owners instead of people providing labour (L). Look at technology like GPT-3, machine learning, smart contracts and other forms of automation. These profits will be given to capital owners. Inequality increases when we replace people providing labour (L) with more efficient use of machinery capital (K).

This is where DeFi comes in. It builds a base layer which is an open-source technological stack (K) that is not owned by a single person. Anyone (L) can tap into this capital available to build innovative products and solutions. It becomes accessible and available to everyone and anyone willing to learn.

6. Is DeFi a solution looking for a problem to solve?

Which brings me to the next point that many people ask. Right now, yes, DeFi is a solution looking for a problem to solve. Today, we still live in a predominantly physical world, with an increasing shift towards the digital world.

Right now, we do not have these problems highlighted in #5, because we are not there yet. However, we know we are getting there. Inching closer towards a predominately digital world every day.

Thus, the problem of inequality of capital owners (K) and labour providers (L) will continuously increase. DeFi looks at innovative ways to align incentives of a distributed system. In the end, we can better distribute value amongst users.
The alternative is for capital owners (K) to hoard all profits and the rest of the world bows down to capital owners.

7. How does DeFi have a role in Web 3.0?
Web 3.0 is an open-source collaborative new world that enables both humans and machine intelligence.

Web 1.0 is generally what we call a read-only database. The

database creates content and as consumers, we consume it. It's like a newspaper. We read newspapers and consume the content.

Web 2.0 increases the users on the network. It is a read and write database. That means we can consume the content and also create content. It's like the newspaper with a forum page or The Economist with letters to the editors.

Web 3.0 brings the web to a new level. It is a read and write database with machine intelligence. It usually talks about machine learning (artificial intelligence), internet of things, robotics and blockchain. 5G network helps Web 3.0 as it allows for more information and data transfer for machine intelligence to work efficiently.

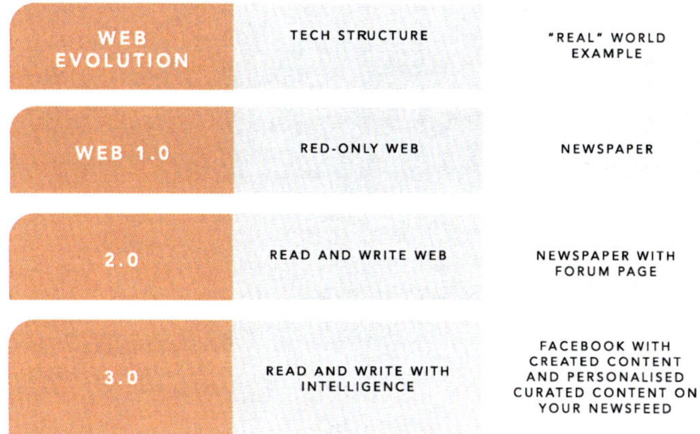

8. Where is the innovation in DeFi?

Most innovation are not absolutely mindblowing. In chapter 13, we dive further into the math of automation in DeFi.

One of the innovations in the space is the use of bonding curves as the core technological stack for these protocols. There are various ways of using bonding curves as discussed in Chapter 11.

9. What is layer 1 and layer 2?

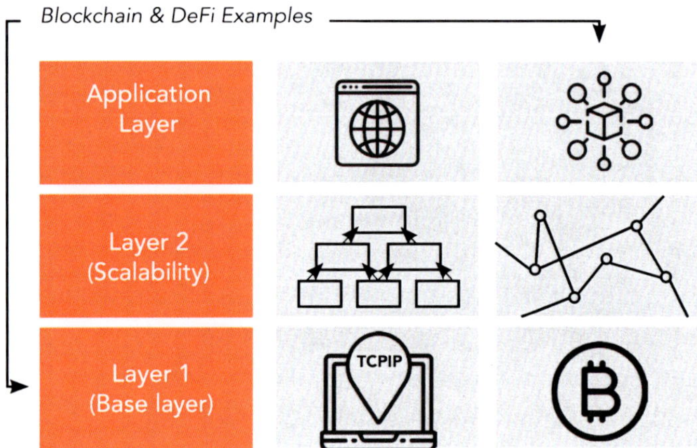

Layer 1 is the core base layer. Instead of a centralised ledger, we use a distributed ledger (aka blockchain).

Layer 2 are scalability solutions. This is because Layer 1 can be slow sometimes or too costly to send many mini-transactions.

Application layer is usually where most DeFi protocols are.
It can be built on Layer 1 or Layer 2. It focuses on producing the solutions to end-users instead of providing the back-end solutions to protocols (Layer 1 and 2).

Box 5: Comparing Traditional Lending with DeFi Lending

If Adam has $100 and Benny needs to borrow $100, how does that work? If you trust each other, you can just lend directly, and maybe Adam charges an interest rate, let's say 5%.

In the traditional finance space today, you don't know each other. Adam puts the money with the bank. The bank pays Adam some interest. Then the bank uses that money to find people like Benny, who want to borrow, and Benny pays the interest to the bank.

DeFi now replaces the role of the bank and solves the problem of "trust" across the world. Instead of trusting the people, DeFi turns that trust into code in the system. How? (1) money (aka Facebook app) is programmable. And (2) the operating system of money (aka your iOS or Android system) is also programmable.

Now, Adam can find all the Bennys in the world **without** having to

1. Trust Benny or know Benny personally
2. Engage with a bank or third party that will take profits away
3. Find a centralised institution

DeFi Lending

We are basically programming code into the money (e.g. $TOKEN). And in the code, we incentivise people to put money in or take money out.

How? We do this by changing interest rates.

This will change people's behaviours by creating loans and to encourage lending or borrowing.

When demand drops, the interest rate drops. People are more likely to demand more $TOKEN now, since it is cheaper.

When demand goes up, there is too much supply. Interest rates increase. People demand less $TOKEN because it's more expensive now.

The change in interest rate is executed by programs and code.

14.3 Economics vs Monetary Value

Tokens are a way to extract the economic value of a ecosystem and to distribute this value directly to the community. In DeFi, tokens to capture the value of the community and redistribute the value. The monetary value comes when tokens with economic value are traded in the secondary market.

In DeFi, where is the economic value coming from? This is similar to Uber when they started. They were paying for users to use their services. They were losing money in every single transaction that the platform processed but it helped to bootstrap the network economy in the long run.

In the marketplace economy, it is always a chicken and egg issue. Without a supplier, you do not attract users to your platform. Without users, suppliers are not incentivised to come. By having a very high reward, you attract both sides i.e. the suppliers and the consumers to come at the same time. Hopefully in the long run, it can grow into a sustainable economy for the protocol.

14.4 Where is DeFi's Economic Value Accrual?

Where is the economic value accrual then? It comes in 3 major areas:

1. Network effects and Positive Externalities
2. Collaborative Commons
3. Interoperable Lego Blocks

14.4.1. Network Effects and Positive Externalities

In networked economies, you have value being created in that economy and the positive externalities that come with it.

> *In economics, a positive externality is additional benefits that affects a third party that did not incur the benefit. For example, in developing a housing market in a rural city, the positive externalities could be improved public healthcare, better local communities and more collaborative commons like weekend markets, libraries and cleaner parks.*

14.4.1.1 Example: Vaccines

Think of vaccines. When a person is vaccinated, they are less likely to catch that particular disease. Because they are less likely to catch it, they are less likely to become a carrier and infect others. Getting vaccinated has a positive externality for the community.

14.4.1.2 Example: DeFi and Fiscal Policy

Similarly, native tokens of each DeFi sector are used to capture the economic value in the system. In DeFi the networked economies are multi-sided so we can create and generate positive externalities in each side of the market. These tokens are used across the DeFi sectors and increase the overall value of the platform.

Since most of the native tokens are a form of governance token, you can think of the community holding governance tokens as government bodies when it comes to fiscal policies. Each platform has its government and decision-making power. Now, they come together to make decisions across platforms. Because they have skin in the game on various platforms, the decisions made are highly likely to increase the overall value of the platforms, and the positive externalities of the community overall.

14.4.2 Collaborative Commons

What are collaborative commons? This is a system that reduces centralised ownership and relies on having sharable economic value that encourages cooperation and collaboration. These DeFi protocols are open source, not owned by anyone. These protocols can then be used to encourage peer-to-peer cooperation and collaboration.

In such systems, we are looking to encourage the maximum value from the protocol without overdoing it. When we overdo it, it becomes an economic phenomenon called Tragedy of the Commons. This is where users extract as much value as they can from shared resources currently, not considering the future cost.

For example, water.

Water is a shared resource between us today, and with now and our future generation. Selfish individuals or firms use water responsibly, depleting or spoiling the resource through their collective actions. For example, South Africa's drought crisis in 2017[3] and fresh groundwater[4] being destroyed or lakes and bodies of water being polluted[5].

Today, we are changing the way we think about common goods. We know that resources can easily be exploited. We can engineer incentives to be in place to reduce that and use the tools available to encourage collaboration instead of exploitation.

14.4.3 Interoperable Lego Blocks

We will share the nine sectors in DeFi. In the same way that you have many areas in finance, you have many areas in DeFi. The fun thing is that they work like Lego blocks. You can stack them on top of each other and the systems can speak to each other.

14.4.3.1 Example: Traditional ETF vs Crypto ETF

For example, you have money (USD) and you can use it to buy a derivative (ETF) in an exchange (NASDAQ) and earn returns (dividends).

You can use programmable money ($crypto-USD) to buy a derivative (an ETF that rebalances automatically) in a decentralised exchange (Balancer) and earn returns (BAL tokens + returns from transactions fees).

14.4.3.2. Example: DeFi Lending

You can use this programmable money to lend out. Someone can borrow it and use it as collateral on another DeFi sector. You gain interest rates as returns and possibly a native token.

Thus, borrowers can stake programmable money in a decentralised exchange with low impermanent loss (Curve vault) and gain both interest rates and native governance tokens ($CRV).

The entire system is a bunch of Lego building blocks that can be stacked on top of each other. That's where the fun begins. And there is a huge positive externality spillover by sharing value between the various DeFi sectors.

Currently, the tokens exist on their own in Layer 1 protocol, e.g. only on Ethereum, on EOS, on Algorand. However, more solutions are coming into the space to solve this problem. Tokens will soon be able to interact and move between all the Layer 1 protocols. Polkadot is one of the protocols looking to solve this problem.

When this is solved, economic value can exist beyond just the Layer 1 protocols. Unlike traditional finance and networks, where collective switching costs hinder positive externality flow, interoperable solutions allow the economic value to flow between various protocols.

Imagine each Layer 1 protocol being a language. Ethereum only speaks English. EOS only speaks Chinese. Algorand only speaks Russian. These are very different languages. If there is a good idea in the English-speaking community, you cannot communicate it to the Chinese or Russian community. So, Polkadot wants to be the translator to allow the three languages to communicate with each other and share ideas. That is where the economic value comes from.

Once the various Layer 1 protocols are able to speak to each other, we can only imagine the immense economic value that will be generated and created for the entire community as a whole.

14.5 Nine Sectors in DeFi

Note: if you are in the financial capital market space, please refer to Appendix A for a comparison chart of the terms used in DeFi.

Finance is a complex market. If you ask someone what they do, and they say finance, you rarely follow up with "which area in finance?". Whereas in medicine, you would be more likely to ask about the specialisation like gynaecology, paediatrician, cardiothoracic surgeon.

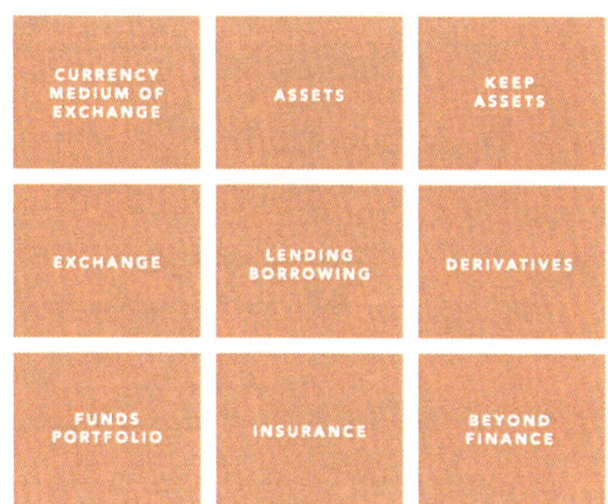

This is because finance is hard and complicated. You have so many sectors and it's difficult to keep up with them. There are many sectors in finance, but here specifically, we will dive into nine sectors. It gives us enough sectors to have a snapshot of the DeFi environment and understand how they work, according to what we have learnt so far.

The nine sectors we want to look at are currency as a medium of exchange, assets, places to keep these assets, exchanges, lending and borrowing, derivatives, funds and portfolios, insurance, and applications beyond finance.

14.5.1 Currency as a Medium of Exchange

Traditional finance's medium of exchange includes examples like USD, GBP, EUR, JYP, RMB.

These are governed by 12 very brilliant monetary economists in the central bank. They decide the interest rates, define the inflation rates and printing money. Check out Box 3 in the previous chapter for more details.

The purpose of the central bank is to ensure price stability and general trust in the currency.

Remember that in DeFi we can codify the business logic with machines and math. What if we can define price stability with math to reduce the political influence that makes money non-neutral? Being built on a distributed ledger, it is possible to outsource trust of the currency to machines and code.

In DeFi we look at currency as a medium of exchange, a way to get access into the various DeFi sectors (aka protocols).

DeFi's medium of exchange are currencies such as $ETH[6], $wBTC, $USDT, $AMPL.

14.5.2 Assets

In traditional finance, the existing asset classes are

- Stock/equity
- Bond/fixed-income investments
- Cash/money market funds
- Real estate/tangible assets
- Futures and financial derivatives

In DeFi, a new asset class is created. Crypto assets like $SNX, $AAVE, $YFI, $MKR can behave somewhat similarly to some types of existing asset classes, but they are unique on their own.

You can have equivalent tokenised versions of the existing asset classes. And a new addition of asset class could be created in the foreseeable future, as we see how the design of this new asset class plays out.

Crypto-assets are still relatively new in this space They have elements of various asset classes like stock, equity or even bonds and some fixed-income instruments. However, they are also very unique on their own.

Currently, the assets are priced from the market through trading and other financial forecasting. As much as we seek to figure out the formula of how to accurately price this new asset class, we are still relying on price discovery and forecasting to estimate its value.

14.5.3 Keep Assets

Now that we have defined the various assets available, where do you keep them?

Assets are kept traditionally in banks like Bank of America, HSBC, Standard Chartered.

There is also a huge movement by fintech banks such as Monzo and Revolut to provide solutions for keeping your assets.

In DeFi, assets are kept in crypto wallets like My Ether Wallet, Metamask, Ledger, Trezor.

14.5.4 Exchanges/Trade

Exchanges in traditional finance are NASDAQ, the London Stock

Exchange, the New York Stock Exchange, and Shanghai Stock Exchange. These systems are basically an orderbook where buyers and sellers place their orders. The trade can be matched when they find the right counterparty, or a market maker comes in to fulfil the order.

For example, I can only sell my cement for steel when there is someone wanting steel for cement (counterparty pairing). Otherwise, a construction company with lots of cement and steel can come in and trade with me (trade via a market maker contract).

In DeFi, there are decentralised exchanges (DEXs) like Uniswap, Bancor, Curve. Instead of pairing with counterparty traders, the machine will execute the trade. To do this, a liquidity pool is introduced, and the math is executed by the smart contract for the amount to be exchanged. The liquidity pool can be known as the market maker in traditional finance.

14.5.5. Lending/Borrowing

People can lend and borrow from traditional banks like Citibank and HSBC, or fintech banks like Monzo. In DeFi, there are lending protocols such as Aave, Maker, Compound.

Back to the example in Box 3, Adam has an extra $100. Benny wants to borrow $100. Now, they do not know each other, so the bank does the trade. Adam puts that $100 in HSBC and the bank pays Adam 1% to safeguard the money.

In turn, the bank will tell Benny, "you need $100, right? I have that

$100. I'm going to lend it to you and charge you 5%". Benny takes the deal and the bank earns 4%.

Now, we can use machines and lending protocols to replace the role of the bank. The lending protocol will define the interest rates via math and provide the option to Benny. Benny can go to Aave, Maker or Compound to view the rates. The one with the best rates will be borrowed from by Benny. And Adam puts his $100 in the lending protocol and waits for trade to happen.

Instead of a bank, we now optimise the business logic with math and code in DeFi's lending and borrowing.

Similar to exchanges and trade, lending and borrowing also exists on two levels, centralised lending (Celsius, Nuo Network) and decentralised lending (Aave, Compound). Both systems provide interest rates to lenders and borrowers to incentivise them to use the platform. There is no fixed formula, it depends on interest rate mechanisms each protocol chooses to use. Each protocol calculates the lending rates uniquely.

14.5.6 Derivatives

Futures contracts, forward contracts, interest rate swaps, options, structured notes, and variance swaps are some examples of derivatives in traditional finance. The derivatives market is the largest when it comes to total value in the entire financial sector. The notional value is 48 times larger[7] than the gross market value.

In DeFi, derivatives are still new and being explored. Marketplaces like Synthetix, Opyn, Hegic, FTX, UMA provide some products in the space. Common crypto derivatives are futures, perpetual futures, options, binary options and variance swaps. While they are mainly focused on $BTC exposure, new products are coming out to also bet on DeFi tokens. New products are coming out like crypto-ETF and DeFi-indexes. We explore that in the next section.

Math is used to define the business logic in simple logic like rebalancing the portfolio and managing a leveraged position. In general, decentralised markets use exchange or interest rates to enable such trade.

14.5.7 Funds and Portfolios

Exchange-traded funds, mutual funds, hedge funds, and municipal funds are some examples in traditional finance. Funds can be actively managed or passively managed either by companies like Fidelity or asset management companies. There are also venture capital funds for other types of risk exposures.

In DeFi, funds and portfolios can be managed traditionally via a VC fund or via a DeFi asset management fund. Alternatively, these can be automated with code and math to allow for trade of the basket of goods or specific assets. For example, there's PieDAO and Balancer.

This is different from indexes, which is another sector that we are not covering. However, the mechanism is similar, in that they use math to define the allocation proportion in the indexes.

14.5.8 Insurance

There are traditional institutions that provide insurance like AIG, AXA, Ping An, AVIVA, Prudential.

Traditionally, insurance started as a peer-to-peer hedge. Farmers pooled money to insure each other. If Farmer Fanny's crops are destroyed due to fire, Farmer Fanny can take the pooled insurance fund to cover the losses. In return, Farmer Fanny has to contribute monthly to the pooled fund.

As globalisation happened and it became more challenging to manage the pooled insurance fund and define the risks, insurance companies came in to aggregate the risk and undertake the risk. In return, people paid a premium to be transferring the risk to the insurance company.

In the DeFi space, insurance is still relatively new and has a huge potential. Payouts can be automated with math and code. Risks can be calculated, given the inputs available with on-chain and off-chain data.

Nexus Mutual provides financial insurance for smart contract errors in the DeFi space. Opyn provides insurance for when you purchase an option contract so that you can hedge your exposure risk.

14.5.9 Beyond Finance

Beyond the finance sector, we use financial products in many ways. Like using money to purchase items in our day to day lives, or to settle accounting issues like balance of payment between nations.

In DeFi right now, the market is still very new. The use of DeFi beyond finance is in arts via NFTs and betting markets. Some examples of NFTs include Aavegotchi, Rarebits, SuperRare and community access tokens. There's also Augur, and Gnosis for betting markets.

Notes

1. Lucas Jr, R. E. (1972). Expectations and the Neutrality of Money. Journal of economic theory, 4(2), 103-124.
2. Coates, I. V., & John, C. (2018). The Future of Corporate Governance Part I: The Problem of Twelve.
3. Tragedy of the Commons in Cape Town's water crisis. (2018, February 2). The Prindle Post. https://www.prindlepost.org/2018/02/tragedy-commons-cape-towns-water-crisis/
4. Aw, shucks! | Center for rural affairs. (n.d.). Center For Rural Affairs - Building a Better Rural Future. https://www.cfra.org/news/131022/water-overcoming-tragedy-commons
5. Industrial water and water pollution. (2020, January 7). Water Pollution. https://www.water-pollution.org.uk/industrial-water-pollution/
6. The other currencies are medium of exchanges for user-to-user exchange of information and data, whereas $ETH is a medium of exchange for protocol-to-protocol exchange of information and data.
7. Source: BIS Dec 2019 report with lower bound estimates using OTC products in the notional value. It is highly possible that the value is much larger in reality due to highly customised structured products as a hedge for market volatility and movement. https://www.bis.org/publ/otc_hy2005.htm

Chapter 15: Ponzinomics

> *Ponzinomics = Ponzi + economics.*

What's ponzinomics? It's the economics of Ponzi scams.

15.1 Economics vs Ponzinomics

Remember, economics is a tool. It can be used for good or bad. It's good when economics is used to incentivise certain behaviour for an economic value. It's bad when it's used to cheat, scam or steal. Don't blame economics. Economics, as a science, is neutral. People can use the tool for bad.

Similar to technology, people can misuse technology. Facebook as a technological platform to connect peers and share information is neutral. But this technological platform can be used for bad, like to spread fake news and propaganda.

Economics has three basic fundamentals.

1. Supply
2. Demand
3. Opportunity cost, which translates to behaviour of people

Ponzinomics also has three basic fundamentals.

1. Supply
2. Demand
3. Funky economics that is an amalgamation of a few things, but mainly to drive FOMO for short-term gains without long-term results

What is ponzinomics? In general, it has three steps. It all starts with the **sell side liquidity crisis**.

15.1.1.Ponzinomics in three steps

1. You have very low supply.
2. Your prices increase somehow. E.g. It could just be you making a lot of transactions to the very little supply and it increases prices. Or it could be you doing some stuff to have this short-term price increase.
3. You create this demand. Start tapping into the FOMO[1].

15.2 Three Ponzinomics Fundamentals

In general, ponzinomics is trying to induce this sell-side liquidity crisis.

What does that mean? Sell-side is the supplier side. Liquidity crisis means there's not enough quantity.

The sell side liquidity crisis means that there aren't enough tokens for sale for everyone to buy. How do we do that? By reducing supply and then increasing demand.

Going back to the economics design framework that I created, it's all about creating robust sustainable incentives within your ecosystem. The system can continue to grow so that the system can be accruing a lot of value. These internal tokens are a way to represent the economic value. The real economic value that's being created in this network. When it's traded in secondary markets, that's how we get price discovery and a monetary value to this economic value.

In general, this system works. It becomes a Ponzi when the monetary value of this internal token only exists because of the secondary market pumps and dumps – limited supply, which drives demand. In general, limited supply driving demand is good. But when you use all these mechanisms in a secondary market to create this kind of artificial demand inflation, these kinds of short-term price liquidity crises, that's how you get Ponzi scams.

The price discovery reflects the price increase. The price discovery is not because of the primary market that's driving the demand and growth. It is just the funky economics that you're doing in the secondary market that is pushing up prices so much. That's where it becomes a scam, so all these are still quite fluffy and technical.

15.3 Case Study: Ponzinomics in Seven Steps

1. Be influential somehow, anyhow. It's easy these days to create a fake account and generate some community interest via social media growth hacking and the likes.

2. Define value using your influence. It could be perceived influence and power by your community. Or in a more strategic way, use your power in Step 1 to get banks or VCs to determine the value to be close to your ideal value.

3. Float a small amount on exchanges. Like 3%.

4. Make, force or influence people to buy the amount available for exchange. See step 1.

5. Total market capitalisation is now defined by that 3% floating. Suddenly, it's very valuable.

6. Using FOMO, people are keen to hold your token, and force trades. This increases the trading volume and pushes prices up more.

7. Dump tokens slowly, you have 97% to play with. Liquidate as much as possible until the market figures it out.

15.4 Ten Ponzinomics Mechanisms

1. Fork something well-known, copying the open-source code. This is not uncommon, but to fork something without changing anything adds zero value to any of these experiments and mechanisms.

2. List token on Uniswap pool with similar symbols but it's fake. Making some transactions in the liquidity pool. This is also not uncommon, when scam and Ponzi projects want to piggyback on the reputation of the legit projects.

3. Build community via Twitter using an anonymous account to promote the project. See the case study above, step 1.

4. Use a similar name for a promising token. This is very common, since new crypto or new DeFi users are confused with the immense amount of information. They are likely to be duped by these cheap tricks.

5. Shill on forums like Twitter, Facebook communities, YouTube comments, Reddit and other forum spaces. Be wary of the information being shared and always do research, do not take their word for it.

6. Rug-pull liquidity move. Rug-pull is when you are standing, and someone pulls the rug out from under you. You lose your balance and you get hurt. Here, rug-pull liquidity is moving liquidity out of the DEX liquidity pool. Users are left with useless tokens because someone has stolen all the collaterals in the liquidity pool.

7. Listing tokens that will never be traded. For example, some tokens are a pure utility token that exists within a successful protocol. Someone else can create the token with a similar name and list it on DEX to cheat users, thinking that the utility token of a successful protocol is traded, when it is not.

8. Switch-a-roo the real token's link with a fake token's link. Always check the token addresses when transacting. Uniswap has a reminder to remind you to check your token address before engaging in any transactions.

9. Presale and slow public token release to allow for private presale to dump tokens. This is a common practice, and the details are in the case study above on Ponzinomics in seven steps.

10. Self-audit of smart contracts by anon creators. Imagine Facebook saying that their books are clean because they have audited their own books. It does not work like that. In these protocols, the audit lies in the smart contract. When they claim that the code is audited, do check who audited it and when.

Notes

1. FOMO means Fear of Missing Out.

Chapter 16: Math of Stable Token

One thing you realise is that in everything mentioned so far, math was highlighted the most. Math is the method used to define the business logic, which is then turned into code for machines to understand and execute.

This is where formulas are important. This is where audit is critical and where regulatory bodies are interested because the code can fail when it comes to execution. Transactions are based on the integrity of the math to automate and execute these business logics.

16.1 Math Concepts of DeFi

> *Do note that there is no "one ultimate formula" in DeFi or in each DeFi sector. It depends on the objectives, the business logic, the outcomes.*

Thankfully, there are general formulae to get started, depending on a few variables.

16.2 Currency as a Medium of Exchange

Money has 3 functions. Here, we want to focus on medium of exchange.

There are three general ways to create currency onchain for the DeFi ecosystem.

- 1-to-1 peg
- Over-collateralisation
- Algorithmical rebalancing

16.2.1. 1-to-1 Peg

General Formula: $y = x$

This is the most straightforward and basic method. 1 new token is minted for every token collateral. This works for strict pegs like $BTC vs $wBTC, $ETH vs $sETH, $USDT vs $aUSD and $ Aave.

Smart contracts can be coded to do this pegged minting and burning instead of trusting a third party to execute. Thus, trust in the math and the code instead of a third party to do custody of your collateral asset.

16.2.2. Over-Collateralise

Over-collateral method is to provide your asset as collaterals, and mint or borrow an amount based on your collaterals.

MakerDAO mints $DAI based on the collaterals you provide. You have to provide 150% worth of collaterals to mint 100 $DAI.

Aave and Compound allows you to deposit assets that can be used as collaterals to borrow against. You can borrow up to a certain percent (about 60-70%), based on your collaterals.

Another interesting note from a monetary economics perspective is the shift towards full-reserve banking[1]. Full reserve banking[2] means that for every dollar that is minted, it is 100% backed by collaterals. DeFi goes a step further with over-collateralisation.

16.2.3. Algorithmical rebalancing

This last method uses math to rebalance the token to ensure that it has a level of price stability. Currently, most tokens are pegged to 1 USD, but this can change as the system matures and it can be pegged to a basket of goods.

The model for AMPL is different from other token projects, because instead of defining your valuation via prices, it is defined by the proportion of network held.

Let's say you own 0.0000618% of the network by market cap valuation. Let's say that is US$1 with 10,000 tokens.

Now, prices increase to US$1.15. The total tokens increase. You also increase your token holding, while the value of tokens decrease. You will still own the same percentage of the network.

The math to think about here is invariant, a constant that the math formula exists by. Basically, it is a variable that doesn't change. The machine knows how to adjust automatically. And in this case, it's the percentage of the network owned. That is the invariant.

Notes

1. Lainà, P. (2015). Proposals for full-reserve banking: A historical survey from David Ricardo to Martin Wolf. Economic thought. World Economics Association, vol. 4(2).
2. The last time we saw full reserve banking in action was in the 19th century. As the capital market and traditional finance matures, banking has also shifted and changed. Today, most banks either have a low reserve or no reserve to back their loans lent out. In DeFi, most on-chain privately issued currency with a peg to fiat currency are over-collateralised. After the global financial crisis in 2008, many economists started toying with the idea of full reserve banking again. While full reserve banking is challenging to implement in banks (especially in 2020), this is possible to implement with DeFi.

Chapter 17: Math of Decentralised Market Maker Mechanisms (AMM)

Bonding curves show the relationship between token A and token B.

How is it done? Via math formulas. All the shapes are pretty much the same (concave shape). But the math formulas differ very much. The similarity in the math formulas is that they use this thing called invariant. It follows a physics formula within the conservation of energy principle.

AMM is great because it facilitates transparent price discovery. We can also explore multi-dimensional graphics instead of just 2D graphs. This is done by having more variables (e.g. tokens) interacting in the liquidity pool.

There are a few innovations in the space, but we will focus just on the basic structure of AMMs.

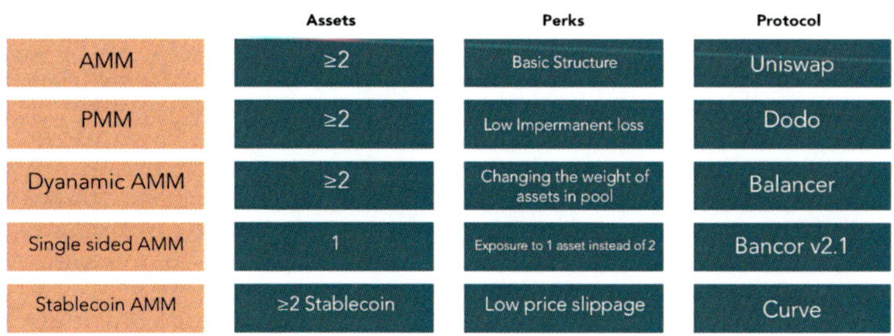

	Assets	Perks	Protocol
AMM	≥2	Basic Structure	Uniswap
PMM	≥2	Low Impermanent loss	Dodo
Dyanamic AMM	≥2	Changing the weight of assets in pool	Balancer
Single sided AMM	1	Exposure to 1 asset instead of 2	Bancor v2.1
Stablecoin AMM	≥2 Stablecoin	Low price slippage	Curve

17.1 CeDeFi vs DeFi

There are two types of exchanges in crypto, a centralised exchange with order books like Binance, Huobi and Kraken. Or decentralised exchanges like Uniswap, Bancor, Curve.

Math is more applicable to decentralised exchanges like Uniswap, Bancor and Curve.

Math is used as the base algorithm for these decentralised exchanges or general autonomous market makers in DeFi. In general, bonding curves are the main mechanism behind all decentralised exchanges. The difference is how they are being executed, which are the algorithms in place.

Instead of bonding curves showing the relationship between token price and token supply, it shows the relationship between token A and token B.

17.2 Automated Market Makers (AMM)

This is important, as the shape of the curve differs from the other use-cases of bonding curves. In decentralised exchanges, the shape of the curves is pretty much the same, a concave shape. But the math formulas differ very much. The similarity in the math formulas is that they use this thing called invariant. It follows a physics formula along the lines of the conservation of energy principle.

The table below summarises the generalised algorithms.

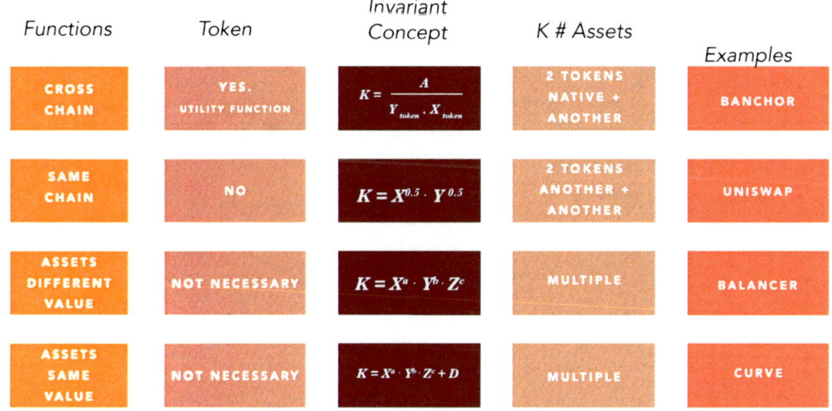

Algorithms for Automated Market Makers

Functions	Token	Invariant Concept	K # Assets	Examples
CROSS CHAIN	YES. UTILITY FUNCTION	$K = \frac{A}{Y_{token} \cdot X_{token}}$	2 TOKENS NATIVE + ANOTHER	BANCHOR
SAME CHAIN	NO	$K = X^{0.5} \cdot Y^{0.5}$	2 TOKENS ANOTHER + ANOTHER	UNISWAP
ASSETS DIFFERENT VALUE	NOT NECESSARY	$K = X^{a} \cdot Y^{b} \cdot Z^{c}$	MULTIPLE	BALANCER
ASSETS SAME VALUE	NOT NECESSARY	$K = X^{a} \cdot Y^{b} \cdot Z^{c} + D$	MULTIPLE	CURVE

17.2.1. Invariant Concept, K

For the AMMs to work, the key factor is to include an invariant. That is something constant. A never changing variable. The concept is that the functions of the variables can change, (token X and token Y), but this variable itself does not.

This becomes the governance in the smart contract code to be able to execute the trade at the price specified by the bonding curve. What it lacks in price perfection is made up in price predictability. As liquidity increases, price slippage is reduced, and it becomes more efficient to trade at a tighter spread.

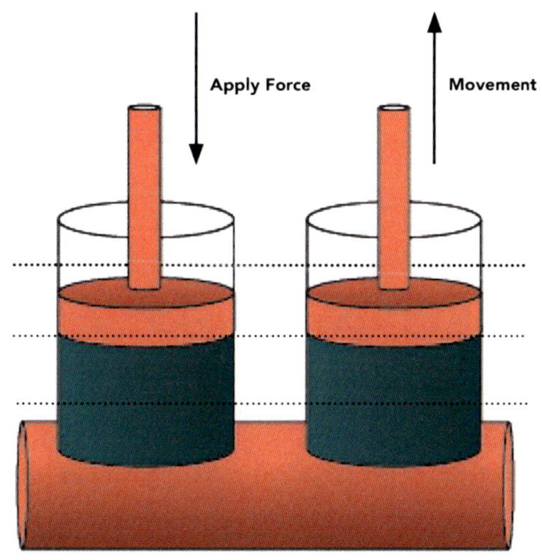

Similar to a hydraulic system, the invariant is the amount of liquid in the press. When one side decreases, the other side increases to maintain a balance.

In the same way, when $TOKEN decreases in quantity, that is because there is $ETH being added into the pool. The product of the number of $TOKENs and $ETH tokens remains the same. That is the invariant.

17.3 General Graph

In general, the graph is a downward slopping concave graph.

Assuming no new liquidity is added in, the graph represents the price at which a token can be traded for another.

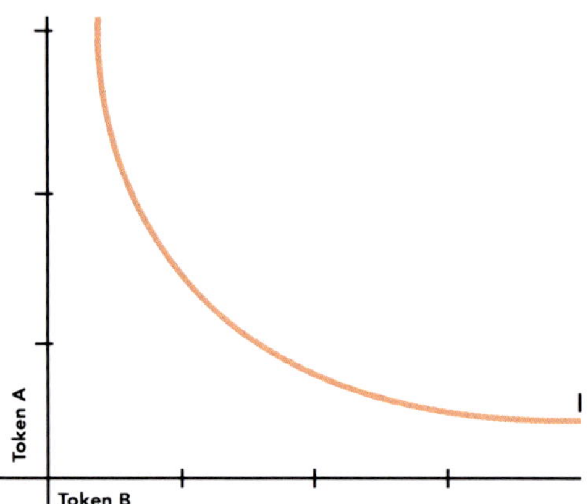

In the graph on the right, at 50 tokens on the x-axis, you get 40 tokens on the y-axis. That means you can trade 50 $TOKEN for 40 $ETH, for example.

Assuming no new liquidity being added, the area under the graph for when I trade any $TOKEN for $ETH is always the same.

Why? Because that is the invariant that we have been talking about.

The system is expandable in terms of the various dimensions it can calculate. Under a 3D graph, anywhere along the surface of the graph is an appropriate exchange rate.

The volume under the curve is then the invariant.

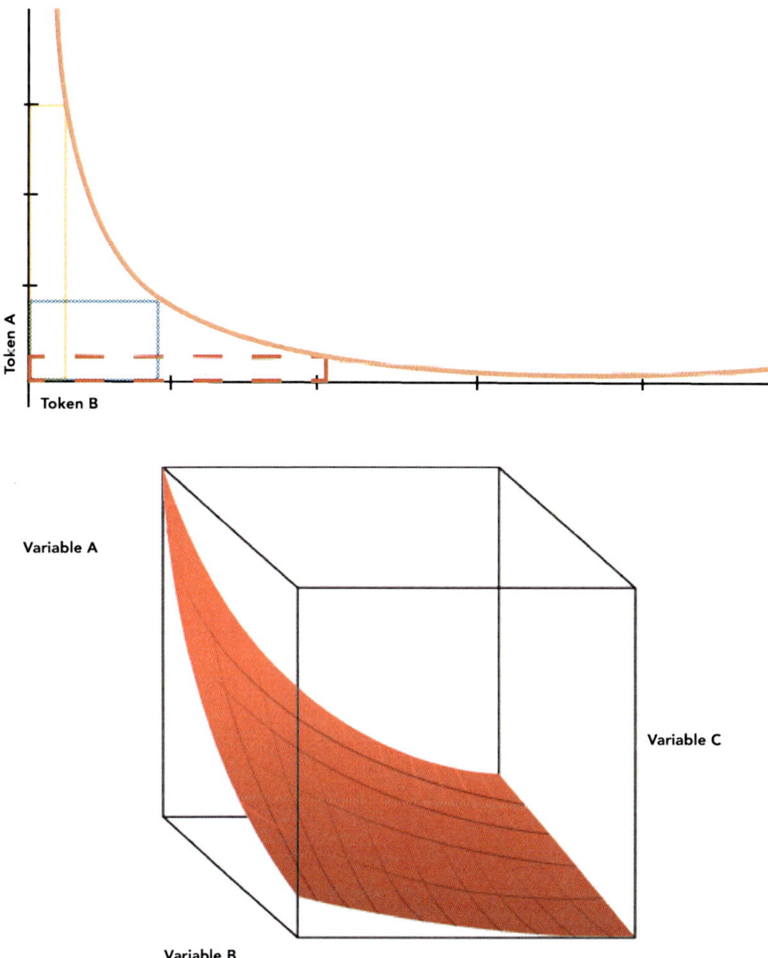

Chapter 18: Fundraising Bonding Curve

Back to bonding curves, another use case is to use bonding curves for fundraising.

18.1 Fundraising Application

As discussed in Chapter 11, a bonding curve mints new tokens based on the collateral it receives. When new assets ($ETH) are added into the collateral pool, new $TOKEN is minted.

The application of bonding curves in fundraising do not follow a general formula, unlike the applications in autonomous market makers. However, there are still questions and variables to consider when designing the right curve for your fundraising.

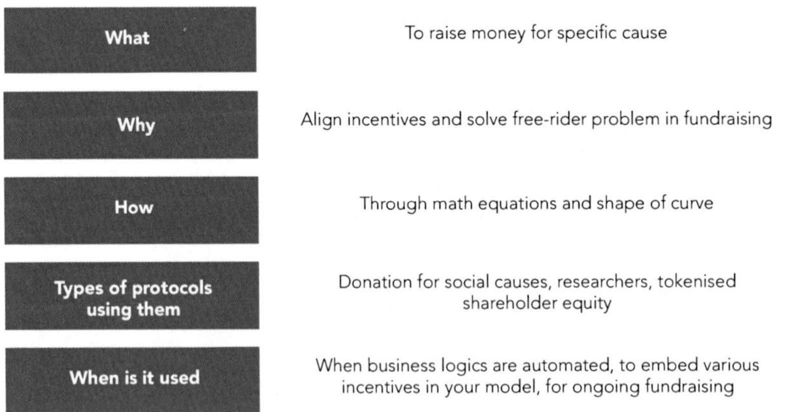

18.2 Fundraising for Token with Utility Function

A token with a utility function is a token which mainly facilitates internal transactions and trade within the ecosystem. It does not interact much with the secondary market and outside world.

In this aspect, we will dive deeper into three different use cases:

1. Donation fundraising to support many different causes
2. Using bonding curves to bootstrap fundraising
3. Fundraising for research projects

18.2.1. Donation Fundraising

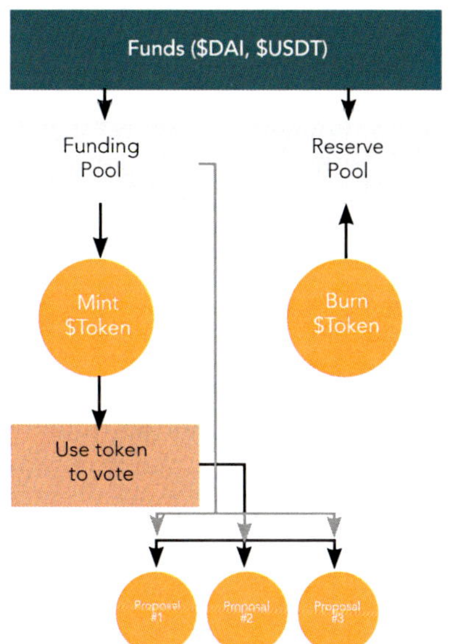

An example of donation fundraising is the Giveth platform. Giveth is an organisation platform that supports a lot of different social causes. Funds are donated to the system, governed by the bonding curve. It is a variation of the usual bonding curve we have been discussing.

How are Funds Collected?

On a high level, the bonding curve works in the same way. Funds, $DAI, are added into the bonding curve and it mints a token, $TOKEN.

When $DAI is added to the system, part of it goes to a foundational collateral pool and another part goes to a funding pool to fund the various social causes. The funds in the different pools are then further allocated for other causes.

The collateral pool is the reserve where people redeem $TOKEN for the underlying $DAI collateral.

Since Giveth is all about social causes, the donated funds added to the funding pool will be used for various functions. E.g. cleaning the beach. Funds in the funding pool will be allocated to these other social causes.

How are funds distributed to various causes?

Various causes are supported by voting. Users submit a proposal to support a cause. The tokens, $TOKEN, can be used to vote for these proposals. Funds donated will then be allocated according to the votes.

In Giveth, the other factor in the bonding curve is time. To prevent early investors from removing their capital in the collateral pool, there is a lock up period of the token pool.

The curve function in the Giveth constant liquidity model is an upward sloping graph. A simple basic model can be $y = mx^2$.

Specifically, for the Giveth platform, we are looking at five variables that will be added to the math model of the bonding curve:

1. Native token ($TOKEN)
2. Collateral token ($DAI or $USDT)
3. Reserve pool
4. Funding pool
5. Time factor: vesting period

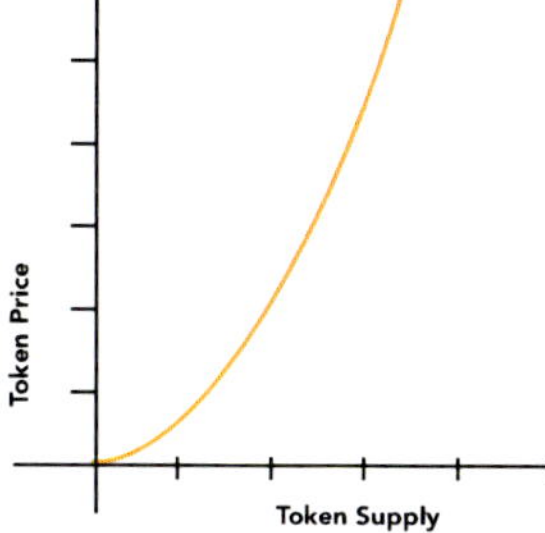

18.2.2. Bootstrap fundraising with Reserve

Aragon mixes both AMM style (see Chapter 15) and constant liquidity (see Giveth example above) in their fundraising method.

The AMM style uses a concave function as we see in the autonomous market maker protocols. It is also a constant liquidity provider since it always has the tokens for someone to exchange. The reserve ratio style that they have created is similar to the AMM style in terms of the formula.

Similar to the Giveth platform, when funds are added to the system, it goes into two different pools, the reserve pool and the funding pool, but they call it a discretionary pool.

The difference is that the platform is governed by a DAO (Chapter 19). Instead of a hard-coded distribution of funds, as seen in a social cause donation platform of Giveth, Aragon allows users to vote on the split of the different pools and also to vote on how to distribute the discretionary pool.

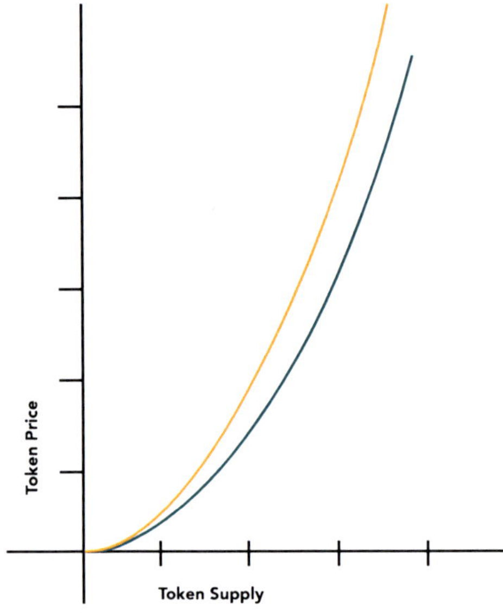

The curve function is similar to Giveth, with an upward sloping graph. A simple basic model can be $y = mx^2$. To visualise, you can also see a similar curve to separate the funding proportion from the reserve proportion. E.g. $y=(m-a)x^2$, where $a<m$.

At Aragon, we are looking at five variables that are added to the math model of the bonding curve:

1. Native token ($TOKEN)
2. Collateral token ($DAI or $USDT)
3. Reserve pool
4. Discretionary pool
5. DAO

18.2.3. Fundraising for Research

Another use case is to fundraise for research. Specifically, for academic research in new fields. The reality of research is that it is funded by someone, a government organisation or company. It is used to promote an idea via research, whether good or bad.

A bad example would be Coca Cola funding plenty of research to drive the idea that the reason why people get fat is due to fats not sugar. That is false.

How can we turn research into a community driven project then? We can use bonding curves to crowdsource funding and fund research that will educate the public with scientific facts.

Molecule is a project focusing on fund-raising for medical research. Instead of the complicated graphs we discussed, it uses two straight lines with a buy curve and a sell curve. The buy curve is higher, which is the price you pay to purchase the tokens. The sell-curve is lower to disincentivise people from selling. This goes back to the idea of incentive alignment and the free-rider problem.

This model incentivises people to hold their tokens and not sell them. This is aligned with the cause of funding public research and this model helps with that. Depending on the objective of the platform, the difference between the buy and sell curve can vary greatly.

In Molecule's case, we have four factors:

1. Buy curve
2. Sell curve
3. Fundraising aspect
4. Ending fundraising

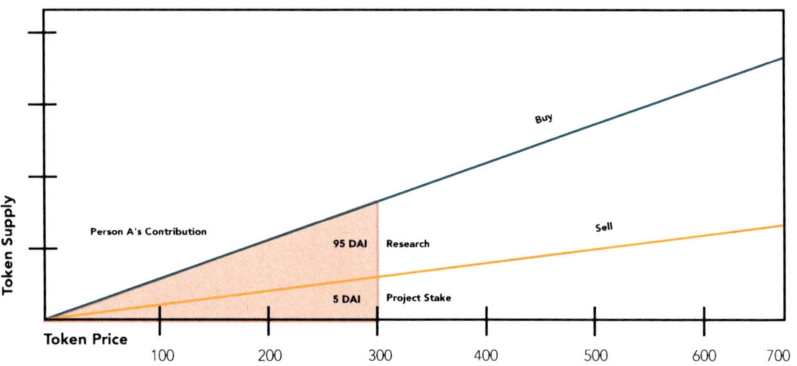

The funds will be used for fundraising, the amount of funds being the difference between the two curves. When 100 $DAI is added to the system, the smart contract calculates the area under the graph to mint the tokens where the sum is 100 $DAI. That is 300 $TOKEN.

Let's say the sell curve is 5% of the buy curve, 5% of 100 $DAI will be allocated to the sell curve. That means 95 $DAI will be supporting the project and 5 $DAI will be used as reserves.

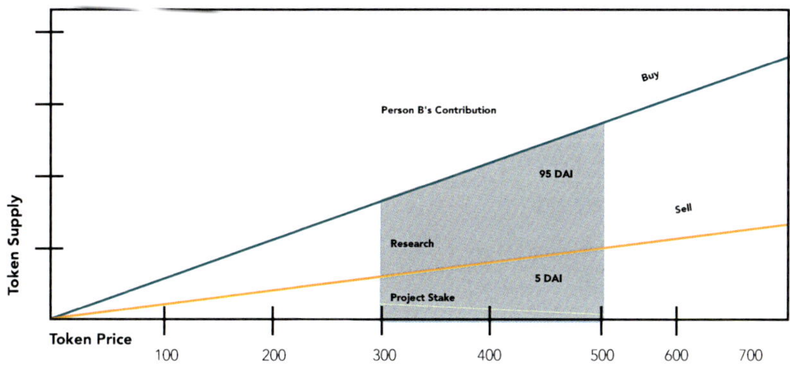

Later, a second person does the same. He/she adds 100 $DAI. The area of the graph is also 100 $DAI worth, but this time the supply minted is only 200 $TOKEN. That is fair as the model incentivises early investors who take the risk and receive more tokens as a result.

Similarly, 5% of the 100 $DAI will be used as reserves and 95 $DAI will be used for the research project.

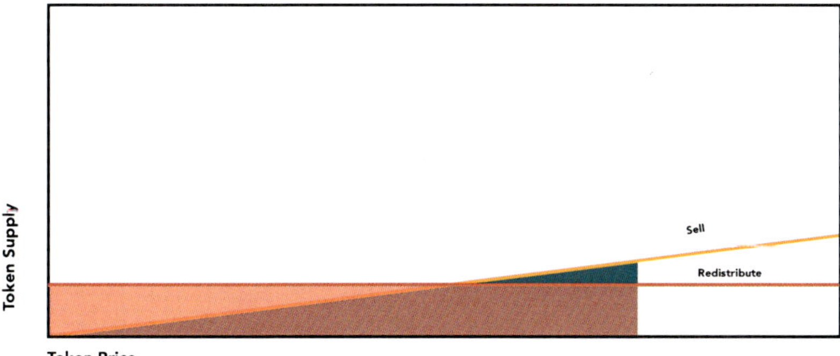

When fundraising ends because the project ends, the funding will be closed. All additional funds left over will be split proportionally to funders in the bonding curve.

If you are thinking about such models, I also urge you to think about giving some form of ownership to these funders when the research is successful. That can create a more long-term incentive for funders to keep funding such public research. I'm experimenting with one such model. See Chapter 25.

18.2.4 Summary

In Giveth, when money enters the system, it is allocated by the smart contract. With Aragon, the allocation is decided by the DAO. Molecule defines the allocation with two independent curves instead.

18.3 Fundraising for Token with Security Function

Previously, we looked at tokens as a utility function just to account for fundraising and any other activities. It's not so much about the token representing any form of income earned. In this subsection, we will see how tokens can have a security function too.

A security token function is where that token also represents an underlying asset. This underlying asset is called financial security. Such an asset can generate income. How do we define that? We can use a bonding curve.

The tokens can now claim ownership to future profits earned by the company. This is similar to the idea of equity, where you are a shareholder with 10% equity, and you get 10% of the company's net revenue.

The key difference between a security function and utility function is the *area under the curve*. In a utility token model, the area under the curve is defined by the general collaterals in the system. In a security token model, the project itself can be generating profits and a portion of the profits is added to the collaterals, aka the area under the curve.

For example, Economics Design raises funds with a bonding curve. That means you get to invest in Economics Design. In return, you get a token that represents part of the revenue of Economics Design. As usual, the earlier you enter the system, the more tokens you are entitled to, based on the curve.

By the end of Year 1, Economics Design earns $X. Of this profit, 20% will be added to the bonding curve. It is not a share buyback model, but it has a similar effect of increasing the value of each token (share) in the market.

How? When more funds are added to the bonding curve collateral, each token is now worth more. The bonding curve shifts outwards.

In this model, there are four ways to trade the tokens:

1. Mint fresh tokens from the reserve by adding collaterals to the system.

2. Buy existing collaterals at market price from existing token holders.

3. Sell tokens at market price: OTC trade or via a secondary market exchange platform.

4. Redeem tokens with the bonding curve of the system itself.

Chapter 19: Crypto Insurance

19.1 Smart Contract Insurance

Since most of the economics rules and incentive mechanisms are defined in code, smart contracts become one of the main failure points. As such, insurance for such internal technical risks becomes crucial.

Nexus Mutual is one such insurance provider. In the monetary policy of NXM, there are two variables that are fixed and two variables that are flexible – A and C are the fixed variables. The variables that change are the MCR and the total capital or capital pool.

> *The variables follow the general formula,*
>
> $$price = A + \left(\frac{MCR_{ETH}}{C}\right) . MCR\%^{4}$$

MCR — Short Term Driver

MCR is the minimum capital requirement. It's kind of like the reserve in the bank. NXM does something similar to banks: if I put 100 $ETH as capital into the NXM pool then a part of it has to go to the reserve and the other part is available.

Total Capital — Long Term Driver

You can think about the total capital increase as the increase in DeFi adoption or DeFi market adoption. As more DeFi protocols are being adopted you can argue that there's a correlation to an increase in the total capital, which is why these two variables are included in this model.

This is very important because MCR is like a short-term forecast or short-term variable to understand the growth of Nexus Mutual's protocol, whereas the total capital variable is a way to look at the long-term growth of Nexus Mutual. The short-term variable is the amount of money or reserve that could be used to do your insurance cover whereas the long-term growth is the total capital which is linked to DeFi adoption.

Three elements in the token bonding curve

1. Total Capital.

2. MCR so the minimum capital requirement and this capital requirement is important so in case anything happens this minimum capital can be used to cover the insurance.

3. MCR ratio is the total capital divided by MCR so the linking between these two variables.

Read more about Nexus Mutual in Chapter 7.

19.2 Impermanent Loss Insurance

One of the greatest risks in decentralised exchanges is impermanent loss. These are losses due to external trading activities when someone puts their tokens in the liquidity pool rather than keeping them in their wallet.

Bancor provides insurance for the impermanent loss incurred, if any. One change in Bancor V2.1[1] is to allow for single-sided liquidity provision. Bancor protocol will then mint the required $BNT to support the liquidity pool. As a result, the protocol is able to earn transaction fees. These fees can be used as the insurance fund to compensate for losses.

If there is a lack of fee in the insurance fund, Bancor will then mint $BNT tokens to compensate for the loss.

Notes

1. Accurate as of October 2020.

Chapter 20: Crypto Derivatives

DeFi is exploding. And this is only just the beginning. The power of DeFi is twofold: (1) Decentralised governance and (2) Programmable codes and internal valuation that can be tokenised.

Tokens are not just a pump and dump scheme anymore. This is not 2017. Instead, tokens represent certain economic value generated by the system (e.g. network tokens) or certain internal value (e.g. leveraged tokens).

In the previous chapters we discussed the math and economics engineering of many of the basic financial products such as bonds. Those were the low hanging fruits of financial products because these were the easiest start in changing the current financial system. In this section, we take a step further to derivatives, which we will refer to generically as synthetic assets. These are more complicated, but also give us more avenues to explore the value add of tokenisation.

I do want to caution that these are more complicated products. It's best to do more research if you are interested to invest in such protocols. For those familiar with traditional finance (TradFi), please refer to **Appendix A** for a comparison of financial terms between TradFi and DeFi.

20.1 Synthetic Assets

> *Synthetic Assets: you create a new asset out of thin air using the collaterals you provided.*

Synthetic assets are basically regular derivatives in traditional finance. These are assets created by referencing the value of an underlying asset. For example, a cash settled corn futures contract.

Like traditional finance, synthetic assets exist in the DeFi world. This is created by having certain collaterals to create a new asset out of thin air and find counterparties to balance the trade. Instead of owning TSLA directly, you own the synthetic version of it, somewhat like a swap contract. The synthetic $TSLA will have very similar economic returns to direct ownership, but it will not actually represent a claim on a company's assets the way Tesla common stock does.

How it is done? You collateralise an asset $ABC to mint synthetic TSLA. This synthetic TSLA moves in the same way as TSLA. The difference is that you find counterparties for your trade and trade on the synthetic TSLA instead.

More specifically, the mechanism of creating a synthetic crypto asset is similar to the creation of $DAI. You collateralise assets ($ETH, $YFI, $USDC) to mint $DAI on the Maker platform (see Chapter 9 for details). The difference now is that you collateralise *the network token* to create the synthetic assets instead of $DAI. This mechanism considers liquidity and slippage issues as seen in DEX, while also maintaining the collateral ratio seen in pegged assets.

20.1.1. Case Study: Synthetix

An example is Synthetix. This is an example of how synthetic assets can be created and the math mechanisms used.

Synthetix is a protocol that issues synthetic assets. The only collateral accepted is Synthetix native SNX tokens, instead of any collaterals. These synthetic assets are then traded on the Synthetix platform. $SNX captures the value of participating in the network and of the fees generated from the exchanges. Currently supported synthetic assets include sUSD, sEUR, sBTC, sETH, sDEFI (index), sGold and sSilver, and inverse versions of some of these.

20.1.2. Collaterals to Mint Assets

Synthetix maintains a 750% over-collateralisation ratio in the system. That means that there needs to be US$7.50 worth of $SNX to mint 1 $sUSD. If the collateral falls below 750%, either more $SNX needs to be added or synthetic assets need to be burned.

Similar to Maker's CDP, a fee is incurred when minting synthetic assets. To retrieve the $SNX locked as collateral, a fee in $SNX is payable and burned. At the same time, by having $SNX locked as collateral (staking), $SNX holders are able to earn the fees generated. This is similar to a saving account in the bank.

20.1.3 Synthetix Debt Pool

The debt pool is an important variable as this determines what is backing the assets in the system. It measures the staker's proportion of the pool and changes caused by new assets minted or burned.

This information is valuable because it constantly and transparently calculates each individual user's debt.

To calculate the new debt owed:
New Debt Minted (Total Existing Debt + New Debt)

User's new debt proportion of the pool when adding new debt:
New Debt Minted x (Previous Debt Pool + New Debt)

When the user repays the debt by burning the synthetic assets, they unblock the $SNX as collateral. This changes the amount of debt owed in the system.

User's new debt percentage after paying:
(Existing Debt - Debt Burned) x (Debt Pool - Debt to be Burned)

This protocol represents a highly novel and unconstrained method of creating synthetic assets. It also rewards users who create synthetic assets and in so doing aligns the incentives that help ensure the system functions as designed.

20.2 Leveraged tokens

> *Instead of a leveraged position, you turn that position into a token to represent your leveraged position.*

Leveraged tokens are just one example of the power tokenisation can bring. The power is in the internal rules and governance are enforced with programmable codes in the tokens.

Other than the usual supply and demand, such tokens can have internal valuation due to the underlying asset it is structured with. And with that comes risks, such as volatility drag on assets, beta slippage on trades, and price movement of the underlying assets.

Leveraged tokens are tradeable synthetic assets that represent a leveraged position of the underlying asset. Instead of physically managing the administrative rebalancing or structuring, this leverage is achieve d using smart contracts to amplify exposure to the underlying. Such tokens can be used to get a leveraged long or short position of an asset.

In general, the types of leverage that can be provided are:

- Long: bet that prices go up
- Short: bet that prices go down

The usual leverage for tokenised long and short positions is 3x. Up to 10x leveraged positions are available in the crypto (OTC) derivative market.

20. 2.1 Benefits of Tokenised Leveraged Positions

A key benefit in tokenising leveraged positions is the ability to reduce liquidation risks due to the automatic rebalancing and compounded leverage features of such tokens. While these features are possible in traditional finance when managed by your broker, they are costly and risky to replicate. Tokenisation allows for the efficient automation of such strategies.

Increase Profits

Profits will automatically be reinvested into the underlying assets. If the leveraged position makes a profit, the leveraged position of 3x will now be on the existing capital, plus the profits made. It is compounded.

Reduce Risks_

When losses are incurred, the position will be automatically liquidated to the degree necessary to cover those losses. If you have a short $TOKEN position and over the course of the period, $TOKEN increases in value, your position will be liquidated like a stop-loss order and your holdings reduced.

20.2.2. Rebalancing Calculation

Let's take an example to understand how rebalancing is calculated. The goal is for the exposure to always be 3x, which is the leveraged position.

- Position: LONG ETH
- Value: $25 K
- Leverage token: 100 ETH/token
- ETH trading price: $400

Net Asset Value (NAV) = Assets - Liabilities

NAV = (100×$400) – $25,000
= $40,000 - $25,000
= $15,000

Exposure = 100 × $ 400 / $15000
= 2.67

Rebalance size = (desired position - current position) × LT outstanding
= (3 - 2.67) × 100 ETH/token
= 33.3 ETH required to be added to the underlying position

This does not include some platform activity fees applicable like trading fees, redemption fees, and management fees. These affect time decay in value.

Leveraged tokens in this form might not be the final form in these kinds of derivative structures. However, combined with other protocols and mechanisms, we can definitely see new creative ways to structure new derivatives.

20.3 Tokenised Crypto Bond

> *You create a fixed-income product using the tools available, either within DeFi protocols or via the futures and spot market.*

As we move on to more complicated financial derivatives, it is less about economics engineering (as we discussed from Chapter 1 to 13 in this book) and more about financial engineering. Tokens and smart contracts are merely a means to an end in such financial products.

20.3.1. Value of Crypto Bond

You can look at bonds as a fixed-income instrument or as a way to crowdsource funding. Depending on the function the bond plays (other than in 007), the way it is structured will be quite different.

With crowdsource funding, you can consider the model of using bonding curves with a financial security function as discussed in Chapter 18.3.

For fixed-income instruments, bonds can be used to structure a product with a varying level of risk. In the financial products discussed in Chapters 16, 17, 18, and 19, these are generally "returns optimising", by trying to find the most alpha.

Beyond yield generation, finance is also about reducing risks. This can be done by structuring the risk profiles in bond-like assets.

20.3.2. Automated Recalibration

Going back to leveraged tokens, I mentioned that the strategy can be combined with other tools to create new models. This can be done with bond structuring use case.

One of the problems in traditional finance is that when all these types of bonds are being created, we do not have the luxury to be constantly calculating and adjusting the risk exposure. Even if we can calculate it, we're not recalibrating it constantly according to the kind of risk exposure that we want in real terms and not nominal terms.

This is something that DeFi can add a lot of value to. Traditional financial products are generally inefficient. Imagine, for example, that risk parity strategies could be implemented using constant-risk leveraged tokens. If such a strategy was seeking an X%

risk exposure, we can look at using smart contracts and math to automate this recalibration of the risk given the new inputs available.

20.3.3. Disclose Structure Strategy

One of the inefficiencies in traditional finance is that regulations ask to disclose a lot of different things (i.e. preliminary official statements by an underwriter). But the problem is that these structures and strategies are complicated.

Not only are they complicated in the creation, it is also difficult to find where the risks are coming from. Smart contracts and decentralisation are an improvement because they are transparent.

The smart contract can be translated to a clean dashboard. There, you can see the constant change in where the yields are coming from and what kind of risks are being diversified into the different protocols. Having a very clear understanding of the structure is very important because it then becomes a lot easier to trace and look at where all these yields and risks are coming from. This helps to reduce information asymmetry and helps people to make better, more informed decisions.

20.3.4. Structure of the Bond

I wish there was a general formula that I can give you. But the reality is that there is none. Bonds are really versatile instruments, and you can customise them in many ways and forms. However, I will add that in building fixed-income bonds, it's important to find pair counterparties to net off the risks.

This is where tokenisation can be helpful in incentivising the party that is holding the risk of the other side of trade. Once again, it depends on how bonds are structured and what sorts of risks and strategies are being deployed.

20.3.5. Case Study: FlexUSD

Whilst is it possible to create various bond-like products using DeFi, this example uses the futures market to achieve the fixed income structure.

FlexUSD is an interest bearing USD that receives its yield from the difference between spot prices and derivatives market. This is especially possible as CoinFlex, the company behind FlexUSD uses physical settlement on their exchange.

Combining the concepts of Repo[1] and perpetual futures, FlexUSD allows holders to earn the interest rates in an 8-hour time period. These interest rates are typically more attractive than retail p2p lending and borrowing.

In traditional finance, Repo exists and is only accessible to banks. Tokenisation allows for retail people to get a slice of the pie, while allowing technology (bots, algorithm, machines) to execute the financial strategy. Retail users do not need to be the ones trading but can still enjoy the massive benefits of attractive yields.

Notes

1. Repo means repurchase agreement. It is a short-term borrowing rate between institutional players like banks and central banks. It typically lasts overnight. Think of this as borrowing and lending, but for banks instead of retail people like you and me.

Chapter 21: Financial Risks of DeFi

There are plenty of risks in DeFi, including that it is not regulated yet, cyber-security risks, lack of smart contract (machine) audits, lack of experts to audit the math, DeFi being in an experimental phase. Those sources of risk are beyond the scope of this textbook.

In this chapter, we will focus more on the financial risks in DeFi.

21.1. Opportunity Cost

The beauty of opportunity cost is that, thanks to smart contracts, it is now a lot easier to calculate your opportunity cost now, because information is more transparent and readily available.

Opportunity cost exists in four areas. Given capital available, you can now choose to place it in:

1. Traditional financial markets (e.g. via low-cost ETF in Fidelity or high yield bonds) via the various risk assets.
2. Money market funds to generate a low but safe return.
3. Crypto market funds like $BTC or $ETH and keep them as it is. Interestingly, we have seen more traditional listed companies like Microstrategy starting to have $BTC exposure in their portfolio.
4. DeFi (e.g. via low-cost DEX in Uniswap or high yield liquidity mining incentives) via the various non-crypto-market funds.

Based on the expected returns, taking into consideration the volatility of various asset classes, it is possible to calculate the opportunity cost of your capital.

21.2 Liquidity Loss

Liquidity loss is most evident in protocols that rebalance like Ampleforth's algorithmically balanced model. Instead of being tied to the internal politics of the US by being tied to the USD, Ampleforth's model is to change its monetary supply based on the global demand for money.

Ampleforth does this with an automated governance using code, by internalising the price volatility in the secondary market.

The code has two math functions: (1) It calculates the price difference between the "ideal price" USD$1 and the actual exchange rate now (e.g. US$1.15). Then it mints more tokens, so that the price goes back down to US$1. (2) It doesn't do this suddenly – token changes happen over a period of 10 days. We call this supply smoothing.

The Ampleforth token ($AMPL) can be used as collateral in many DeFi projects. It is not strictly pegged to a fiat currency (e.g. $DAI with USD) which makes it more independent and useful in the long run. Basically, Ampleforth is a new global currency without a central bank.

When the model internalises the price volatility in secondary markets and alters its supply directly, it creates this risk called liquidity loss.

Why? The model for AMPL is different from other token projects, because instead of defining your valuation via prices, it is defined by the proportion of network held.

Let's say you own 0.0000618% of the network by market cap valuation. Let's say that is US$1 with 10,000 tokens. Now, prices increase to US$1.15. The total of tokens increase. You also increase your token holding, while the value of tokens decreases. You will still own the same percentage of the network.

When prices increase, the total token quantity increases to reduce the price of each token. This is commonly known as debasement. The risk also flows the opposite way. When prices are too low, tokens will be burned proportionately which will cause a reduction in token holding of all $AMPL token holders. The proportion of the network held is still the same.

This liquidity loss in tokens disappearing becomes a risk in more complicated financial structures.

21.3 Price Slippage

When it comes to Autonomous Market Making (AMM; see Chapter 15), there are two main risks associated with them. Quick recap: AMM is a method to allow for tokens to trade between each other. We use the model called invariant, which is a constant, to facilitate the trade.

Although we use mathematics to define the trade, there are still risks involved due to things outside of the math, such as:

1. An internal risk when you trade, called price slippage.
2. An external risk when you don't trade and prices change

outside, called Impermanent Loss.
What about risks if you ARE trading?

This risk is called price slippage. Price slippage is the difference between the expected price before the transaction and the actual price when the token is transacted. That is why on Uniswap, you have this variable of "minimum received" and price impact.

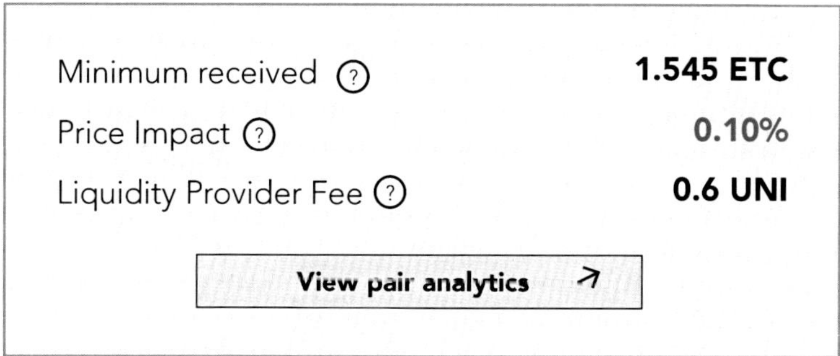

Where is price slippage coming from?
DEXes are continuously trading. The price for token #1 is different from the price of token #2 because of the autonomous market maker model. The larger the transaction size relative to the liquidity, the higher the slippage.

That means when you want to trade 9,000 tokens and there are 10,000 tokens in the pool (aka 90% of the liquidity), the price slippage will be higher. That means the risk of actual amount received vs expected amount received is larger.

Is there a way to prevent it?

Short answer:

1. Increase incentives to encourage more people to stake liquidity. The larger the liquidity pool, the lower the price

slippage.
2. The use of oracles to get a valid price value by comparing other prices.

Long answer: Well, not really. An alternative is to pay higher gas fees, so your transactions are prioritised, but that's going to be costly on your side. The transaction fee might be even more than the price slippage.

Another way is to choose liquidity pools where your trade is a small percentage of the pool. If you want to trade $COMP for $ETH, you can go to Balancer, Uniswap, Bancor. Choose the pool with the greatest liquidity and trade there instead!

21.4 Impermanent Loss

> **When does it Exist?** It exists only when the liquidity providers withdraw their funds from the liquidity pool. Liquidity pools exist in decentralised exchanges like Uniswap, Bancor, Curve and Balancer.

> **Where does the loss come from?** If you have some capital, then there are 2 ways to go about it so the first one is to keep it in your wallet and the second way is to keep it in these liquidity pools. Trade happens and the tokens in the liquidity pool are lost. Loss comes from the difference of that vs what you keep in your wallet.

What it is really, is the potential loss on paper that exists. It only becomes "real" when you withdraw the tokens from the liquidity pool.

Let's say I own a Tesla stock. And it went from $500 to $400. The loss is $100 on paper. Until I sell that Tesla stock, the loss is not realised yet, it's just the value that has changed. The value could go up to $500 again and I have no realised loss. The concept is similar for impermanent loss.

The Tesla example shows what loss is. A real loss. In impermanent loss, the loss is not fixed yet, because AMM changes too quickly according to price movement and recalculates at the moment. The loss is not permanent. Yet.

So, we talked about loss. We talked about the idea of "impermanent". Now let's go back to our crypto liquidity pools.

A Uniswap Example

Let's use Uniswap as an example because it is easier.

Assume Uniswap has no transaction fees. A pool has two tokens, ETH and USDT tokens.

Currently, 1 ETH = 400 USDT. This is calculated for tokens available INSIDE THE POOL only.

Now, let's say outside the pool, people are trading 1 ETH = 420 USDT. e.g. on Binance.

How can you profit from this?

Arbitrage traders use 400 USDT to buy 1 ETH. Then go to Binance and sell it for 420 USDT. That means 20 USDT for free! Yes, this is legal. And yes, this is done in traditional "real world" finance too.

Where is the loss coming from?
These traders buy and sell ETH until the exchange rate in the liquidity pool is 1 ETH = 420 USDT.

Now you're thinking, ok that is the normal price anyway. How does it affect me? During this period, this is what happens:

Beginning of state: amount in the pool 25 ETH and 10,000 USDT.

Token	Quantity	Price	Value in USD
ETH	**25**	**400**	**10,000**
USDT	**10,000**	**1**	**10,000**

Constant product = 25 * 10,000 = 250,000
When price goes up to 1 ETH = 420 USDT, arbitrages come into trade.

This is the result:

$$eth_{liquiditypool} = sqrt\left(\frac{constant_{product}}{eth_{price}}\right) = = 24.3975$$

$$usdt_{liquiditypool} = sqrt\ (constant\ product * ethprice\ ) = = 10246.95$$

Let's say we own 10% of the pool, so you are entitled to 2.43975 ETH + 1,024.695 USDT.

The value of that in USDT == 2.43975 * 420 + 1,024.695 = 2049.39 USDT

If we kept that 10% in the hardware wallet instead, we still keep out 2.5 ETH + 1,000 USDT.

The value of that in USDT == 2.5 * 420 + 1,000 = 2050 USDT

Value loss = 2050 - 2049.39 = 0.61

21.4.1. Calculating Impermanent Loss

$$impermanent_{loss} = 2 * \left(\frac{sqrt(price_{ratio})}{(1+price_{ratio})} \right) - 1$$

This is the general formula to calculate the LP loss in Uniswap. Do note that this formula is only relevant to Uniswap and it does not include the trading fees.

Impermanent loss is what happens independent of you trading. It is the opportunity cost of leaving your tokens in the liquidity pool vs keeping them in your wallet. A good measure is to calculate the expected returns via trading fees and minus the risk of impermanent loss.

Another thing to note is that this assumes that only one side is changing at one time. E.g. $ETH moves, but $USDT remains the same. In reality, when you are trading pairs like ETH-COMP, both tokens are correlated and can move more, but in the same direction. This could potentially reduce the impermanent loss if two tokens are positively correlated.

Chapter 22: DAO, The Future of Governance

> *The philosophy of distribution is not just about distributing power. Spiderman said that with power comes responsibility. The future is distribution. Both distribution of power and distribution of responsibilities. How is this attained? Via governance coordination.*

Imagine the Senate, but instead of politicians going around campaigning and getting votes, the Senate is made up of the people of the country. And instead of relying on people executing the law, machines do that.

22.1 Improvement to the Current System

Do you see where this is an improvement?

Politicians have an incentive to be re-elected and they might not always have the best policy for the long-term economy. That might mean, for example, increasing taxes and cutting spending when times are good. This helps the economy in the long run, but politicians have a short-term government contract. So, the incentives are not aligned.

Politicians could also have a limited view of the entire picture. The policies in place are not the best for everyone and could be only short-term focused. The policies only benefit a certain segment of people.

Or inefficiency in executing a policy or law. It could be due to an inefficient workforce or human error, just to name a few.

So, what is a possible solution? Decentralisation and autonomy in decision making. And when it comes to execution, we use machines to automate the business logic, whenever possible.

And that brings us to this new creation, DAO. DAO is a decentralised autonomous organisation.

While we mainly talk about blockchain, the fact is that a DAO can exist on both blockchain and non-blockchain technological stacks. It can also work in any digital ecosystem, platform or ledger.

> *DAO is governed by people (token holders) and executed via smart contracts.*

A DAO is mainly a new way of governance and decision making. It can also combine with automated execution via smart contracts.

22.2 Crash course: Smart Contracts

Smart contracts are just digital contracts that do what they are told automatically. For example, if three people sign and agree to transfer $100 from fund to Chen, then $100 will be transferred to Chen". The "thing" that does the action of approving and transferring is the smart contract. It's digital and automated.

So, these smart contracts are programs. They embed rules (send money) so they can execute (to Chen) when specified conditions are met (three people signed).

Now, with this system you don't have to call up your accountant, show that three people have signed, confirm that the three people are who they say they are, verify the account of Chen and then make the transfer.

This is a rule programmed in the smart contract.

Of course, you can complicate it with more programmable business rules, getting inputs from IoT devices and stack smart contracts above each other. But let's just keep it simple for now.

Going back to where we left off. A DAO is a new way of governance and decision making. Once decisions are made, they can be executed by smart contracts.

What decision making are we talking about here? We will discuss these decisions in detail later, but to get your head around DAO, these are some common decisions:

- How to allocate funds
- Which projects to support
- What to do with funds

As mentioned, DAO is a new way of organising decisions. That is part of governance. And it is a very important part of governance, especially in decentralised ecosystems. In centralised ecosystems, you can always rely on the board of directors or the Senate. In decentralised ecosystems, you are part of the board and the Senate. That is why organising decisions is an important evolution of digital economy.

Step 1: making decisions.
Step 2: executing decisions.

Decisions can be different, like we mentioned just now. These decisions will be told to the smart contracts, with programmable rules.

22.3 Example: How to Allocate Funds

Like in board of directors and the Senate, you have to submit a proposal of how you want to allocate the funds. Let's say the proposal is to give $5k to fund a project to allow for interoperability with Ethereum. You submit this proposal to the DAO.

The DAO will then vote on this proposal — yes or no. There are three things to consider here, but we will not go into detail here.

1. What is the voting structure like: is it a static or continuous vote?
2. Who gets to vote: proxy vote, any user, user with specific tokens, user with minimum token threshold?
3. What is their voting power: 1 vote per address, vote power based on percentage of tokens held, vote based on reputation?

Let's say the DAO agrees, yes, we will give $5k to fund the initial step of this interoperability project (Step 1).

The proposal includes a smart contract. When the vote is yes, the smart contract will be executed and $5k will be taken from the pooled fund and given to the interoperability project.

This gives you a rough idea of how DAO works. It is an organisation to coordinate decision making.

Now that we have the general picture painted, let's go back to answer the main question: What is DAO?

Imagine a community swimming pool. Everyone from each household brings a pail of water to fill the pool. Everyone gets part ownership of this pool. Now, the pool slide is on fire.

Everyone gets to vote if they should use the swimming pool's water to kill the fire. Everyone decides yes, let's use the water. Some water is used, and now everyone gets to enjoy both the slide and pool.

In the same way, the DAO is where people in the ecosystem pool funds together and get part ownership of the fund. Being part owners, they get to vote on how the funds will be used. When there are returns, it goes back to the fund. As part owner of the fund, you get part of the returns too.

Of course, the DAO can execute other decisions instead of just fund allocation.

That being said, there is no 100% decentralised and autonomous organisation. Centralisation and decentralisation are not a dichotomy, but a spectrum. Each ecosystem has their own governance rules and differing level of decentralisation.

DAO is architecturally decentralised with individual participants in different countries. But the execution logic is centralised, which is the protocol.

22.4 Economics of DAO

Now that we have a better understanding of DAO, let's dive into the economics of DAO, since this series is about economics.

Economics is more than just supply in demand. In DAOs, we will discuss these three economics:

- Economics of trust
- Economics of coordination
- Economics of allocation

22.4.1 Economics of Trust

Without going too much into the history of trust, we need trust to transact and trade in an economy. Beyond that, we need to be able to trust decisions made in the ecosystem.

In the digital world today, we want to be able to trust the parties we are interacting with.

Let's go back to the swimming pool example again. Everyone living in the community can get a bucket of water, contribute and enjoy. If they want to sell their ownership because they are moving to another country, they can sell it to the new homeowner.

Here's the problem. Not everyone can get access to this pool. There is a massive level of trust required to maintain the accounting. What if someone destroyed the pool or contaminated the water? There are possibilities for negligence and malice.

With blockchain, instead of trusting someone to manage the

account, it will be managed via smart contracts. The group (DAO) will just focus on making the right decisions and execution of those decisions will be done by machines.

Instead of trusting people to execute, we trust the code. We codify the trust into programmable rules.

An example is PieDAO.

PieDAO is a DAO to manage crypto index funds. The decision that the DAO makes is to vote on the creation and parameters of pooled index funds. The funds will then be created via smart contracts. Instead of trusting that someone will not be a fraud and take your money away, you can safely trust the machine and transparent smart contract, and you will also be part of the governance system to decide how you want your money to be managed.

22.4.2 Economics of Coordination

Economics is about coordinating the various participants in the economy. Who teaches the new generation, who grows food for the population to eat, who will take care of the sick and elderly, who will create policies to make the economy better?

In DAO, we are talking about coordination of decisions.

Coordination is hard. Even if we manage to coordinate activities, how do we ensure that people will cooperate? People naturally do not cooperate, unless there is an incentive to do so.

Each decision-maker follows their own goals. Now, we want to be able to allow interactions between decisions-makers so that they will coordinate their decisions. Otherwise, we could end up with a decision that is undesirable.

Instead of trusting people to coordinate by themselves, we do it via the DAO.

An example is MolochDAO.

MolochDAO is a grant-giving DAO to fund Ethereum public infrastructure. The decision that the DAO makes is to vote on allowing new people in and to issue new stocks to them. Each stock is 1 vote. They also get to vote on which project to invest in.

This mechanism makes it easy for people to leave or defect. If you truthfully do not want to be part of the DAO anymore, destroy your stocks, get the capital and leave. This is good in terms of coordination, because those who do not wish to coordinate will exit. Now, we can have a group of participants who are willing to coordinate.

22.4.3 Economics of Allocation

Lastly, it is about allocation. This is similar to how governments collect tax revenue and decide where to allocate it. It could be education programs, fixing roads, building better lights, improving healthcare.

In any ecosystem this is also what governance is about. For example, how to design tax revenue systems, how to evaluate programs. The blockchain equivalent is how to design transaction fees and how to evaluate proposals for the community fund.

Instead of a central government deciding this, we decide via a DAO.

An example is KyberDAO.

Kyber is an on-chain liquidity protocol. KyberDAO governs the Kyber ecosystem. Users get to vote on how the network fees accrued are allocated. It could be allocation of tokens earned, burning of tokens or rewarding them to other types of participants in the system.

22.5 Other Types of DAO

The list is still growing as projects test out various types of DAOs. In general, it can be broken down into the following: asset management, protocol management and project funding.

Asset management: PieDAO

DAO is used in asset management to decide how assets will be managed. Machines are good at executing tasks, but decisions are still reliant on human inputs. The DAO makes decisions on how to manage assets.

PieDAO manages and monitors tokenised index funds on Balancer protocol. They create different asset pools and the DAO gets to vote on the parameters of the pools. Think of it like a decentralised ETF. The DAO is a social layer to manage the pool and balance the assets in the pool. DAO holders get to redeem the fees earned by the pool from the underlying asset.

Protocol management: MakerDAO & KyberDAO

DAO can also be used in larger management like protocol or ecosystem management. Although these decentralised ecosystems do not have a central governance, decisions still need to be made. That is done via DAO.

MakerDAO and KyberDAO are the two protocol management DAOs for their ecosystems. Token holders can participate in governance decisions to make a change in the protocol. This is important as it is a step towards giving governance power to the users of the ecosystem.

Project funding: MolochDAO, LAO, Dash, Aragon

Lastly, DAOs can be used to allocate funds. This is done by coordinating resources to issue grants. Participants pool their resources and allocate them to fund development. These participants can also get access to the returns by the fund. This becomes tricky when we look into the regulations and legality space.

MolochDAO and Dash are two DAOs that allocate funds for investment decisions. There are is also Limited Liability Autonomous Organizations (LAO) which have been created to include the legality piece into DAOs. LAOs all work in the same way, allocating funds towards investment projects. A LAO, however, is set up as a traditional legal entity that protects LAO shareholders from liabilities.

Dash is similar, except that it does not use individual money to allocate funds. The fund comes from the network. People have to pay to propose and voters have to stake tokens to vote.

Chapter 23: Economics of Yield Farming

Yield farming is part of token distribution and user acquisition. It is increasing the supply of tokens and distributing it to users of the protocol. For example, when users execute trade on the protocol, they are rewarded with the native tokens, independent of the trade returns. This is attractive because it is possible to get a 100% APY. But it comes with risks.

> *Liquidity mining and yield farming are similar. Yield farming is the general umbrella term. Liquidity mining is a more specific term, where you receive new tokens by adding liquidity into the system. For example, in decentralised exchange and in lending protocols.*

23.1 Projects Using Yield Farming

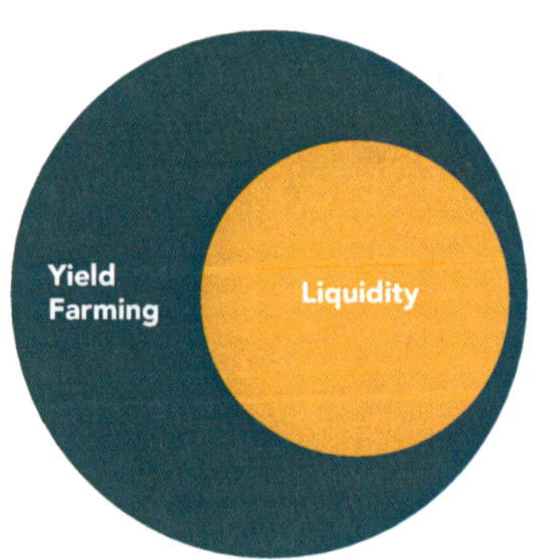

These projects and strategies exist or at least existed when the book was being researched and written.

- **Synthetix**: Issues $SNX to liquidity providers. It was successful because $sETH make up 1/3 of Uniswap's liquidity pool.

- **Curve Finance**: Issues native tokens like $SNX, $REN, $BAL, $CRV to liquidity providers.
- **Compound**: The total assets under Compound has surpassed Maker, the top DeFi app. It is the primary market for a decentralised money market. Daily $COMP are issued to users based on trading volume. It was successful because 1 billion new assets have entered the Compound market.
- **Balancer**: Weekly $BAL are issued to users based on trading volume. Before distribution was introduced, volume had generally been under $2 million. Since the distribution, it has generally been around $4 million. But on Sunday, June 28, volume shot up to $14 million.

23.2 Good Bad Ugly

Yield farming is not perfect. Yield farming as a strategy to increase transaction activities are not something that is sustainable for a long-term. In general, the tokens issued via yield farming have a utility function, specifically governance.

23.2.1 The Good

It works. This native token is an incentive for liquidity providers. This is exactly what exchange platforms are doing with their native tokens too, by incentivising market makers. It works for users because they are rewarded with extra tokens. It works on the platform because they are onboarding new users.

Projects like these are way beyond the stage of just a whitepaper. We have a working product that can be used, and this is the first step towards getting a user base.

23.2.2 The Bad

This is still a short-term incentive that is not sustainable. What happens when the hype of trading is gone? Or when transaction fees are too expensive, and it makes no economic sense to trade? Or when tokens are all given out?

So far, it seems like the yield is a zero-sum game. If you don't know how to play, you should not participate. It may change in the future by increasing the size of pie, but for now, it is a beautiful zero sum. It means do not be the last sucker standing because you are going to suffer all the losses. If you don’t have insider knowledge or strategic advantage, you are not earning yield. You are the yield.

Market capital drops immediately once incentive stops. Uniswap introduced liquidity mining and distributed $UNI tokens. On Nov 17, Uniswap stopped the liquidity mining. This brought the total capital in Uniswap down to $1.8 billion, from $3.3 billion 24 hours early, when the $UNI yield mining incentive was active.

23.2.3 The Ugly

The real ugly part is the hidden strings attached. Due to all the trade going on in Ethereum, gas fees have shot through the roof. So, beware of gas fees, slippage fees, asset volatility, impermanent loss.

Leveraged trading can be good to secure greater upsides, but the downside can also be quite steep, especially since the market is so volatile and you can get squeezed out quickly, if you have all your liquidity tied up in the DeFi apps.

Because there are so many transactions (that may or may not be inflated), the transaction fees have soared. As a result, Ethereum is looking to increase the block size. This is great for validators in the short run to increase their returns, but this is an ugly risk in the long run because the Ethereum network can be more vulnerable to attacks on the network.

23.3 Economics of Yield Farming

Let's use the economics design framework to analyse the economics of yield farming.

- Token Design: Self-reinforcing mechanism. The token incentives create liquidity which starts a feedback loop.
- Valuation: At the end of the day, this method just encourages network effects without providing any real economic value. For protocols and projects to succeed, the need is for builders and users to stay on the platform for a long time, and not just during this movement. In the short term, we are also seeing an increase in token value.
- Token supply: There is a token supply increase, or supply inflation. It is also distributed to users with the highest volume. Instead of people paying for tokens, it is earned via the platform.
- Return of tokens: These tokens are not exactly free. Early investors of the tokens have invested and received tokens. They are happy for tokens to increase in value to cash out their returns. However, unless you have a strategic plan for using tokens to gain returns, you are just part of the plan. (Similar to IPO Pop[1])

- Transaction activities: Borrowers are keen to borrow more because with the native token distribution, it is almost like they are subsidised to borrow. The increase in trading results in higher transaction fees and attracts better returns for lenders.

23.4 Value of Yield Farming

In general, yield farming is a great way to bootstrap a decentralised community.

The native tokens issued usually have a governance function. This is a great way to distribute governance to users instead of hoarding the governance function within the founding team or give the governance power to venture capital firms.

Depending on the protocol and financial function (exchange vs lending), the native token issuance serves different purposes.

In exchanges, due to impermanent loss, native token issuance via yield farming makes it attractive to be a liquidity provider despite the potential of impermanent loss.

In lending and borrowing, native tokens attract capital to the platform so they can be lent out and the platform can be earning profits.

Native tokens issued via yield farming enters an interesting asset class. It combines both stock equity (with voting rights) and dividends (earning cash flow from using the protocol). Since the "dividends" are in a different currency from the transactions, it does not take the structure of an interest return.

E.g. Lending $USDC on Compound gives me interest returns with $USDC and $COMP native tokens by the system.

23.5 Summary

Yield farming has a value. It is also a great mechanism to bootstrap the community. However, it can be challenging because volume drops once the incentive stops. This can be mitigated by creating stickiness during the yield farming period and to prove to users that it is a great product worth staying with.

Notes

1. IPO Pop is a situation where the value of the stock increases when the stocks are listed on an exchange. Early buyers of the stock can profit from this trade. For example, nCINO jumped 195% upon listing on Nasdeq in July 2020. Baidu was the largest IPO pop on Nasdqa in 2005, with 354% increase on Day 1. https://www.nasdaq.com/articles/ncino-jumps-195-in-biggest-ipo-pop-for-a-us-tech-company-since-the-internet-bubble-2020-07

Chapter 24: {Case Study} Binance

Token economics is the concern of the ecosystem within which the tokens exist. It is more than just the tokens themselves. Just like in economics, we focus on more than just the economics of money.

There's a specific field for that, called Monetary Economics. In economics, we discuss many things like building the ecosystem (or a country) within which the money exists.

The specific field in token economics that only talks about token is called token design or token engineering. It is slightly different, but the general idea is similar.

Let's dive into Binance as a case study to analyse, using the economics design framework.

24.1 Market Design

Market design is the design of the environment within which the tokens exist. In market design, we also understand the primary objective of the token, so as to design the right market for it.

24.1.1. Objectives

When we start designing anything, it's like calculating the optimisation function in calculus. You need to know what to optimise. Or it's like dating. If you don't know who you are and what you are looking for, anything goes.

Back to the BNB token. What is the main objective of the BNB token? The main objective, at least for now, is a utility token for discounted trading fees. This objective might change in the future, but this is the objective now. And this is the objective to focus on.

Of course, there are secondary objectives such as:

- Holding it as a store of value due to its deflationary feature
- Trading it with other crypto tokens as a medium of exchange
- Spend it on other goods like in-store purchases
- Donate to charity

All in all, there are over 20 use-cases of BNB tokens. That brings me to the first factor in market design – thickness.

24.1.2 Thickness

Thickness is the prerequisite to achieving network effects. Since Binance, like all exchanges, is a 2-sided platform, this means we have to achieve thickness from both ends of the user-base. In an exchange specifically, it is market makers and market takers. But in the token ecosystem, we are talking about businesses accepting BNB tokens and the value-add to the users themselves.

Business

Binance, being one of the top few exchanges, can tap into their network to establish partnerships.

Instead of engaging intermediaries to fulfil token exchange, Binance engages directly with their partners who accept BNB tokens in their network.

These could be for activities like travel, paying bills, earning interest on stakes, shopping, etc. There are 31 partners in total.

Of course, these are just secondary objectives, as mentioned. The main objective is still to use tokens to get a discount on trading fees on Binance. We will discuss the token design later in the next section.

Users

Binance launched the BNB tokens with an ICO. That has been the only distribution of tokens, and the rest are kept. To attract users to increase thickness, BNB tokens are deflationary, which increases their value in the long-run and attracts people to hold them.

There are also many use-cases to attract different types of users, beyond traders. For example, Binance has its own incubator and launch pad. There, transactions are only done in $BNB.

The token is also traded on Binance, which provides price discovery and a monetary value to the token. The deflationary feature and price discovery incentivise profit seekers to hold BNB tokens.

24.2 Token Structure

Token structure is part of token design. In token structure, we will dive deeper into a token's monetary policy and valuation.

24.2.1 Supply

There is a max supply of BNB tokens at 200m tokens. 100m has been distributed to the public via the ICO, 80m to the team and 20m to investors.

24.2.1.1. Change in Supply

Unlike Bitcoin, there is no slow increase in supply. The 200m tokens were distributed and that is it. There is no increase in supply as more assets and securities are bought.

Instead, BNB has a decrease in supply. Every quarter, Binance will burn some BNB until 100m BNB are destroyed, which is 50%.

Token burn is where a token is destroyed and can't be used again. For example, it can be sent to a wallet address, but the wallet's private key does not exist. The point is that the tokens are permanently taken out of the circulating supply.

What does this mean? This is similar to a share buyback in the equities market. Companies use their profits to buy shares to increase the value of each share. In the same way, Binance burns part of its profits to increase value for the remaining tokens in the market.

Where is the profit from? Remember that the main objective of using BNB is to reduce trading fees? Well, Binance collects these BNB as their profits, but at the end of each quarter, they will burn some tokens.

24.2.2. Monetary Policy: Hyper Deflationary Structure

$BNB has a deflationary feature. What does it mean? It means that the number of tokens decrease but the value of the tokens increases with time. This is done through burning of some existing supply of BNB tokens.

24.2.2.1 Burning BNB

Initially, BNB burned was in proportion to the profits generated from the exchange. For example, 50% of BNB tokens used to pay for trading fees were burned each quarter. But now, as the use cases of BNB expands, the amount of BNB burned is not based on its profits but self-reported volumes. This has caused some controversies in the space, since we are all about transparency.

Let's break this down into economics design's two foundational principles: (1) supply demand and (2) behavioural economics.

24.2.2.2 Supply Demand Explanation

Basing solely on the main objective, let's say BNB tokens are only used to reduce trading fees. The more the use-cases of BNB tokens, the better this explanation.

The more people use BNB tokens to reduce their trading fees, the more tokens are burned, hence the increase in value of each token. Simply, when we have 10 apples and 10 bags, then each bag will initially contain 1 apple. When we burn five bags (50%), now, each bag will contain two apples. Each bag is more valuable now.

With each burn, the value of BNB tokens increases. That being said, it does not mean monetary value, just value to the user.

24.2.2.3 Behavioural Economics Explanation

For people who see value in the long run, they will hold BNB tokens and pay in other tokens first, like USDT. The other inflationary tokens reduce in value in the long run, so long-term believers will buy and hold BNB tokens.

There are also people who see value in the short run. This could be a trader making a huge trade, and the discount in trading fees using BNB tokens generates a better value than holding BNB token in hopes of price appreciation in the future. They rather use it now.

There is also a collective group behaviour. When people see more users paying trading fees in BNB tokens, this signals a reduced confidence of BNB prices in the future. Even if the rational structure is a deflationary mechanism, the behavioural model says otherwise.

Having transparency in the BNB burning is a double-edge sword. On one hand, we have full transparency of how many tokens are burned, for accountability purposes. On the other hand, when in some quarters significantly more are burned than others, it shows other traders that BNB tokens are not so valuable to hold, and you are better off using it now. Or when trade volume in BNB is too low, it could also signal a low value in using BNB tokens, hence it is not worthy to buy a stake in for price appreciation.

Considering that there are so many other use-cases of BNB (31 so far), it makes sense that Binance now calculates burn volume via their internal metric rather than just trading volume. BNB might generate more value in other markets than using it for trading fees.

24.2.3 Current Status

As of Q4 2020, in the 13th quarterly $BNB burn[1], there are over 26m $BNB burned. Since the value of $BNB fluctuates, the value burned also differs.

24.2.4 Valuation

The value of BNB token has fluctuated but remains one of the strongest altcoins so far. There is also some research using price-earnings ratio (PE ratio) to determine if BNB is over or undervalued. All the reports I've read so far show that it is undervalued. But I'm not here for that.

We use the PE ratio to determine the **relative value** of a company's shares (equity) compared to other companies' shares or historical data. It is a good enough metric to consider when valuing the token price. However, do remember that BNB is not an equity or share.

My issue is not about the PE ratio value. Rather, I view BNB as being similar to airlines miles. BNB price is directly connected to the achievements of Binance as a business. Like airlines miles, BNB has no legal obligation to protect the value of BNB, the way a company might be if they were responsible to their equity shareholders.

Airline miles are independent entities from the airline itself. They can accrue value from within the ecosystem and extract that value via network partners like hotels and car rental. But the truth is that no matter how independent they are, the success is still very much linked to the fundamental business, the airline itself. When airlines are going bankrupt like we see today, the airline miles go down with them. Technically and legally speaking, they are separate entities. But in reality, it's hard for airline miles to survive when the airline is bankrupt.

With Binance, the success of $BNB is conditional on Binance's success. The PE ratio might be undervalued today, but there should be other factors and metrics to consider when valuing the token, more than from just an independent price-point level.

Also, as much as deflationary mechanisms increase value, this is not a guarantee. Burning tokens only affects the supply side. You also have the demand side to deal with. Just because there are less tokens in circulation does not mean that the market will pay more for the remaining ones.

How then, can we attain a decent price for BNB? By ensuring that there is demand for it. Which moves us to the last section – financial incentives.

24.3 Financial Incentives

24.3.1. Platform Activities

Financial incentive is one of the pillars in token design. In the case of Binance, each trade incurs a standard fee of 0.1%. Traders can use $BNB to pay for trading fees and get a discount.

The discount follows a decreasing schedule. In 2017, paying in $BNB gave traders a 50% discount. It halves every year until 2021. It's 2020 now, so the discount received is 6.75%.

That is quite a significant discount. Going back to the point above on burning BNB accruing from trading, you can see why Binance shifted to other reporting values than just trading. With 6.25% discount, deflationary pressure and plenty of other use-cases, users are more likely to use $BNB in other avenues than for discount on trading fees.

That is why by 2021, $BNB will not be used to receive a discount anymore. The use-case of $BNB will expand to other platforms like staking and redemption of other services.

When Binance allowed users to use BNB to get a reduced fee, they were basically doing a "pre-sale" during their ICO period. Users purchased BNB tokens to be used later. There was a real use-case, instead of just purchasing the tokens in hopes of price appreciation.

When traders trade in large volumes, they are incentivised to purchase BNB to reduce their fees. There is a monetary gain in that trade.

Using BNB tokens to pay for trading is also not too costly for the exchange. Sure, it is diluting one of their revenue streams, but the value is going back to their early adopters. Since it is their token that they created from thin air, there is not much to lose for allowing a discount in trading fees with BNB tokens.

24.3.2 Staking (Return on Stake)

At the end of the day, the staking mechanism affects the supply of tokens while allowing the market to dictate the demand. Another way Binance is encouraging supply change is via staking on the platform. High-volume traders must hold certain $BNB in their accounts to unlock more discounts.

Think of it like a subscription model. I subscribe to the newsletter by locking up $NEWS[2]. The tokens are frozen and cannot be touched. I am not losing out. In fact, this gives me access to all the items related to Economics Design.

Similarly, for high-volume traders, this subscription model is better than using $BNB to get discount on individual trades. This locking up of tokens further reduces the tokens available. As of May 2020, 33M $BNB tokens are locked up, taking the total supply minus tokens burned minus lock up, to about 147M $BNB tokens circulating today.

Staking for traders aside, BNB holders can also stake $BNB to get returns on their asset, via their new update in April 2020. Binance blockchain is moving to a staking-based consensus mechanism and to also run smart contracts. Gas fees will be paid in $BNB. Validators will collect the gas fees from transactions. Validators have to stake $BNB before becoming a validator.

And of course, there are other partners of Binance that provide returns on $BNB.

24.4 Conclusion

This native token is created by the company. Instead of recycling it by putting the token back into the ecosystem, some are burned. Recycling it is also known as the multiplier effect. Like you pay money for fried chicken. The fried chicken company uses it to pay their suppliers and money is just spread into the system. Instead, the money you pay for fried chicken is a specific type of money, and part of that money is burned. It reduces the total available money in the ecosystem. Burning doesn't affect prices directly, but it does in the long run.

Is this a good mechanism? Sure, it exists to serve the objective and purpose of the BNB's role in Binance's ecosystem. But is it the best system in the world? It is hard to say. Deflationary assets have other issues and it might not be suitable for your use-case.

Ultimately, why is this mechanism used? It is definitely not possible to keep buying back and burning the tokens forever. Instead, this mechanism gives Binance more lead time to build community, reward early adopters, thicken networks and develop other real use-cases to serve the ever-changing dynamics of users. Instead of using a loss leadership to grow and attract users like MoviePass did, Binance issued its own native token to attract users while continuously attracting value from the ecosystem.

Notes

1. The 13th quarterly burn happened in October 2020, https://www.binance.com/en/support/announcement/4db101d45b204c3a9206c057f0f6856a.
2. This is an example token. As of Q4 2020, this token does not exist.

Chapter 25: {Case Study} This Book

This book is tokenised. No, this is not one of the "tokenised collectable" books. Rather, I am tokenising the publishing rights. This is an experiment of tokenising rights like intellectual property rights, distribution rights and licensing rights.

25.1 Thoughts Behind This Idea

This is an experiment.

Tokenisation is to way to represent the value of something. As we discussed mostly in this book, we are usually tokenising the economic value of an ecosystem. That is a huge topic on its own. You can probably guess that after going through so many chapters. And, there are other values that can be tokenised. This is what I am experimenting with.

This experiment is inspired by two people. One saying to me "you should tokenise this book since this is what you are teaching" and the other I have been having an ongoing discussion with about tokenising financial securities in the form of non-fungible tokens (NFT). The right idea at the right time, here we are.

25.2. Distribution Rights as an NFT

Firstly, this token is only available to publishing houses. It is not for everyone.

Secondly, this token is a form of accounting for the books sold. This is very important because it defines how we design the token moving forward.

Thirdly, you can bet your crypto-portfolio that I am going to use bonding curves.

25.2.1 Why NFT?

The value that the token represents is the right to publish and distribute this book in various geographies. I chose NFT because there could be a possibility of embedding some form of token rules (e.g. maximum number of books sold) into the token. That means each token could be unique on its own.

25.2.2. Why tokenise?

I believe very strongly in only tokenising something if the token version of it adds real value. In the publishing world, you have two ways to get a book published. Either going to a publishing house or self-publishing.

The publishing house route is great since they specialise in such business. However, they also have to take on the risk and many are not willing to do so. This is especially true for new areas of specialisation. I know this because I spent two years speaking to publishers and failing miserably. They either find it too technical, too niche, too complicated or they are simply uninterested. Their main fear is understanding the market demand for such books.

That brings us to the second option, self-publishing. That means doing everything on your own. While it is good to give you full control of how the book will be, you lose out on having the specialised skillset to bring the book to new heights. For example, campaign strategies, PR network, and greater distribution reach.

Thus, I saw tokenising publishing rights as a solution. I can help a publishing house get a better grasp on the market demand with actual market demand and for self-publishers (me) to tap into their specialised skillset and network.

25.2.3. Why now?

The idea of tokenising publishing rights is still very new. Conversations are usually around tokenising reputation, a community or a digital good. However, the reality is that everything that is discussed in this book is still undergoing experiments. Everything is continuously evolving. Hence, tokenising publishing rights in this book is to focus on testing[1] and improving the concept of tokenising publishing rights.

This idea has been brewing in my mind since Q2 2019, when I learnt about bonding curves. One technical issue, which is still not solved, is aggregating off-chain worlds to on-chain smart contract execution. That is the main focus of my worry. I figured, why not get this experiment started first, and I will update with new solutions as time goes on and I update this book with a new version.

25.3 Economics Design of this NFT $EDBK

$EDBK represents this Economics Design Book.

The general idea is to:

1. Limit publishing rights of physical books to specific geographical regions
2. Price publishing rights in accordance to the perceived risks
3. Use the token to account for distribution of additional income

The main fear by publishing houses is to not know the market demand for the book. Thus, $EDBK signals the demand to decrease information asymmetry. Since $EDBK is an NFT that represents the right to resell and publish the book, the only difference is in the details. For example, how long they have the rights for, the geographical area and quantity of books.

The price of the $EDBK is determined by a bonding curve. The earlier a publisher purchases the token, the cheaper it is. That means, they take on the risk to be the first mover and in return, pay a cheaper fee as a publishing house. As market demand for the book increases, this encourages other publishers to get the rights. Now, the publishers are certain about the market demand of the book and there is less risk to publish this book. Thus, they pay a higher fee to buy the rights to publish the same book.

The publisher pays royalties to the author, me, and keeps the mark up. Part of the royalties will be added to the pool and distributed to the $EDBK holders proportionally, including any other sales by the self-publisher (me). These rules and agreements will all be embedded into the bonding curve, via a smart contract

25.3.1 Market Design

Market design is the design of the environment which $EDBK and token holders exist in. Since I limit the token to an NFT and holders to publishing houses, this greatly constrains the environment. Similar to permissioned blockchains, the participants are verified off-chain. Thickness of the market and congestion is less of an issue in such environments.

When it comes to safety, the idea is for tokens to represent the level of risk and market demand. This provides useful information for publishers to determine when they are interested to enter the market and distribute the books. The social proof is in the price of $EDBK.

In terms of calculation, computation and data will be aggregated and executed by an open-source smart contract. Currently in Version 1, I will be collecting the relevant data and calculating the distribution of additional income publicly. This is because the off-chain world uses Web 2.0 technology while the on-chain world uses Web 3.0. Until we are able to find ways to verify off-chain data for on-chain computation, I will do it publicly for now.

25.3.2. Mechanism Design

Currently, I have no intentions of embedding any other non-token rules into the system. A popular incentive is governance and the right to vote. Since the vote would be mainly to vote on the distribution of additional revenue or to vote out a potential competitor, I do not see any economic benefit by allowing voting. This does not align the incentives of the various agents and it can cause more problems and produce solutions.

In the **token economics revamp 2.0**, we can explore some other ways of mechanism design. When data from the off-chain world can be integrated into the on-chain smart contacts, I can imagine a function of validators and stakers. This increases the need for proper governance and mechanism incentives.

Until then, this experiment is good on its own.

25.3.3. Token Design

The token will be minted via a bonding curve. Within the token, various elements will be embedded, such as:

- Duration that a publisher has the publishing rights
- Minimum or maximum quantity of books to be distributed
- Exclusive geographical area of distribution

We can do this as a bonding curve while having the asset as an NFT because the underlying variable is the same: a book.

An important note is that $EDBK only includes physical books[2]. That is why the bonding curve has a revenue stream and that is the sales of eBooks. A publisher owning $EDBK also has access to profits generated by the eBook sales. This is because publishers also advertise the book. This information advertised becomes a public good to all publishers.

To reward the public good, distribution of the eBook revenue via a bonding curve is implemented. As this experiment matures and tragedy of the commons appears, quadratic compensation will be considered with respect to the NFT and the marketing budget. In the **token economics revamp 2.0**, this can be embedded and calculated via the smart contract, which is a value add of tokenising and using smart contracts for computation and distribution.

> *So, if you are a publishing house keen on participating in this experiment, please reach out to book@economicsdesign.com!*

Notes

1. It's about improving experiments instead of finding perfection. It is easy to focus on finding the best and most perfect mechanism. The reality is that such mechanisms continuously evolve. We should focus on experiments instead of perfection.
2. Property rights is a component in the architecture of the token. And in the specific NFT case of $EDBK, the property right of owning $EDBK is to be able to distribute and resell the physical book.

Chapter 26: The Future of Tokenised Ecosystems

To conclude, we are just getting started. We are building and experimenting with the base layer infrastructure of tomorrow. This will change the way we do things, the current system that we are used to, and the underlying principles that we have been following.

26.1 What's Next in the Economics of Token Engineering and DeFi

DeFi and token engineering is still in an experimental phase. Ideas and concepts are being tested out. Being technology agnostic, one can see the DeFi space as a test net for the future. It has a healthy growing number of new entrants into the space to test the impact of using tokens in various aspects, such as:

- User acquisition
- Incentive alignment
- New fundamental mechanisms

The next step is to bring these benefits to the physical "real" world instead of residing on-chain only. From a practical point of view, the next step is to work with regulators to regulate the space before these systems are adopted in the "real" world.

26.2 Sectors To Look Out For

What sectors will continue to mature as we look ahead?

Insurance has the potential to keep growing. Either to build upon the existing crypto-insurance infrastructure or to create new mechanisms to align incentives of agents.

Web 2.0 is limited to the division between the on-chain world and the off-chain "real" world. As we continue to advance, we can see more protocols connecting the two worlds together. It could be **oracles**, standardisation of data structures or new mechanisms to get information in the off-chain world.

The book has mainly covered fungible tokens so far. The next sector to explore are the various ways to design **non-fungible tokens.**

Tokenisation of traditional financial securities is next in line. Currently, DeFi is tokenising the lower hanging financial services like lending, borrowing and trading. We are likely to see more tokenisation mechanisms for financial securities. Regulations are important here.

Tokenising unique assets like intellectual property, access rights, property rights and other types of intangible assets. DeFi comes into the picture with distribution of returns and potentially incentivising the various behaviours of token holders. All the DeFi chapters discussed in this book are just the tip of the iceberg.

26.3 An Ideal Future

I imagine a world where we exist digitally, transcending geographical jurisdictions and creating digital economies to suit ourselves. Digital governance rules on its own and with the ecosystem's people. You can decide which governance rules you prefer and exist in that digital ecosystem. Then, we are not bound by race, nationality, skin colour or language, but by philosophy and ideology. Then the market will decide which autonomous organisation will succeed.

The future is extremely exciting. Every day we are experimenting and building interesting concepts and mechanisms that can make the future a little brighter. This is just the start. The future is in the hands of people like you and me. May the future be slightly less flawed then the system we have today.

What's Next

I want to keep myself updated:
Next, you can sign up for my weekly newsletter on economics design at www.economicsdesign.substack.com. I share about a case study, interview with protocols or a topic on economics.

I want to educate myself more:
Alternatively, you can sign up for the digital course on the economics of token engineering at www.education.economicsdesign.com.

I am an investor and I want to learn more about fundamentals:
If you are keen on fundamental reports, you can find out more at www.economicsdesign.com. We publish market reports and protocol specific reports.

I am an information junkie. Give me more raw information:
For other resources, I keep an open-source resource list at bit.ly/tokenomics-resources.Check it out!

Appendix A

Financial Terms

These are analogies, not equations.

Traditional Finance	Decentralised Finance
Agreement	Consensus mechanism
Availability of market makers to provide liquidity	Liquidity pools
Bad trade	Rekt
Bank account	Wallet address
Bank accounts	Wallet
Banks borrowing and lending from each other	P2P lending (e.g. Aave, Compound)
Board of Directors	DAO
Broker that executes trade on your behalf	Smart contract
Buy and hold strategy	Hodl
CDO, Bond, Money Market Fund. Anything where you add assets into a product as an investment strategy	Vault, pool
Collateral	Staking
Database, ledger	Blockchain
Derivatives	Synthetic assets
Earning returns denominated in another asset	Liquidity mining or yield farming
Equity holders with voting rights	Governance token
ETF	PieDao
Exchange (e.g. NASDAQ)	Autonomous Market Maker (e.g. Uniswap)

Appendix A

Financial Terms

These are analogies, not equations.

Traditional Finance	Decentralised Finance
Futures contract rollover	Perp Futures
Interest bearing assets	aTokens, interest bearing assets on Aave that accrue interest from P2P lending
Investor with significant holding	Whale
IPO	ICO, IDO, IEO
Long	Moon
Lottery	No-loss lottery (e.g. PoolTogether)
Market maker	Liquidity provider
Money (e.g. USD)	Stable coin (e.g. $DAI, $USDT)
Money markets	Aave, Compound, Curve, Maker
Penny stock	Shitcoin
PIN	Private key
Portfolio manager	Non-custodial portfolio manager (e.g. Balancer)
Repo	Borrow against stake or collaterals, yield farming
Returns	Yield
Roboadvisor but only focusing on investing in the best interest rates in money market funds	Yearn finance
Stock buy-back	Token burn
Third party data source	Oracle
Transaction fee	Gas fee
Unrealised loss	Impermanent loss
Using collaterals to create an asset (similar to CDO mechanism)	CDP

Glossary

Economics Related

1. **Allocation mechanisms**: how do we allocate products to the right participant. Example: auction market, voting.
2. **Behavioural economics**: newest school of thoughts in economics. It understands that people are irrational. Looking at ecosystems that are decentralised, one has to consider the behavioural aspects. Bluntly, this is the attempt to influence people's behaviours through economics.
3. **Cooperative game theory**: participants work together and cooperate and behave in certain ways. For example, everyone agrees to trade on-chain and no one agrees to make private transactions off-chain.
4. **Crypto economics**: economics behind blockchain ecosystems. This includes token ecosystems and economics of blockchain platforms themselves.
5. **Deflation**: the value of money increases in the future. While this is good, it prevents other economic activities like using that money to invest in other value-adding activities. It is better to hold on to the money instead.
6. **Dominant strategy**: a strategy that is always better than the rest of the strategies possible. For example, I have three possible strategies: eat a Kobe beef steak, murder a person, get eaten by a shark. The best strategy is to eat a Kobe beef steak, so that is the dominant strategy.
7. **Economies of scope**: efficiencies formed by variety, not volume.
8. **Economic efficiency**: pareto optimum. No one can benefit more without another party losing out.
9. **Economic models**: models to represent reality. No model is

perfect, and having a model is better than none. It can be used to predict the future or to analyse the past.

10. **Egalitarian mechanism**: a mechanism that is fair to participants in games. There are criteria to determine if a mechanism is egalitarian.
11. **Fiscal policy**: Government spending and taxation designed to affect the monetary market. More government spending could boost the economy. Fiscal policy also decides taxation rates.
12. **Game theory**: strategic decision making. Used to analyse options to make decisions or analyse why such decisions are made
13. **Governance**: the rules in which people (or tokens) have to play by when in a space (e.g. digital ecosystem, game, theme park, country).
14. **Government bonds**: contract issued by the government to borrow money from people and to return the money (with interest) at a later date.
15. **Incentives**: rewards to encourage certain behaviour. This can be financial or non-financial based.
16. **Incomplete contracts**: Since contracts usually cover the solution when a situation happens, contracts are thus incomplete, because they do not include every possible situation that can potentially happen, as well as the solutions.
17. **Inflation**: decrease in value of money, because there is an increase in supply. For example, I could use £1 to buy a chocolate bar. There is a 50% inflation, and now for the same chocolate bar, I have to use £1.50 for the same chocolate bar.
18. **Interest rates**: amount charged when you borrow something or lend something. For example, interest incurred when you borrow money from the bank. And the bank pays you some interest when you leave your money with them.

19. **Markets**: place where consumers and producers come together to buy/sell, change prices and outputs until equilibrium market prices and market output levels are determined.
20. **Macroeconomics**: decision making for an economy as a whole.
21. **Market design**: designing the environment, which the market interacts in. It can be anything from organising organ donation to token ecosystems or platforms like Amazon and Airbnb.
22. **Market failure**: when the market does not function as it is supposed to. For example, oversupply of products, inability for people to transact with each other, etc.
23. **Mechanism design**: reverse game theory or rules of the game. Instead of participants choosing a strategy based on the outcome of their choices, mechanism design is the rules of the game, to constrain the behaviours of participants, towards a desired outcome.
24. **Microeconomics**: analyse, model and understand individual behaviours (e.g. market design, Nash equilibrium).
25. **Monetary economics**: economics of money. Central banks make decisions regarding money in general; policies are set by the central bank to control the movement from a high level.
26. **Monetary policy**: central bank changing interest rates and money supply to manage the economy.
27. **Moral economies**: an economy that is based on goodness, fairness, and justice, as opposed to one where the market is assumed to be independent of such concerns.
28. **Multi-stage game**: the opposite of multi-stage game is a single-stage game. A single-stage game is where everyone plays together once, and then they leave and do not interact anymore. So, a multi-stage game is a game form, where there is a sequence of one game after another.
29. **Nash equilibrium**: steady state where everyone will not

change their decisions because you don't benefit from changing the state.

30. **Non-cooperative game theory**: cooperation is tough. People naturally do not cooperate unless there is an incentive to. Hence, non-cooperative game theory is the natural state of people. We use this state to analyse behaviours and actions of participants.
31. **Pareto efficiency**: a state of how things are allocated. The allocation is known as pareto efficient if you cannot increase someone's benefit without someone suffering or paying for it.
32. **Price**: an allocation mechanism for goods and services.
33. **Private information**: information that is not public, like insider information, analysis, private observation, etc.
34. **Property rights**: how the good is used and owned. It is usually a socially enforced construct.
35. **Repugnance**: the social constraints preventing exchange from taking place at positive prices. Basically, markets that prevents us from having a monetary price tag to it. For example, assassin market or organ donation.
36. **Required reserves**: amount of physical cash (reserve) that needs to be in the bank. This amount is stated by the central bank.
37. **Resolution mechanism**: different mechanisms to resolve disagreements within the ecosystem. For example, specific codes in smart contracts, TCR.
38. **Savings function**: the relationship between income and savings. It shows the willingness to save, given the amount of income.
39. **Schelling point**: natural point that everyone tends towards without communication. For example, Let's meet at the metro station in New York at noon. It is helpful when we have decentralised ecosystems and need to make a decision based on everyone's little decisions.

40. **Social choice**: a collective decision that is the best for everyone.
41. **Token**: anything that represents value.
42. **Token economy**: an environment in which participants interact with each other in a digital space, facilitated by tokens or a unit of measure.
43. **Token economics**: the economics underlying a token economy. It sets forth the architecture of the token economy, including the governance mechanisms, token monetary policy, property rights, and thus determines the structure of the overall token governance and ecosystem design.
44. **Token policy**: how tokens are governed and managed.
45. **Zero-sum game**: someone wins at the expense of another.

Finance and DeFi Related

1. **Algorithmic rebalancing**: rebalancing to an agreed upon value algorithmically.
2. **Autonomous Market Maker**: a system to allow exchange between assets using math.
3. **Bond**: debt security with an obligation to repay.
4. **Bonding Curve**: a curve (equation) that connects two or more variables mathematically.
5. **Composability**: A system design principle that deals with the inter-relationships of components. A highly composable system provides components that can be selected and assembled in various combinations to satisfy specific user requirements.
6. **DeFi**: decentralised finance is a movement that uses decentralised networks to transform the financial system as we know it, by removing the intermediaries.
7. **Derivatives**: a contract that gets its value from the assets in

the contract.

8. **Digital currency**: a category of currency that exists digitally. You have two types: legal tender and non-legal tender.
9. **Discount rate**: interest rates when a commercial bank borrows from a central bank.
10. **Effective lower bound**: used to be zero-lower bound. Now it is the effective low interest rates that are at zero. There is little that central banks can do to further reduce interest rates.
11. **ETF**: index fund that is traded on the stock market. Typically purchased and sold by brokers.
12. **Exchange rates**: the amount of currency A needed to pay to get currency B.
13. **Flash loan**: a loan that you can secure through a smart contract from the DeFi protocols liquidity pool. It allows the smart contract to execute in many protocols, to borrow, use and repay the loan in a single transaction.
14. **Futures contract**: legal agreement to buy or sell an asset at predetermined price at a specific time in the future.
15. **Hedge fund**: an investment fund that invests in assets using complex strategies and financial instruments to improve the returns of the fund.
16. **Howey test**: Howey test is a test created by the US Supreme Court to determine if a certain transaction qualifies as "investment contracts". If they are considered a financial security, the investment is subjected to disclosure and regulation requirements.
17. **Impermanent loss**: if you have some capital, there are two ways to go about it. The first one is to keep it in your wallet and the second way is to keep it in these liquidity pools.

Trade happens and the tokens in the liquidity pool is lost. Loss comes from the difference of that vs when you keep it in your wallet.

18. **IPO Pop**: a situation where the value of the stock increases when the stocks are listed on an exchange. Early buyers of the stock can profit from this trade. For example, nCINO jumped 195% upon listing on Nasdaq in July 2020. Baidu is the largest IPO pop on Nasdaq in 2005, with 354% increase on Day 1.
19. **Market maker**: institute that always buys and sells on the exchange.
20. **Monetary policy**: how money is governed and managed.
21. **Leverage**: a financial strategy to use of funds to increase exposure to your trade. For example, I have $10 and the leverage I receive is 10-times. So now, I have $100 worth of leverage position that I can use to trade.
22. **Liquidity**: ease of changing an asset into cash.
23. **PE Ratio**: current stock price divided by earnings
24. **Perp-futures**: perpetual futures contract to buy or sell an asset at predetermined price without an end date.
25. **Ponzinomics**: economics of Ponzi scams.
26. **Physical delivery**: in terms of options and futures contract, which requires the actual underlying asset to be delivered upon specific date, rather than offsetting with cash transactions.
27. **Present value**: current value of future sum of money, given a specific rate of return.
28. **Price discovery**: overall process of setting spot price or price of an asset, financial security, commodity or currency.
29. **Price stability**: prices are consistent over time.
30. **Price slippage**: Price slippage is the difference between the expected price before the transaction and the actual price

when the token is transacted.

31. **Quantitative easing**: printing more physical money. This reduces the price level of each piece of money.
32. **Repo**: repurchase agreement. It is a short-term borrowing rate between institutional players like banks and central banks. It typically lasts overnight. Think of this as borrowing and lending, but for banks instead of retail people like you and me.
33. **Venture capital**: a form of private funding in exchange for equity. This is usually for start-ups with high growth potential.
34. **Yield**: returns from investment.

Technology Related

1. **Data**: raw records.
2. **DApp**: decentralised applications. These are applications built on blockchain.
3. **DPoS**: delegated proof of stake is similar to Proof of Stake. But instead of everyone having a chance to put their name into the box to be a validator, we limit those that can put their names in the box. That means we delegate the validation tasks to a group of people. This can help to increase transaction speed because there are fewer validators. It can also increase safety because to appoint these delegated validators, there is usually some checks and criteria to meet.
4. **Fork**: copy the source code, make changes to it and run the code independently.
5. **Fungible token**: tokens that are replaceable. For example, 1 Bitcoin. Non-fungible tokens are unique tokens that are not easily replaceable. For example: a crypto kitty.
6. **GPT-3**: machine language that uses deep learning to produce human-like text.
7. **Information**: transformed data (clean).

8. **Intangible assets**: assets that typically involve the development of specific products or processes, or are investments in organisational capabilities, creating or strengthening product platforms that position a firm to compete in certain markets.
9. **Interoperability**: the ability for different systems to speak to one another. For example, an app running on iPhone can send data to another app running on Android.
10. **Knowledge**: the ability to connect information with evidence and reflect or analyse the results to form a coherent an understanding.
11. **Layer 1**: the base technology layer.
12. **Layer 2**: a layer above Layer 1, usually to resolve scalability problems in Layer 1.
13. **Merkle tree**: a way of organising information in cryptography. It looks quite like a business organisational chart.
14. **Operational rules**: rules that govern distinct operations in the ecosystem, institution or organisation. They are usually hardcoded, in black and white. For example, hardcoded algorithms, law or standard operating procedures.
15. **Plasma Cash**: imagine you eat a lot throughout the day. And you like to count your calories. Every hour, you will eat something, like an apple, banana, chocolate bar, etc. Now, it's very annoying to keep adding up the calories you eat every hour. So, you just tabulate what you eat at the end of every day, instead of updating your app every hour. That is how Plasma Cash work. It aggregates all the transactions and updates Ethereum mainchain at once.
16. **Plasma Chain**: a form of childchain to Ethereum. It is designed specifically to increase transaction speed to 1-3 seconds.
17. **PoS**: proof of stake. Think of a lottery. You have a chance of winning if you buy the lottery ticket. Similarly, PoS is where

you place your name and stake (some tokens) into a box for a chance to be a validator. Meaning you get to approve the transactions and be rewarded in block rewards or transaction fees. A stake must be added to prevent bad actions. For example, if you validate an empty block, you will lose your stake.

18. **Protocol**: the language that systems run on. Protocols are codified and systemised processes and steps to do something. Instead of listing Step 1, Step 2, Step 3, the protocol writes that in the code. Systems then follow the steps and execute an action.
19. **Roll-up**: Layer 2 scalability solution in blockchain, by aggregating transactions over a period and updating all the transactions at once on the mainnet.
20. **Sharding**: instead of keeping a physical cup, imagine smashing it on the floor and giving each friend a small piece of the cup. One scalability solution is sharding, which is to break information into small pieces and having different validators keep these pieces. Only the owner of the data can retrieve the information through the private key held.
21. **Smart contract**: digital contracts that do what they are told automatically, when something is triggered.
22. **Sidechain**: imagine you are a financial trader and you use two monitors. The main monitor is for you to do your regular work and the side monitor shows the graphs and details of the market. You can move your window from the side monitor to the main monitor, and they are all connected in the overall computer system. Similarly, sidechain is like the side monitor. It is a separate set of blockchain networks and allows transactions and tokens to be used. You can move the tokens and transactions to the main chain (aka main monitor)

whenever you want. We usually use sidechains for scalability solutions or to increase throughput speeds.

- We have security from the main chain (aka whatever virus-free software is on your computer systems)
- We have speed from the side chain (e.g. your side monitor runs specific programs very quickly like a Raspberry Pi)

23. **Private key**: password in the crypto world.
24. **Protocol**: an operation or set of rules that is defined and written down.
25. **Sybil attack**: individual splits themselves up by creating identities on a P2P network. Imagine a person creating multiple Facebook account to like their own post.
26. **ZK-rollups**: an application to ZKP. It aggregates transactions and update the mainnet, significantly reducing transaction fees.
27. **ZKP**: zero knowledge proof. It is a cryptography protocol developed in the 1980s.
28. **ZK-SNARKS**: a category of ZKP. It allows one party to prove an action is done without identifying the specific individual.

Acronyms

AI	Artificial intelligence
AMM	Autonomous market makers
BIC	Bayesian Incentive Compatibility
BoE	Bank of England
BoJ	Bank of Japan
CBDC	Central bank digital currency
DEX	Decentralised Exchange
CDP	Collateralised debt positions
CHF	Swiss Francs
DAO	Decentralise autonomous organisation
DLT	Distributed ledger technology
DSIC	Dominant Strategy Incentive Compatibility
DSR	$DAI Saving Rates
EEA	Ethereum Enterprise Alliance
ELB	Effective-lower bound
ENS	Ethereum Name Service
ETF	Exchange Traded Fund
FED	Federal Reserve (US Central Bank)
FI	Financial Incentive
FOMO	Fear of Missing Out
GBP	British Pounds
GPT-3	Generative Pre-trained Transformer 3
HKD	Hong Kong dollars
HSBC	Hong Kong Shanghai Bank Cooperation
ICO	Initial Coin Offering
IoT	Internet of Things
IPO	Initial Public Offering
IM	Instant messenger
IP	Intellectual Property
IPR	Intellectual Property Rights

IT	Information technology
KYC	Know your customer
LAO	Liability Autonomous Organizations
LP	Liquidity provider or liquidity pool
LPC	Liquidity provider contract
MAS	Monetary Authority of Singapore
MCR	Minimum capital requirement
MVP	Minimum viable product
NFT	Non-fungible token
OSM	Oracle Security Module
OTC	Off-the-Counter
PBoC	People's Bank of China
PE	Price-earning
POA	Proof of Authority
QE	Quantitative easing
RFID	Radio-frequency identification
SEC	Securities and exchange commission
SGD	Singapore dollars
TCR	Token Curated Registry
UIUX	User Interface, User Experience
VC	Venture capital
VPN	Virtual private network
ZLB	Zero-lower bound

Protocols and their Token Names

AMPL	Ampleforth
BAL	Balancer
BNB	Binance
BNT	Bancor
BTC	Bitcoin
COMP	Compound
DAI	Stable coin soft-pegged to USD using

MakerDAO	Maker
$DAIBNT	DAI-Bancor liquidity pool in Bancor
EDBK	Economics Design Book, this book
EOS	EOS, a Layer 1 platform
EREP	Fake token created for examples
ETH	Ether
KNC	Kyber
LTC	Litecoin
MakerDAO	Maker
MEOW	Unicat
MKR	Maker
NXM	Nexus Mutual
PETH	Pooled ETH
SNX	Synthetix
TOKEN	Fake token created for examples
UNI	Uniswap
USDC	Circle's stable coin
USDT	Tether

Recommended Economics Books

You'd think I would leave without giving you more resources to learn more? Here are some great books, both academic and easy reading.

1. Keynes, J. M. (2018). *The general theory of employment, interest, and money.* Palgrave Macmillan. https://doi.org/10.1007/978-3-319-70344-2
2. Friedman, M. (2020). *Capitalism and freedom.* University of Chicago press.
3. Von Mises, L., 2016. *Human action: A treatise on economics.* Lulu Press, Inc.
4. Kahneman, D. (2011). *Thinking, fast and slow.* Farrar, Straus and Giroux.
5. Kingma, B. R. (1969). *The economics of information: A guide to economic cost-benefit analysis for informational professionals.* Library and Information Science Text Series. Libraries Unltd Inc.
6. Haskel, J. & Westlake, S. (2018). *Capitalism without capital.* Princeton University Press.
7. Sharpio, C. & Varian, H. R. (1998). *Information rules.* Harvard Business Review Press.
8. Posner, E. A., & Weyl, E. G. (2018). *Radical markets: Uprooting capitalism and democracy for a just society.* Princeton University Press.
9. Posner, E. & Weyl, E. G. (2018). *Radical markets: Uprooting capitalism and democracy for a just society.* Princeton University Press.
10. Roth, A. E. (2016). *Who gets what – and why: The new economics of matchmaking and market design.* Eamon Dolan/Mariner Books.
11. Vulcan, N. & Roth, A. E. (2015). *The handbook of market design.* Oxford University Press.
12. Evans, D. S. & Schmalensee, R. S. (2016). *Matchmakers: The new economics of multisided platforms.* Harvard Business Review Press.
13. Schumpeter, J. (2012). *Economic doctrine & method: An historical sketch.* Martino Fine Books.
14. Pan, S-L. & Sandeep, M. (2018). *Digital enablement: the consumerisation & transformational effects of digital technology.* WSPC.

15. North, K, Maier, R., & Haas, O. (2018). *Knowledge management in digital change: new findings and practical cases*. Springer.
16. Rifkin, J. (2015). *The zero marginal cost society: The internet of things, the collaborative commons, and the eclipse of capitalism*. Griffin.
17. Shiller, R. J. (2020). *Narrative economics: How stories go viral and drive major economic events*. Princeton University Press.

Made in United States
North Haven, CT
16 October 2021